THE NEWANTIQUES

THE NEWANTIQUES
Bevis Hillier

TIMES BOOKS

*For Pascal and James
recalling happy days in Beverly Hills*

Acknowledgement and thanks for their help and cooperation in making available illustrative source material are due to the following: James Barron, page 134; the Brighton Museum, page 173; Vernon C. Brooke, page 192; Kenneth Clark of Banstead, page 45; the Ethnographical Museum, Palermo, page 177; the Fine Art Society, page 63; the Gilbert Collection, page 171; the Gordon Wigg Collection, page 195; Bevis Hillier, frontispiece, pages 49, 51, 118 and 200; John Jesse, page 83; John May, page 131; Sotheby's, page 214; the Victoria and Albert Museum, pages 91, 94, 97, 134 and 189; Harriet Wynter, page 187. The following have kindly granted permission to reproduce copyright material in the text: John Murray, for extracts from *The Collected Poems* of John Betjeman, pages 72 and 197; Jonathan Cape, page 210; Hodder and Stoughton, page 211; the Journal of the National Book League, page 160; *Punch*, page 14; Dorothy Stroud, page 101.

Illustrations by Jim Robins
Designed by Sally Muir

First published in Great Britain by Times Books, the book publishing division of Times Newspapers Limited, New Printing House Square, Gray's Inn Road, London WC1X 8EZ
© Times Newspapers Limited 1977
ISBN 0 7230 0152 9
Printed and bound by Hazell Watson & Viney Ltd, Aylesbury, Bucks

Publisher's note: all prices given in this book are approximate.

Frontispiece: A late nineteenth-century Dresden porcelain caricature of a *Times*-reading Englishman

Contents

Introduction

My first article on antiques for *The Times* was published in 1960, when I was twenty and in my first year as an Oxford undergraduate. The article, which was about John Turner, an eighteenth-century imitator of Wedgwood, was accepted by Iolo Williams, then Museums Correspondent of *The Times*. I still have his handwritten letter, which came from the old 1874 building: *The Times* has had two changes of address since then. I was in the cockiest phase of early achievement. In the previous term I had had part of an unfinished novel published in *Cherwell*, and had received a letter from Evelyn Waugh's literary agent asking if he could handle my work. I had just won a *Punch* competition for an imaginary art criticism and had proudly hung on my study wall my prize – a Thelwell cartoon – 'The Age-old Custom of Beating the Balm-cake at Abbots Dawdling', which illustrated the commercialization of village tradition with a neon sign blazing 'ANTIQUES! ANTIQUES! ANTIQUES!' at cigar-smoking, camera-festooned American tourists.

My pleasure at having an article accepted by *The Times* was marred by two things: first, articles were still anonymous, so I had to appear under 'From a Correspondent' instead of a by-line; and second, the sub-editor who wrote the caption for my photograph of a Turner tea service called it 'a Wedgwood tea service', when the whole point of the article, which was titled 'Justifiable Fame for an Imitator' was that Turner's works, although remarkably similar to Wedgwood's, had their own individual style.

Two years later, when I was about to come down from Oxford, I read in *The Times* of Iolo Williams's death. His obituary paid tribute to his versatility: he had not only written what remains one of the best books on English water colours; he was also a botanist, a bibliographer and an expert on folk songs and the Welsh language. On the same day as the obituary appeared I wrote to the Editor of *The Times*, Sir William Haley, saying: 'I hope it is not too indecently early to ask whether Mr Williams's death has created vacancies lower down the scale?' – meaning, of course, could I have his job? Cheek is one of the most important qualities of a good journalist: without it, the awkward questions that draw revealing answers would never be asked. I believe it was my cheek, as well as the fact that I could already claim to be a *Times* contributor, that won me an interview with the personnel officer, who told me: 'You can't just walk into Iolo Williams's job, as you are not trained. But we do offer one traineeship a year, and you can apply for that.'

Then followed three more interviews. In one, with the Arts Editor, I was asked to criticize some works of sculpture he had in the room. In another, with the News Editor, I was told: 'Of course, Iolo is irreplaceable. You know, he was our Kew Gardens Correspondent as well as our Museums Correspondent. You couldn't take that on, could you?' I admitted that I could not. 'And again', the News Editor continued, 'Iolo got us the Piltdown skull, you know. He used to read some obscure scientific periodical, and when he read in it an exposé of the Piltdown skull fraud, he knew he had a wonderful scoop for *The Times*. We kept the story out of the early edition, so the *Telegraph* would not get on to it. Do you think you could get us scoops like that?' I mumbled that I probably could not.

But I got the job. After my training and a period as a Home News reporter, covering stories from race riots in Southall, Middlesex, to 'Goldie the Eagle Escapes Again', I became Sale Room Correspondent. As a specialist, I must have seemed an exotic and rarefied figure to my colleagues. I moved in a world where the hottest news was several hundred years old. My predecessors in the job tended to produce long lists of prices 'realized', 'fetched', 'made' and 'brought' (even, occasionally, 'commanded') by the sale room antiques. This pleased the dealers, who gained a conspectus of the market, and the auctioneers, who thought people would be encouraged to bring their heirlooms to them when they saw the high prices; but it can have meant little to the million regular readers of *The Times*, who did not know the difference between Ming and Capodimonte, a Stevengraph or a *kakemono*. I decided instead to describe two or three of the things sold each day in detail, treating them very much as the news reporter treats the events he covers, but also appending a shortened list of the day's prices for the benefit of dealers. At first, auction houses were upset by this change of policy, and even in one case suborned eminent museum men and dealers to write to the Editor in protest; but the more far-sighted sale-room press officers realized that the change would eventually be to their advantage: people whose eyes had formerly skated uninterestedly over a list of prices might now read the column out of interest.

I worked on the principle that people are interested in people, not things. I began as Sale Room Correspondent on 1 January 1968, and the early sales I had to cover – the light *hors-d'œuvre* of the season – contained no works of startling artistic importance, and no record prices. But I still found interesting an album kept by Beatrice Stuart, who modelled for many well-known artists before and during the First World War. It contained different versions of her features by Sir Frank Dicksee, Dame Laura Knight and Sir Alfred Munnings, the last of whom had added a verse:

> Most of your portraits are wrong,
> Some of them only a mess;
> Lambert has made your fingernails long,
> But Dicksee's is quite a success.

Beatrice Stuart, who had one of her legs amputated at seventeen because of a bone disease, was the model for the figure of Peace in Adrian Jones's Quadriga group which dominates Hyde Park Corner from the Decimus Burton arch on Constitution Hill. I also enjoyed reporting a sale of Tassie medallions in which descendants of the original subjects bid for their ancestors; the sale of teapots from the collection of Mr Tom Williams of Newquay, who hoped to finance a visit to Yi-Hsing near Shanghai (his Mecca) with the proceeds; and the sale, for £1,200, of E. H. Shepard's drawing of the picnic from *Winnie-the-Pooh*. ('It was a case of "hush, hush, whisper who dares", as bidding, which began at £200, jumped up by £50 bids to this surprising total.') *Punch* picked up the story and turned it into a funny poem à la Pooh:

> Sotheby, Botheby, tiddeley-pom,
> A sketch of my picnic has sold for a bomb.

As the auction season gained momentum, schoolboy sketches executed at Charterhouse by Sir Max Beerbohm fetched £480; a great silver tankard engraved with scenes of the Battle of Culloden and probably commissioned by the Duke of Cumberland, the royal Commander-in-Chief, was sold for £12,000; a bronze figure of Juno at Sotheby's was identified as a Cellini; letters of A. E. Housman were sold, giving new insight into his sex-life; and Sotheby's held a sale of instruments of torture, leaving not a rack behind.

In reporting the sale of the Housman correspondence, I created another precedent at *The Times* by writing the opening of the story in lines of verse parodying Housman's manner:

> At Sotheby's the hammer raps
> Like drum-taps for a slaughtered lad,
> And autographs are sold to chaps
> With half the heart their authors had.
>
> O never fear the poet's curse:
> His corpse, must rot his soul may burn:
> Like him, the copies of his verse
> Are sold 'not subject to return'.

There were people who found something shocking in my way of treating the world of antiques as a continuous source of entertainment. By so doing, however, I was actually acknowledging the seriousness of the subject. To me, a few hundred words in a daily newspaper was not the place for a parade of scholarship, or laborious exegesis. I was quite prepared to undertake such work: the subject of my 1960 article in *The Times*, John Turner of Lane End, was later developed into a book of the more-footnotes-than-text kind. But anyone who imagines that it is possible to learn about antiques from a newspaper article or television programme is in for a disappointment. Indeed, anyone who imagines it is possible to learn about 'antiques' will be disappointed; for the longest human lifetime is not long enough to master all the information on even so circumscribed a subject as English porcelain: the different decorators; the beguiling differences between the factories' 'pastes'; the evidence of archaeology which every year expands the subject; who was apprenticed to whom; who shipped blank wares to be decorated in Holland ... and so on. Attempting to gain a smattering of knowledge about antiques in general may be all very well for someone who wants to run a small general antiques' shop in the country; but to my mind, early and con-centrated specialisation is essential to the collector who wants to achieve more than dilettante dabbling. The profound appreciation of a subject, and the pleasantly exclusivist feeling of knowing more about it than anyone else on the face of the earth, come only with specialis-ation. One may perhaps compare the two kinds of collecting by a consideration of the difference between promiscuity and deep love for a single person. If I had to say how my essays fitted into that particular metaphor ... Well, perhaps one might think of this book as the files of a discriminating marriage bureau. Here are the varied beauties assembled; their pictures, their pasts, their whereabouts now, and – ever so discreetly – their financial standing. Some have had spouses who died or divorced them; others are entering the arena for the first time, with the bloom almost of youth upon them – Miss Art Deco and Miss Austerity/Binge, for example. But naturally we hope you will want to learn more about them before taking the plunge.

When I was asked by John Higgins, the new Editor of *The Times*'s Saturday Review, to contribute a fortnightly antiques' column, I approached the task much as I had tackled the sale-room column. First, I asked myself, who are my potential readers? 'Top People', if the notorious old *Times* advertising campaign was to be believed. Maybe – but 'Top' in what sense? The constant stream of letters I received asking the value of a chipped vase or a single copy of the *Strand Magazine* suggested that not all were gilded parasites lounging in stately homes. It is significant that the antiques' article which attracted more letters than any other was about Dr Gregory Scott, a young G.P. who had set out to make a collection of all the early Penguin paperback books. He had bought most of them for about 5p apiece, and his collection is now worth about £500 – far more than he had paid for it – because things acquire additional value when the aggregate or 'set' into which they are placed assumes a significance transcending the mere accumulation.

I envisaged my audience as well very educated, but at best shabby-genteel. I decided to take my own by no means princely financial position as the norm: that meant, in terms of expenditure on antiques, up to £10 without turning too many hairs; up to £50 for an especially desirable treasure; up to £100 for something I desperately wanted; and considerably more (if necessary with bank loans) for something that I knew was worth far more in the sale room. I occasionally mentioned in my articles prices much higher than £100 for the benefit of those who could afford them, or to indicate to those who could not, what to look for in the bargain tray.

What is the best subject for the more modest collector? The answer is, he should create his own subject: ideally, he should begin collecting something which no one has ever collected before. In one of the essays in this book, I suggest that a novel way of collecting would be to specialize in the artefacts of one calendar year. I chose the year 1874 as an example; and later I devoted *The Connoisseur* of January 1974 entirely to objects from 1874, with an historical introduction by Professor Asa Briggs, an article on the Criterion Theatre, London (built in 1874) by Sir John Betjeman, further articles on silver, porcelain, paintings and even American toys of 1874; and – because '74 had been the birth year of Sir Winston Churchill – Lady Spencer-Churchill, his widow, contributed a foreword. One could equally well collect the year 1900 with a view to showing off the collection at the millennium; or any other year which took one's fancy. Among other subjects I wrote about which were not widely collected were Victorian travel books; family photograph albums; book-plates (once avidly collected, but now a faded hobby); Victorian memoirs; smokers' requisites; book blurbs and dedications; antique packaging; old magazines; relics of the Raj; dog collars; mosaics; puppets. Not all the subjects I discussed were new antiques, but even when tackling the more conventional antiques, I tended to write about tokens rather than coins, Art Nouveau silver rather than Georgian. A selection had to be made for the purposes of this book, and it seemed intelligent to give some kind of theme by choosing the articles on the more off-beat subjects. The more conventional topics on which I wrote, T'ang pottery and Chinese porcelain, for example, can be studied in many books; some of the subjects which I discussed have no other literature.

The collector I deprecate is the mere magpie or accumulator. The collector at whom *this* book is directed is the 'archaeologist without a spade', who is prepared to research his subject deeply, root out old documents which enable him to date or otherwise categorize his pieces. It is to this kind of collector that 'new antiques' present such a rewarding challenge. He is also likely to be the kind of collector who sees his examples not just as pretty things to hoard in a cabinet and gloat over, but as talismans of history which have something to tell us about the people who made, used or displayed them.

This is why I cannot think of 'antiques' as a phenomenon that suddenly cuts off in 1830 or 1876, with a 'now-you-see-it, now-you-don't'. The world wags on; the strands of society weaken, thicken or twine; and it is (chrono-)logical that the frontiers of the antique should move steadily nearer our own day. We are all in the privileged position of being able to buy the antiques of the future, to meet their makers and be their users — the position Wedgwood's contemporaries were in during the 1760s and '70s, but which so few of them were able to exploit. I have written about the Art Deco period, which my parents lived through, and the Austerity/Binge period, which I lived through; and I am eagerly preparing to welcome Joan Hassall engravings, Laurence Whistler glass, miniature weather-forecasting stations and models of spaceships into the cabinet of New Antiques.

Bevis Hillier

17

Collecting by the year

In 1972 I bought a child's scrapbook, dated 1874, which gave me an idea for a new type of collecting. The owner, little Miss A. A. Scarlett, who had pasted her photograph to the cover, cannot have been more than nine or ten, but she had a flair for page layout. Most of the pages were decorated with glossy Victorian scraps sold as such: one page was covered with scraps of sports, including a man on a penny-farthing bicycle. Miss Scarlett also stuck her Christmas cards in, and there was an elegant 'Almanack for 1874' in the form of a floral fan.

Having bought this nucleus of good illustrative material, I decided that I would make up a 'Scrapbook for 1874' of my own, more on the lines of the BBC's 'Scrapbook for 1940'. I would find out what wars were fought in that year, what books were published, what new inventions were patented, who died and who was born. If the year turned out to be interesting enough, I thought I might persuade a publisher to accept a book on the subject, colourfully extra-illustrated with A. A. Scarlett's scraps, and photographs of pottery, pictures and prints of that date.*

The quickest way to find out the main things that happened in that year was to turn to G. M. Young's *Victorian England*, of which the appendix gives the main events of the Victorian years. The most striking event of 1874, it seemed, was the Ashanti War. If one can be callous enough to speak of any war as 'picturesque', this one was: fought against Kofi Karikari ('King Coffee'), who habitually drank from the skull of a former British governor; won triumphantly by Sir Garnet Wolseley; covered in the newspapers by Winwood Reade and H. M. Stanley, who had found Livingstone in 1871.

No one very significant died in 1874, apparently; but when I checked on births from another reference book I found that the following strange crib-fellows came into the world in 1874: G. K.

---

* In fact, the material was eventually published as an entire '1874' issue of *The Connoisseur* in January 1974

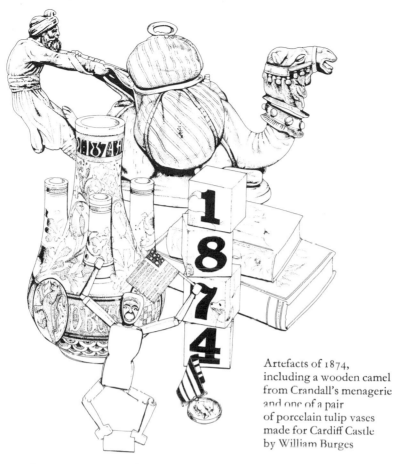

Artefacts of 1874,
including a wooden camel
from Crandall's menagerie
and one of a pair
of porcelain tulip vases
made for Cardiff Castle
by William Burges

Chesterton, Somerset Maugham, Gertrude Stein, Houdini and, in November 1874, Winston S. Churchill. Perhaps my book could be called 'Scrapbook for Churchill's Birth Year'.

Thomas Hardy's *Far from the Madding Crowd* appeared anonymously in serial form in the *Cornhill Magazine* in 1874; some reviewers attributed it to George Eliot. The sensation of the Royal Academy exhibition was Elizabeth Thompson's *The Roll Call*. The subject was the Crimean War, twenty years in the past; it showed a sergeant of the Grenadiers calling the roll after a battle heavy in casualties. The effect of the painting was well described by Raymund Fitzsimons in the *Saturday Book* (No. 28).

When *The Roll Call* came before the Selecting Committee, the members rose to their feet and gave this painting and the painter three rousing cheers. The painting had been commissioned by a Manchester manufacturer, and the Prince of Wales tried, in vain, to purchase it from him. When the exhibition opened, the crowds before the painting were so dense that a policeman had to be posted to keep them moving. The Queen had *The Roll Call* abstracted from the exhibition for a few hours so that she could contemplate it privately at Buckingham Palace. She expressed a wish to purchase the painting, and the owner reluctantly agreed to sell it to her.

I gradually added to my store of 1874-iana. From Sanders of Oxford's costume print exhibition I bought some splendid fashion prints of that year from *The Queen* and other magazines, for £4 each. Mr John Saumarez Smith of the Heywood Hill Bookshop found me an unused leather-bound diary of 1874 – 'being the thirty-seventh year of the reign of Her Present Majesty'. It contains lists of the House of Lords, the House of Commons and the principal officers of state. For £1.50 I bought, from a junk stall at Cambridge Circus, the *Piccadilly Annual* for 1874, full of racy stories and cartoons such as 'Mr Green Horne's Dilemma' (a man emerging naked from bathing, only to find a slavering mastiff sitting on his clothes with bared teeth). At the Handley-Read exhibition at the Royal Academy I saw the marvellous ceramic vases designed by William Burges with the date of 1874 painted in decorative Gothic characters on the body of the ware. Sotheby's Belgravia sold some handsome silver, including a cup presented by the Duke of Devonshire to the winner of the Eastbourne Hunt Races. The Criterion Theatre in Piccadilly is an 1874 building. The first commercially successful typewriter was designed by Christopher Sholes in 1874; Mark Twain lavished praise on the newfangled machine the following year.

One continually came upon desirable things from 1873 and 1875, and the temptation to cheat was enormous; but I was ruthlessly sticking to 1874. The most original candidate was some 1874 Château Lafite and champagne from the cellars of Sir William Gladstone, which came up at Christie's.

The great advantage of collecting 'by the year' is that one can buy the widest range of different kinds of antiques: pottery, pictures, silver, books, wine. It is like sinking a shaft in history. Why not start laying down a good year yourself? Of course, it helps if you can find a Victorian scrapbook ready-made as a starting point. You could start collecting now for a centenary volume of 1984. A century is a very comforting interval. As an old colonel I knew said when *The Times* jettisoned its '100 Years Ago' column in favour of '25 Years Ago', 'Dammit, before you know where you are they'll be printing yesterday's news today.'

Hitler's signature for £125

What is an autograph? The question is not as simple as it seems. When Mr Rawlins (author of *Four Hundred Years of British Autographs*, Dent 1971) was fifteen years old he asked the then Duke of Devonshire for his autograph. Rawlins had been collecting autographs for some time and had no doubt that His Grace would oblige him with a signature. Instead, the Duke took the book, wrote in it 'You are a nuisance', handed it back and turned away. Rawlins thought him rather unkind, and pointed out that he had not signed it. The Duke took the book again and added his signature 'Devonshire', saying that Rawlins had not asked for his signature but only for his autograph, which he had given him.

The Duke was quite right. The unsigned statement 'You are a nuisance' was as much his autograph as if he had signed it. Every lady is a woman, but not every woman is a lady; every signature is an autograph, but not every autograph is a signature. If you merely write the word 'no' that is also your autograph. If a long, type-written document has one initial only at the end, that is still an autograph of the person concerned. Mr Rawlins cites two examples of minimal autographs: the letter 'N' frequently signed by Napoleon on documents, and the adjective 'bon' often written on petitions by Louis XV.

A third word, holograph, is sometimes used by the collector of autographs. This means something written entirely in the hand of the writer. In sale-room catalogues, the abbreviation 'A.L.s.' means 'autograph letter signed', while plain 'L.s.' means 'letter signed', in which case only the signature is in the signatory's handwriting. The abbreviations 'A. Docs.' and 'Doc.s' follow the same pattern except that in this case one reads 'document' for 'letter'.

In spite of the fact that Mr Rawlins' book is an entertaining and informative introduction to the subject of autographs, it disappoints a little because only the signatures of letters are reproduced in it. The serious collector tends to look down on this as scalp-hunting; it would have been more interesting to have fewer signatures and more extracts from letters. The dedicated autograph collector is not interested in the mere ouija-board scrawl of pen on paper.

A dealer I visited, John Wilson, remarked that in his opinion it was the content of a letter which was all-important. He was especially proud of a Dickens' letter for which he was asking £400, and which he had bought cheaply from another dealer who had thought it an inconsequential letter addressed to someone called 'Fred'. It is in fact a stern letter to Dickens's brother Frederick, in which the author advises him to break off his engagement. The letter is at present unpublished and its value would be reduced if I were to publish the full text or a substantial extract. Dated 1847, its first sentence mentions Mark Lemon, Douglas Jerrold and John Forster (Dickens's biographer). Dickens goes on to say of Frederick's fiancée, Anna Weller, 'I am confident your engagement is one of the greatest mistakes that was ever made, even in a matter so liable to mistake as that', and ends the letter, crushingly, by remarking that the 'matter' is probably best forgotten if Frederick feels no hesitation, and that only a complete transformation of Miss Weller could alter his own opinion. (Needless to say, Fred did marry her.)

Autograph collecting is the ultimate democracy: politicians are far less valuable than authors. A typical Gladstone letter costs about £25; a typical Disraeli approximately £45 – but you have to bear in mind that Disraeli was a novelist, too. As little as £25 was recently asked for one of Lloyd George's diaries of 1912, although the entries were few and laconic in the extreme: 'Write Galsworthy'; 'Budget'; 'Lady Glenconner', and so on. Letters from the Duke of Wellington are relatively inexpensive because he lived for a long time; a Nelson letter of comparable interest is usually worth twenty times as much. At a dealer's I visited a few years ago, you could have bought one of two small letters from Thackeray for approximately £125: one, addressed to Adelaide Procter and inscribed in the form of a heart, accepted an invitation from Adelaide's mother; the complete text of the other simply read: 'My Dear Evans? W. M. T.' (Bradbury and Evans were the publishers of *Vanity Fair*.) You might, on the other hand, have preferred a letter from Beau Brummell to one Broadwood (of piano fame?): 'The snuff is perfect. I have already rammed at least an ounce up my half-starved nostrils for I have recently been rather short of such delectable weeds. Truly yrs. George Brummell.' A note from Ezra Pound to Florence Farr which merely read: 'Book ripping. E.P.' cost £45. For £15 you could have bought a letter by Kitchener written in 1901 in which he requested details of his bank balance from Cox's Bank of Pretoria. That kind of letter is interesting because the bank clerk often wrote the actual balance on the letter in pencil. It was not so of the Kitchener example, but at £45 there was a letter from Sir Arthur Sullivan to Barclay's Bank (dated 7 August, 1899) with the clerk's pencil note: '£471'.

The wicked, of course, command higher prices. A signed photograph of Hitler was priced at £125. Royals can be cheap, because there were so many of them. People threw away their Keats' letters when he was unknown, but saved their royal letters out of snobbery. For £20, there was a letter from Edward VII when Prince of Wales: 'My dear Billy, I am so glad to know that you are in Town.' (Sucks to Nancy Mitford, who believed it grossly non-U to refer to London as 'Town'). Another, signed 'Uncle Bertie' and addressed to an obscure German princess, fetched £30. It goes without saying that the farther back in history you go, the more expensive the royal letters become. £2,000 was asked for a document signed by Henry VIII, in which he ordered fifty-seven bits and fifty-seven 'hedstaulles' from the 'Maister of our Horse'. The same dealer lent me, for photographic purposes, an order addressed to the Keeper of the King's Wardrobe for green buckram, and signed by Henry VII. Clutching it on the Northern Line (and at £1,800 I might well clutch it) I experienced a faint flush of the divinity that doth hedge a king. Could this really be a spoor of the man my history book described as 'circumspect and cunning' and whom some scholars think may have murdered the Princes in the Tower, exculpating Richard III? There was something sublimely anachronistic in walking past a Wimpy Bar with what must once have caused the Keeper of the Wardrobe to tremble in his hose.

And this, I suppose, is the lure of autographs. No species of collecting gives one such a feeling of direct contact with an historical individual. Here, on this fragment of paper, once rested the very hand of Keats or Byron. This cabbalistic scrawl is the last recorded signature of Castlereagh before his suicide; that group of sepia hieroglyphics represents Admiral John Byng, shot on his own quarter-deck *pour encourager les autres*. The fine academic script of the boy-king Edward VI reveals the tutorship of his writing-master Roger Ascham. The sprawling hand of Charles II makes one wonder how with so little use for the aesthetics of calligraphy, he could be a connoisseur of pictures. Dickens's superabundant energy often runs on into a set of hairpin bends beneath the signature; Queen Elizabeth I's signature is coldly ornamented with meticulous figure-of-eight flourishes.

One should collect for love of a particular author or movement, and not for monetary gain. At the same time, autographs are still one of the most undervalued parts of the antiques market. At the time of writing, one of the highest prices paid at auction for a single letter (in which George Washington discusses the proposed Constitution of America) is £15,000. Washington is not rare, but he is one of the most 'desirable' names of all; America is the centre of the market (with such dealers as Ken Rendell and Paul Richards of Boston, and Mary Benjamin of New York) and he is arguably the greatest American. For investors, Victorian artists are still quite cheap (good Pre-Raphaelite letters can be bought for under £25); the leaders of modern freedom movements have maintained a steady price; and science and medicine are within range of the average pocket – though these are already rising steeply. Amongst modern writers, Joyce, D. H. Lawrence, and Dylan Thomas are in strong demand: a six-page manuscript of a Dylan Thomas radio talk may cost upwards of £1,500. At the rock bottom of the market at the moment is the Church; so if you foresee a religious revival, go out and buy your Dean Inge or Cardinal Wiseman now. Who knows, the last may be first.

And finally, I shall say a word about the under- (a different) hand practice of forgeries. The principal ways of recognizing forgeries are, first, that the writing is too even on the page and that there is too little variation of light and shade; and second, that the contents are often too good to be true. I was told of a letter of Browning's in which he states that he was not specifically referring to Wordsworth when he wrote *The Lost Leader* – and that as far as he was concerned, bygones were bygones. I have seen a Dickens' forgery, possibly by 'Antique' Smith or the 'South Coast Forger' whose artefacts turn up in embarrassing numbers in Brighton. They are valueless.

So it is a mistake to try to collect autographs without doing a lot of homework first. You might begin with chatty books like Mr Rawlins's or A. M. Broadley's *Chats on Autographs* (1910), and then progress to such works as Mary A. Benjamin's *Autographs: an aid to collecting* (1966). Later you will have to progress to such specialist works as W. A. Churchill's *Watermarks in Paper* (Menno Hertzberger, Amsterdam, 1935) or *Composers' Autographs* (Cassell, 1968). If you intend to collect early material, you will need to study palaeography. The dealer whom I mentioned earlier, John Wilson, specializes in letters and autographs. He trades from Middle House, New Yatt, Witney, Oxfordshire.

Art Nouveau silver

One of the first indications that Art Nouveau silver was beginning to be appreciated properly was an exhibition at the Victoria and Albert Museum in 1970 of the silverware and original designs of Archibald Knox. The work of Knox, who was born in 1864, belongs to the later phase of Art Nouveau, when the wild 'whiplash' style of the 1890s was giving place to a rectilinear style which drew heavily on the taut, interlaced motifs of Celtic art. Born of Scottish parents at Tromode, on the Isle of Man, Knox was passionately devoted to Celtic traditions. A large part of his work for Liberty's – he made over 400 designs for them – was produced for their 'Cymric' range of silver and jewellery and their 'Tudric' pewter manufacture.

The Cymric range was launched in 1899. Liberty's policy of anonymity for its designers was enforced as strictly as was Wedgwood's in the eighteenth century. This, coupled with the loss of the firm's records in the Second World War, has made it difficult to attribute work to individual artists with certainty. The Celtic influence was so powerful and pervasive that it could mask individuality; furthermore, others of Liberty's artists, such as Reginald (Rex) Silver (b. 1879), worked in a style similar to Knox's.

A few early twentieth-century magazines pierced the anonymity, however, and illustrated some of Knox's works for Liberty's. The designs and tracings which were exhibited at the Victoria and Albert and which were later presented to them by Mrs Denise Wren, a former pupil of Knox, are another aid to identification. Most of these drawings relate generically to pieces illustrated in the Liberty catalogues of Cymric and Tudric wares. We can assume that Knox submitted many designs and that these particular examples are the rejects – the only ones that survive, since the Cymric and Tudric designs which were accepted disappeared during the Second World War.

Some Victorian and Edwardian aesthetes looked down on Liberty's. In a well-known Du Maurier *Punch* cartoon of 1894, an Upper Tooting hostess comments: 'We are very proud of this room, Mrs Hominy. Our own little upholsterer did it up just as you see it, and all our friends think it was Liberty's.' The visitor mutters, *sotto voce*, 'Oh, Liberty, Liberty, how many crimes are committed in thy name!'

The Knox exhibition, however, showed how distinguished the firm's products could be. The V. & A. were especially proud of a silver casket set with opals, which bore the Birmingham hallmark for 1903 and the maker's mark of 'Liberty & Co. (Cymric) London'. This piece was documented by a Liberty's receipt which recorded that it was designed by Knox. The Celtic motifs were beautifully controlled and integrated within the simple box shapes. Equally accomplished, and in the range of rather more collectors, were the commemorative spoons and buckles which Knox designed for the Coronation of King Edward VII in 1902.

Knox's silver takes its place beside the furniture of Charles Rennie Mackintosh in the period of high Art Nouveau, the austere and recti-linear phase. But when does Art Nouveau begin in silver? The question is difficult because there is no real agreement among scholars as to the inception date of Art Nouveau itself. Some push its origins as far back as the flaring designs of William Blake, others to children's book illustrations by Walter Crane, and others again to Grainger's Worcester porcelain of the 1850s in shapes derived from nature. The majority, however, would not consider that Art Nouveau proper be-gan before the 1880s, and certainly the 1890s were the years of its first full flowering.

I was interested, therefore, to discover one day at Frank Partridge's in New Bond Street, a silver-gilt inkstand of 1863 by George Fox, in which the Art Nouveau style seemed already fully formulated. The centre was in the form of a water-lily, that characteristic Art Nouveau flower. The stand was chased to simulate a watery surround, with a taper holder in the shape of a lily bud. What really gave it away as proto-Art Nouveau were the elaborate tendril handles, which one would more expect to find on an 1890s' example. It was priced at £500 in 1970, but the price would be approximately double that now. At the same time, Partridge's had on display a similar inkstand of an even earlier date. It was in the form of a water-lily in a circular pond, with a small lily bud which formed a pen-holder, and was made by E. and J. Barnard in 1857. The base was inscribed: 'M.S. the last gift of the Prince Consort Xmas 1861'. The price was £400 – again, far less than the same piece would realize today.

Both of these pieces relied strongly on accurate copying of the forms of nature. That was a prime characteristic of Art Nouveau, which was, in essence, a reaction against historicism in art – the unfortunate Victorian habit of 'reviving', that is pastiching, the Renaissance, the Baroque and just about every other style of the past.

Another good example of the back-to-nature impulse in silver is a pair of silver-gilt pomanders in the form of poppy-heads, which I bought from S. J. Shrubsole of 43 Museum Street, London, WC1 in 1969 for £130. They were made in London in 1884 – again an early date – and the maker's initials were 'C.H.'. The ends remove so that the pomanders can be filled with perfume-drenched wadding or spices.

Two names for would-be collectors to look out for are Dr Christopher Dresser and C. R. Ashbee. Shirley Bury of the Victoria and Albert Museum, who is an expert on Art Nouveau silver, has written authoritative articles on both of these in (respectively) the Christmas 1962 issue of *Apollo* magazine and the January 1967 issue of the *V. & A. Bulletin*.

Dresser was a formidable polymath. He designed furniture, textiles and metal-work, was associated with the Bretby pottery factory, and received his doctorate from Jena University for work on botany. The dominant influence on his silver was Japan, which he visited in 1876. His firm, Dresser and Holme of Farringdon Road, London, imported 'Japanese art metal-work'. He himself designed a toast rack in electro-plated copper (1881) of spiky Japanese form, while a glass claret jug with silver mounts by him, bearing the London hallmark of the same year, is of such ruthless simplicity that it could easily win a Design Award today. He designed for Tiffany's, Dixon's of Sheffield, Elkington's and Heath of Birmingham. Dresser began serious production of silver in the late 1870s and continued until shortly before his death in 1904.

Charles Robert Ashbee (1863–1942) kept his metal workshop continuously engaged on Dresser's designs from 1888, the year in which he founded the Guild and School of Handicraft at Toynbee Hall in the East End of London, until the dissolution of the Guild as a limited company in 1908. Shirley Bury has described Ashbee's works of about 1900 as 'virtually unique among English silverware of the time in expressing the mannered elegance of Continental work'.

Apart from the passive pleasure of owning something attractive which may also be a good investment, the collector of Art Nouveau silver can enjoy it as an active hobby. The study of these comparatively recent wares is still in its infancy, and by searching into old magazines, company records or the lives of individual collectors, it is possible to make a further contribution to the subject.

London shops where Art Nouveau silver is obtainable are: John Jesse, 34d Gloucester Walk, London, W8; and Chiu Antiques, 10 Charlton Place (Camden Passage), Islington, London, N1. If you are in New York, visit Lillian Nassau, 220 East 57th Street, who has a wide selection. Alain Lesieutre, at 2 rue de Tournon, Paris, also has a good stock. Shrubsole and Partridge, although they get the odd spectacular piece of Art Nouveau silver, mainly sell earlier works.

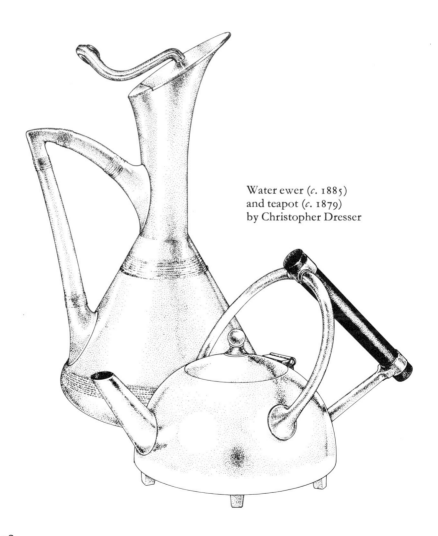

Water ewer (*c.* 1885) and teapot (*c.* 1879) by Christopher Dresser

Pipe dreams

An enjoyable collection of tobacco stoppers – those small seal-like objects, mainly of eighteenth- and nineteenth-century origin, with which you pack the tobacco into the pipe – has been formed by a 'city gentleman' who writes under the name of A. Pinckard. He must have been collecting for years to have gathered together such an impressive range of examples, nearly all of which are of high quality. They include 'scrimshaw' stoppers, worked by sailors in whalebone with incised designs; Shakespeare busts carved in boxwood; *memento mori* skulls; little porcelain figures, and elaborate designs in silver. The one I most covet is a figure of William of Waynflete, Bishop of Winchester and founder of Magdalen College, Oxford, in 1458. The silver base of the wooden stopper is engraved: 'Mag Coll great Oak'; the stopper was probably cut from the tree soon after it fell in 1789. Another piece of historical interest is a silver anti-papist design with reversible heads: the Pope becomes a devil when turned upside down, and the cardinal a fool. Seeing this collection gave me the idea of writing about smoking antiques in general.

Some of the cheapest items one can acquire are clay pipes of the nineteenth century, including those made by Gambier of Paris which bear heads of such well-known figures as Disraeli, Queen Victoria and the prophet Jacob, which last bears the motto 'Je suis vrai Jacob'. These range from £15 to £20. If one is looking for more expensive items, meerschaums dating from *c.* 1820 to 1900 are of interest. In general, they range in price from £16 to £40. Other subjects carved in meerschaum include mermaids, Gainsborough ladies, skulls, skeletons, hands holding bowls, and voluptuous legs.

The meerschaum starts life creamy white in colour; smoking turns it an orangey-brown. A good anecdote relates how one proud owner of a meerschaum pipe determined that it should be coloured to perfection. Knowing that the only way to colour it was to smoke it, and also being aware of the fact that to be stained consistently the pipe

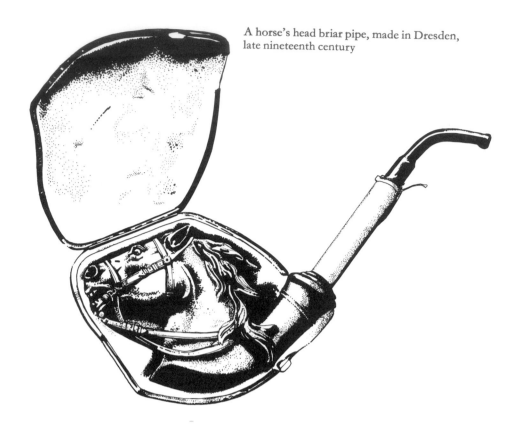

A horse's head briar pipe, made in Dresden, late nineteenth century

must never be allowed to cool while the process is taking place, he arranged that the precious pipe be handed over to a regiment of soldiers who passed it from mouth to mouth for seven months without ever allowing it to go out. At the end of this time, he got the pipe back, tanned to an ideal shade – with a £100 bill for tobacco.

I was informed by a dealer that tourists tend to go for the calabash (the curly pipe which is the subject of so many seaside postcard jokes about nudist camps – 'Oh, Mr Smith, I've never seen a curly one like that!'). The tourist usually asks: 'Please 'ave you the pipe of Sherlock 'Olmes?' They sell for between £4 and £6. A bisque tobacco jar in the form of a French general's head (1914–18 period) can be bought for approximately £20. Porcelain pipes, mainly Bavarian and Austrian, fetch from £12 to £15. Novelty ashtrays are popular, especially the rude ones of reclining women which upturn to reveal brass bottoms. You can buy a hookah and live the mystic oriental life of a Bulwer Lytton for £14 to £15; an amusing pipe-rack; or brass plaques which extol the pleasures of smoking – 'Better to smoke here than hereafter'.

Good reading for beginners is Amoret and Christopher Scott's little book *Discovering Smoking Antiques* (Shire Publications, 1970). This gives you all the historical background to smoking: the Raleigh anecdotes, James's I *Counterblaste* and so on; and contains informative sections on the main classes of smoking relics: foreign pipes, clay pipes, meerschaum pipes, porcelain pipes, briars, jars and paraphernalia, matches and matchboxes, lighters, and the antiques associated with cigars and cigarettes.

In the Antiquarius antiques market, King's Road, Chelsea, there is a stall devoted exclusively to the antiques of smoking. It is run by Brian Tipping, an actor who served as Lord Kitchener's batman in *Young Winston* and played the part of a Scottish soldier in the Christmas Eve fraternization scene in *O What a Lovely War*.

The oddest pipe Mr Tipping had in stock when I visited him was a Siamese opium model in bamboo, fitted with medallions. 'As smoked by Deborah Kerr and Yul Brynner in *The King and I*', commented Mr Tipping; but quickly added '– no, I'm joking!' Harriet Wynter, who specializes in scientific instruments (352 King's Road, London SW3), also sells smokeana. I saw there a lovely tobacco rasp in French ivory, *c.* 1710, possibly showing the Dauphin. (The silver rasp, unfortunately, was missing; the price would now be approximately £200–£300.) She also had in stock a glorious Louis XVI boxwood pipe with classical carvings which carried an inscription in brass inlay: *Charles Duprey, Père à Montreuil-sur-Mer*. I also examined a lead tobacco jar which showed the influence of the Adam brothers and bore the arms of the City of Leeds.

The moral of this story, surely, is: don't let your money burn a hole in your pocket. Let it go up in smoke.

Book-plates: a faded fad

Collecting book-plates, or *ex libris* – labels of ownership pasted into the fronts of books – has almost completely gone out of fashion. There was a great vogue for them in the 1890s and the early years of this century. It began with Warren's *Guide to the Study of Book-plates* (1880), the first book on the subject. In 1890 the Ex Libris Society was founded in England; its handsomely illustrated journals and exhibition catalogues (you can consult them in the Victoria and Albert Museum library) are still among the best works on book-plates. Zealous collectors invented a special argot to describe and classify their prize plates – 'Chippendale', for example, for those in the rococo style.

Why has the craze petered out? The answer is, although Mr Muggeridge will find it hard to believe, that we have become more civilised. Opinion turned against collecting book-plates because it meant taking them out of books. Consider, for example, a run-of-the-mill classical text bearing Gibbon's book-plate. The main interest lies in the knowledge that Gibbon owned this book, and may have drawn on it as material for *The Decline and Fall*. Without the book-plate, the book is worth little; without the book, the book-plate is not worth much. The question was already being argued over at the height of the book-plate craze. The *Daily News* of 3 January 1895 declared:

> The book-plate collector is the worst of all. The amateur of Natal Blues does no harm. The amateur of book-plates divorces the plate from the book, whereas what interest book-plates have entirely depends on their connection with the volume and its original owner. A plate of Pepys or Garrick on a book from their libraries makes a literary relic. The collector sponges off the plate, and gums it into an album. He talks, we learn, of 'Chips' and 'Jacs'; still, his craze is a kind of idiotic retainer of antiquity, the court fool of history or art.

Is there any answer to this tirade? My own feelings about it are ambivalent. On the one hand, book-plate collecting reminds me of the really sacrilegious practice of a collector I once met. He collected china marks: china *marks*. Having bought up pieces of eighteenth- and nineteenth-century china, sometimes damaged but still fine examples of their kind, he would cut out the mark on the bottom with a glass-cutter, retaining a marked disc the size of an old half crown to be hoarded in a coin cabinet, and consign the rest of the teapot or saucer to the dustbin.

At the same time, book-plates have (as ceramic marks seldom do) an artistic value of their own, and the interest of a specific historical association. And as someone pointed out in reply to the *Daily News* writer, many book-plates are found on junk stalls in damaged and grimy books ripe for the pulping machine. In such instances, sponging them off and mounting them is not really equivalent to throwing away the baby and treasuring the bath water.

The earliest known book-plates are three south German examples, all of them about 1470. One, of Hans Igler, bears a hedgehog (Igel) motif; the second belonged to Hildebrand Brandenburg of Biberach, a monk of the Carthusian monastery of Buxheim, and marked books given by him to the monastery; the third, bearing the arms of Domicellus W. von Zell and his wife, was in a book presented to the same monastery.

Many would regard as the greatest of all *ex libris* Dürer's magnificent woodcut book-plate for Bilibald Pirckheimer. Dürer also designed one for Johann Tscherte (*c.* 1521); the satyr in the design is a rebus, for the Bohemian word 'tscherte' meant satyr. Dürer's book plate for Hector Pomer (1525) bears the motto 'To the pure all things are pure' in Hebrew, Greek and Latin.

The French had a less glamorous book-plate tradition, partly because the outsides of valuable French books were often richly heraldic, so that there was no need for book plates. Their great contribution was the invention of the rococo style, which began as a reaction by certain royal designers to the oppressive grandeur and symmetry of the baroque. I bought the beautiful rococo eighteenth century bookplate of Dr Thomas Smyth, archdeacon of Glendalough, in Dublin as the bonus to a 2½p book; the connection of the obviously very fashionable, if not Erastian, Dr Smyth with primitive-Christian Glendalough of the grey round tower and St Kevin's Kitchen is delightfully incongruous.

On 20 June 1793 a decree suppressed all titles and armorial emblems in France. The pretentious book-plate became a menace to personal safety. This is clearly reflected in the changing book-plates of the

Vicomte de Bourbon-Busset. The first, dated 1788, has four lines of engraved braggadocio to proclaim its owner's titles; that of 1793 has nothing grander than a single line in plain type: '*Bibliothèque de Louis A. P. Bourbon-Busset, Citoyen Français*'. Like the *faïence parlante* (pottery with mottoes) in which people expressed their changing fears and aspirations, this aristocratic souvenir of the Terror is the kind of magpie morsel which would serve as a good illustration to academic interpretations of the French Revolution.

The earliest known English book-plate is that of Sir Nicholas Bacon (d. 1579), whose books were presented to the University of Cambridge. Another early dated one is that of Sir Thomas Tresham (d. 1605). Bacon's son was the great Francis Bacon. A son of Tresham's was involved in the Gunpowder Plot with Guy Fawkes. A *pons asinorum* for beginner collectors is the splendid armorial book-plate of Sir Francis Fust. It was not engraved until 1728: the date 1662 which it bears is that of the creation of the baronetcy.

Hogarth designed four plates, including one for George Lambert (d. 1765), the landscape and scene painter. From 1740 to 1770 the 'Chippendale' style dominated, although other conventions such as the pile of books and the library interior were introduced. The follies of the rococo were superseded by those of neo-classicism. One of the finest neo-classical plates is that designed by Agnes Berry for Anna Damer, the sculptress: both were intimate friends of Horace Walpole, whose own book-plate is much in demand in spite of the doldrums of book-plate collecting

Thomas Bewick's woodcut plate for Robert Southey is a good example of the landscape *ex libris*. An even more desirable, and earlier, landscape vignette is that for John Bullock, who served under Wolfe at the capture of Quebec: it shows the fortress of Quebec and the attacking troops. Famous designers are just as important to a collection as famous owners: Millais designed a St Christopher plate for Sir Christopher Sykes; Thackeray designed Edward Fitzgerald's simple *ex libris*; Brangwyn designed Sir Henry Newbolt's.

Warren's book of 1880 began a revival in *ex libris* design. The Dürer manner – apocalyptic heraldry – was a favourite. It was used, for example, in W. E. Gladstone's book-plate by Erat Harrison, which was based on the coat of arms of the family of Gledstanes – gled, kite; stanes, stones (a Hawarden kite, of course).

I have the book-plate of Gladstone's son, Herbert: an almost grotesque exercise in filial piety, since it depicts the old man poring over books in his library. There are some good Art Nouveau book-plates: for example, Anning Bell's design for Professor Walter Raleigh or the exquisite designs by Harold Nelson which were shown at Hartnoll and Eyre's in London in 1972.

The latest book-plate in my own sample collection is Rex Whistler's neo-rococo one for Duff Cooper, which contains a portrait of Lady Diana Cooper as the goddess of the chase. Even today there are artists, such as Joan Hassall and Reynolds Stone, producing fine woodblock plates, and no doubt these will one day be collected too.

A new introduction to book-plate collecting is much needed. The best one at present is still a book privately printed in Sydney, Australia in 1932 – P. Neville Barnett's *Armorial Book-plates*. It is not, of course, readily available. I often receive letters from art students asking for help with such 'projects' as the history of ice-cream parlours or of neon lighting – worthwhile subjects, I suppose, but surely less historically and artistically valuable than a history of the book-plate would be.

There are few shops that make a point of selling book-plates. One that does is Thomas Thorp of 170 High Street, Guildford, Surrey, where the *ex libris* are arranged in drawers under the names of the original owners. Christopher Mendez, of 51 Lexington Street, London W1, is a print dealer who also sells book-plates.

Such stuff as dreams are made of

Bury St Edmunds somehow seems a suitable place to find a seller of stuffed birds and animals. There is something lowering and macabre about its atmosphere. You enter the town past a jail; in the museum you can read an account of the trials of William Corder, the Red Barn murderer, bound in his skin.

There is nothing sinister, however, about Christopher Frost, who sells stuffed birds and animals from his mother's house ('The Enchanted Aviary', 3 Nelson Road, Bury St Edmunds, Suffolk), even if some of his wares – a stuffed mongoose savaging a stuffed snake, for example – give one pause. Mr Frost, who is in his late twenties, left school at nineteen and worked as assistant stage manager at the Theatre Royal, Bury. He was already a collector of stuffed birds – he bought his first at the age of five – and he now began to deal in them on the side. In 1972, having become stage manager of the theatre, he decided to leave and deal full-time. He issued a catalogue and advertised both locally and in such magazines as *Exchange and Mart*, *Country Life* and *Shooting Times*. He sold almost everything from that first catalogue, and later realized how woefully little he had charged. Since then the business has grown rapidly, and he is now one of the leading dealers in the country. Most of his customers are private collectors, but he also sell to museums and stately homes. He emphasizes that he is not a taxidermist, but merely sells birds stuffed in the past. Many of the birds he sells are now protected, including a wonderful snowy owl.

Collectors of stuffed birds and animals look out for the work of well-known taxidermists: T. E. Gunn of Norwich, who specialized in birds, Cooper of St Luke's London, who mounted stuffed fish in bow-fronted cases, and James Gardner, who was taxidermist by appointment to Queen Victoria. In some cases it is possible to acquire work by a given firm ranging over a long period. For example, Mr Frost had a case of five roach in one of Cooper's bow-fronted cases with the gilt inscription: 'Taken in Hampshire by W. Wilshire, August,

1884. Total weight 8lb 6oz. Largest fish 2lb.' An almost identical case containing a tench bore an almost identical style of gilt inscription: 'Tench. 4lb 6oz. Caught by E. L. Woolaston, September 1, 1927.' The 1884 example cost £95, the 1927 one, £58.

The Leicester Museum has published a useful booklet, *British Taxidermists: a historical survey*, edited by Sue Herriott (1968). It was issued as a tribute to the work of Mr A. E. Williams, who retired after almost twenty-three years as taxidermist to the Leicester Museum. The booklet was the first attempt to list British taxidermists and identify their work. Mr Frost is hoping to complete a much larger work on the same lines, and there is every hope that it will not be entitled *Great Stuffers of the World*.

Sue Herriott records that taxidermy as we know it today – an art by which animals' skins are preserved and arranged in a lifelike manner – did not begin to develop until the middle of the eighteenth century. She believes that the first treatise on the subject was that written by R. A. F. Réaumur in 1749. French and German workers developed the early techniques many years before comparable work was done in Britain. The Zoological Collections received by the British Museum from Sir Hans Sloane in 1753 contained many mounted birds, but none has survived, so it is not possible to assess the standard of taxidermy except by default.

The methods described in a pamphlet of Johann Reinhold Forster in 1771, *Short Directions for Collecting, Preserving and Transporting all Kinds of Natural History Curiosities*, make it clear why early specimens have not survived. To preserve a bird, the entrails, lungs and craw were removed. It was then washed with a liquid containing arsenic, and dried with a powder mixture of tobacco, sand, black pepper, burnt alum and arsenic. The body was stuffed with tow, its eyes replaced with painted putty, and it was dried in an oven. 'The preservative used', Miss Herriott concludes, 'can have had little effect on the large amount of flesh left in the bird, so that it probably soon decayed.'

A successful early worker was Charles Waterton (1782–1865), the eccentric squire of Walton Hall near Wakefield, on whom Sydney Smith wrote amusingly. His methods were unique: he mounted birds and animals without using stuffing, moulding the hollow dried skins into the natural shape with great care. His collections have survived in good condition, and are in the Wakefield City Museum. He described his methods in *Wanderings in South America, the United States and the Antilles* (1828).

By the end of the eighteenth century, taxidermy was being practised commercially. One case label records: 'All sort of Birds and Quadrupeds curiously Preserved in any Attitude like life, by I. Cornelias, No 11, Little White Lion Street, Seven Dials, London'. The art was fostered by the Great Exhibition of 1851: British taxidermists learnt from their Continental colleagues. The Great Exhibition also introduced the vogue for animals arranged in human situations and clothes – the 'Anthropomorphic' school led by Hermann Ploucquet of the Royal Museum, Stuttgart, and reaching its most obsessional repulsiveness in the cat tableaux of Walter Potter of Bramber, Sussex.

Victorian wealth gave some sportsmen the chance for extensive travel and big-game hunting. Preservation of large animals made new techniques necessary. One pioneer of big game mounting was Rowland Ward, who was taught taxidermy by his father who had studied with the American naturalist, Audubon. Ward used lifesized models of the animals, on to which the skin was moulded. He created magnificent groups, such as 'The Combat' of 1871. His book, *The Sportsman's Handbook to Practical Collecting, Preserving and Artistic Setting-up of Trophies and Specimens*, was published in 1880. He also stuffed smaller animals: Mr Frost had a glass case of grey squirrels in a natural setting for £55. He also had a full-sized lion at £875. He found it in an antique shop 'in the wilds of Norfolk' and had it cleaned up in London. He thought he might be able to sell it to someone with a large pub. Once he bought a stuffed man-eating tiger (also from a Norfolk village). He fixed it standing up on his car roof-rack, glaring out over the tail-lights, a startling vision to drivers behind who caught it in their headlights.

In addition to stuffed animals and birds, Mr Frost sells books on taxidermy and animal lore. He lent me two examples to read. One was *The Taxidermist's Manual* by Captain Thomas Brown (1859), which is not something to read at bedtime. It contains gruesome engravings of gutted cats and fiendish steel instruments, with instructions about fastening lips with pins and cementing eyes: 'If rage or fear is to be expressed, a considerable portion of the eyeballs must be exposed'. Another useful tip: 'When it is wished to preserve Hedgehogs, rolled into a ball, which is a very common position with them in a state of nature, there should be much less stuffing put into them than is usual with quadrupeds, so that they may the more easily bend.'

One feels sure that Captain Brown knew how to make a porcupine look fretful; but he admits being stumped by that vexing species, Man, 'who justly ranks at the head of the animal kingdom. Numerous have been the attempts of mankind to preserve the skin of their fellow-creature. The very best of these have been most disgusting deformities, and so totally unlike "the human form divine", that none of them have found a place in collections'.

The other book was very different. *The Hunter's Arcadia* by Parker Gillmore (author of *Great Thirst Land*, *A Ride Through Hostile Africa*, *The Amphibian's Voyage*, *Gun, Rod and Saddle*, etc.) conveys the exhilaration of the hunt and the attitude of mind of the hunter. 'Despised brute though the baboon is by all the human family, he is gifted with wonderful instincts' . . . 'I have heard it said that "men are often unjust to one another, women always so", but I am certain they cannot be more so than the porcupine is to the aardvark' . . . 'Bechuana women are ever ready for a scamper across the veldt when aught is to be obtained by it, and a wide, voluminous skirt cannot fail to be found a great inconvenience when perpetrating such pranks; so the females, forgetful of their adornment, gather up their skirts to an elevation which cannot help bringing upon the wearers ridicule instead of respect.' Such is Gillmore's usual manner; but when he really gets on the trail, he falls into that naturally good literary style which nearly all experts have when on the subject of their expertise:

> I was about to shut up my glass, when over its focus passed a new object. It was not for a moment to be doubted what it was, for the erect tips of horn, supported by several spiral twists told at once the tale. No, there was no room for doubt; it was the splendid adornments of a Koodoo bull . . . Women, in all your freaks of fashion, it matters not whether you wear chignons or puffs in your hair, cut it short behind like schoolboys, or frizz it over your foreheads after the manner of Skye terriers, I can admire you in all and every type of *coiffure*; but, with nervousness, I almost hesitate to say that the head adornments of that koodoo absorbed my longing for their possession more than ever did the golden locks or chestnut tresses of sprightly, vivacious New York belles or more developed, Cleopatra-like Anglo-Saxon beauty.

Gillmore, to his everlasting regret, missed his kudu; but Mr Frost had in stock a fine head of a Greater Kudu mounted on a wooden shield at £75.

Tokens of respect

While coin prices have soared dizzily, the prices of eighteenth- and nineteenth-century trade tokens have remained fairly static throughout this century. According to a coins' expert whom I consulted at Spink's, the art and antique dealers of King Street, St James's, London W1, you would have paid approximately 7s 6d for a nineteenth-century token in 1900, and about eight guineas for a five guinea piece – a large gold coin of the reign of William and Mary or George II. Today the five-guinea piece would cost approximately £2,000; but the token has only risen to £1 or £2.

Trade tokens were originally introduced to make good an acute shortage of small change in the 'regal' coinage issued by the Crown. Queen Elizabeth I considered it beneath the royal dignity to issue regal coins in base metal. Copper coins were seldom in use until the reign of Charles II, and there was a constant shortage until the reign of George III. As late as September, 1811, the High Bailiff of Birmingham wrote a memorial to the Privy Council at the request of the city to the effect . . .

> That trade suffereth great and serious evils from the want of small change . . . That there are in this town and neighbourhood many thousands of persons whose weekly labour does not produce more than from three to ten shillings, and that their employers being compelled to pay several together in pound notes, they are under the necessity of going to public-houses to get change, where, of course, some of the money must be spent to induce the publicans to supply them therewith, or they must buy some articles which they do not want, or in many cases must take the articles of food on credit at an extravagant price . . . Your memorialists, therefore, must earnestly request that your Lordships will speedily order a coinage of copper penny and half-penny pieces . . .

On this occasion, as so often in the past, the government was slow to respond to the appeal, and (as also in the past) local initiative came to the rescue: with the issue of tokens.

In his *Numismata* of 1697 John Evelyn wrote:

The Tokens which every taverne and tippling house (in the days of the late Anarchy among us) presum'd to stamp and utter for immediate exchange, as they were payable through the neighbourhood, which though seldom reaching further than the next street or two, may haply in after times, come to exercise and busie the learned critic, what they would signifie, and fill whole volumes with their conjectures, as I am persuaded several as arrant trifles have done, and still do, casually mentioned in Antient Authors.

Evelyn obviously thought that England had seen the last of tradesmen's tokens. In this opinion he was quite wrong: the most interesting period of tokens from the collector's point of view is the late eighteenth and early nineteenth centuries, the central period of the Industrial Revolution. In the late 1780s the lack of small change was again desperate. A proposed Mint recoinage of 1787 was thwarted by a sharp rise in the price of copper and it was this development, it seems, which decided Thomas Williams of the Anglesey Copper Mines Company to issue its first penny token, which appeared in that year with a druid's head on the obverse and the cypher 'P.M.Co.' (for Parys Mines Company) on the reverse. Although it was not exactly the first of the new breed of tokens, it was the first to be struck in large quantities. Williams's coins, like those of other reputable issuers, were of full weight, struck with crisp definition, and well designed. They were the forerunners of a vast series.

The early issuers of tokens were big industrialists. Like Williams, John Wilkinson, the great iron-master, began to produce a long series of tokens in 1787, some of the later ones being struck by Matthew Boulton at Birmingham, who himself had large interests in copper mining and smelting. Lord Liverpool wrote in his treatise on coins of 1805:

Many principal manufacturers are obliged to make coins or Tokens to enable them to pay their workmen and for the convenience of the poor employed by them; so great is the demand for good Copper Coins in almost every part of the Kingdom.

The concentration of large numbers of workers in a single industrial plant (itself made possible by the improved water and steam-power technology of the Industrial Revolution) created the need for a means of ready payment. It was principally for this reason that tokens continued to be issued. One could hardly pay industrial workers, as one could reward agricultural employees, in kind; however, canny industrialists, and sometimes benevolent ones, built shops to serve the factory staff.

At the same time, there grew up a craze for collecting tokens and it was to serve this market that the little book, *The Virtuoso's Companion*, was issued in the 1790s. Such coin dealers as Thomas Skidmore of Holborn and Peter Kempson of Birmingham issued series of tokens on a variety of subjects: architectural studies, churches, public buildings, Oxford and Cambridge colleges and so on. Thomas Spence, an eccentric radical, issued tokens of political propaganda. 'Token-mania' coincided with a rise in the price of copper. This enlarged the profits to be made from melting full-weight coins and tokens, and encouraged re-mintings of flimsier money. In 1797 the government finally took action against the deteriorating situation by authorizing a large official re-coinage, reinforced by terrible legal threats against counterfeiting.

From Boulton's Soho Mint, under contract to the Treasury, poured more than 1,000 tons of the massive 'cartwheel' twopenny pieces during the next two years, driving most tokens out of circulation. Tokens were again issued in large numbers in the early nineteenth century, including the interesting silver tokens of 1811–12, which were designed to complement an issue of poor regal silver. This issue of silver tokens was a pointed indication of the way the state was shirking its responsibilities: permission for issuing private silver tokens was withdrawn by an Act of Parliament in July, 1812. The Mint, meanwhile, was totally re-equipped and modernized under the direction of Boulton. The outlawing of copper tokens followed soon after, in a bill of July, 1817.

Looking through several drawers of tokens at Spink's, I was favourably impressed by the artistic appeal of many of them – and, of course, by their relative cheapness. That issued by the Low Hall Colliery, Cumberland, in 1797 (now worth approximately £80) has on its obverse a delightful scene of a 'horse-wheel' at work. A fine portrait of Charles James Fox, from a political series (worth approximately £18) bears the legend:

> Glory be thine, Intrepid Fox,
> Firm as old Albion's Battered Rocks;
> Resistless Speaker,
> Faithful Guide,
> The Courtier's Dread,
> The Patriot's Pride.

One of Thomas Spence's cranky political satires, showing a cat and

open book with the legend 'In Society Live Free Like Me' (1795) would perhaps cost £40. Among the seventeenth century tokens was a Tiverton, Devon, farthing of Thomas Fowler, 1652, which might cost between £2 and £15. A Hull Lead Works token of 1812 would cost between £3 and £25, according to its condition.

Most of the books on trade tokens have been written from the numismatic point of view. There are, however, two books which I can recommend to the beginner collector, which deal with tokens from the historical viewpoint. *English Trade Tokens* by Peter Mathias (Abelard-Schuman, 1962) carries the sub-title 'The Industrial Revolution Illustrated'. The writing and the historical insights are masterly; the photographs of tokens, by A. C. Barrington-Brown, are beautifully clear. A more recent book is *Trade Tokens: A Social and Economic History* by J. R. A. Whiting (David and Charles, 1971).

The man who keeps his eye on the barometer

Mr Nigel Coleman, the leading dealer in barometers in the south-east of England, has a large antique shop in the High Street, Brasted, near Westerham, Kent, where he keeps a large and constantly changing stock of barometers. He describes his ideal customer as 'rich, with a sense of humour' and he has this advice for buyers of antiques: 'People should realize that if you say something outside a shop window, it can be heard inside. "Couple of brass handles and it'd be twice the price" is the sort of comment you hear.'

Mr Coleman also restores barometers. He emphasizes that those he sells are in no way reproductions; but most of the barometers he buys are in need of some reconditioning. Before visiting his shop I was taken to a workshop where the barometers are restored. Barometers of lustreless wood and tarnished dials are strung from the ceiling like hams. The dials are screwed to the turntable of a kind of home-made 'potter's wheel' and a compound containing silver nitrate is applied which, by chemical reaction with the dull brass, gives an attractive silvery surface with a restrained sheen.

Nearly all the dials have the same set of weather markings: Fair, Set Fair, Very Dry, Stormy, Much Rain, Rain and Change, though Mr Coleman has had in stock a barometer in burr yew by A. Bellamy, Poultry, which included the legend 'Doubtful' among the usual set.

A barometer, (the word derives from the Greek *baros*, weight) is an instrument for measuring the weight of the air. Its domestic application as 'weather-glass' is incidental. The best book on barometers – Nicholas Goodison's *English Barometers, 1680–1860* – is one of the most outstanding ever published on a particular kind of antique. It was published by Cassell in 1969, but is now out of print. For the beginner, the essay on barometers by H. Alan Lloyd, F.S.A., in *The Connoisseur Concise Encyclopaedia of Antiques* (Sphere Books, 1969) makes a good introduction. Like Mr Goodison, I shall avoid writing about the early development of the barometer (or 'barascope' as it

44

was known) by the scientists of the seventeenth century, and confine myself to the domestic mercurial barometer.

Mr Goodison illustrates and writes about such rare and beautiful variations as the angle-tube barometer made, apparently to the exclusion of any other type, by Charles Orme of Ashby-de-la-Zouch, Leicestershire (1688–1747). But the two main types which the average collector is likely to encounter are the 'stick' barometer and the banjo variety.

From Mr Coleman I was able to gain what no book tells one: an approximate idea of current prices. Both prices and quality cover a wide spectrum: a six-inch barometer with convex mirror, c. 1840 by Ashforth of Birmingham might cost £200; an eight-inch barometer by Curtis of Bristol c. 1790 with a beautifully engraved face and prominent shell inlay on the case, £550. In the larger varieties – i.e. ten-inch dials – prices range from £260 for an instrument by Spelzini c. 1840, again with a convex mirror, to £555 for a fine-quality, cross-banded example by Guanziroli of London (c. 1830); whilst a twelve-inch barometer by Zanetti of Manchester of superlative quality would fetch £560. Six-inch barometers are very hard to find: the price of such an instrument by Kalabergo of Banbury might be £425. Stick barometers range from £225 for a model by Braham of Bath (c. 1840), to £365 for one by Bennet of Cork. More unusual items include a Pit barometer made by Davis of Derby in 1870 at £250. Finer stick barometers are sometimes available at between £600 and £700.*

In the course of my visit, I examined a banjo barometer in rosewood, c. 1840, with a six-inch dial, which was made by Heald of Wisbech. Mr Coleman assumed that Heald, like Caminada of Taunton, was probably an assembler of barometers rather than the maker of the entire artefact: the case would have been constructed by a cabinet-maker, the engraving done by a professional engraver, and so on. One of the most valuable parts of Goodison's book is its list of makers. Looking up Heald of Wisbech, I found that Goodison suggests he was 'probably Alfred Heald, watchmaker, clockmaker, optician and silversmith, High Street, Wisbech, 1851'. Incidentally, some makers, such as A. Bellamy of the Poultry, who made the 'Doubtful' barometer, do not appear in Goodison's long list. This suggests that there is still scope for research and detective work by enthusiastic collectors.

As the description of Alfred Heald implies, many of the barometer

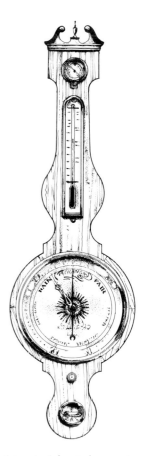

A ten-inch banjo barometer of satinwood c. 1835 by F. Amadio & Son, London

* Further information about banjo barometers can be obtained from an article which Mr Coleman contributed to the January, 1977 issue of the *Antique Collectors' Club Journal*

45

makers (or assemblers) doubled up as opticians; Mr Coleman had in stock a handsome ebony example made by 'C. W. Dixey, Optician to the Queen, 3 New Bond Street'. Goodison informs us that he was Charles Wastell Dixey (1798–1880), who was in partnership with his twin brother George from 1821–38, but on his own from 1839. He was at 335 Oxford Street in 1821; at 78 New Bond Street, 1822–23; and at 3 New Bond Street, 1825–60. So Mr Coleman's example dates from the latest period of Dixey's business. Goodison also records that there is a wheel barometer by Dixey, in a French clock case, at Buckingham Palace.

Many barometer makers were Italians who settled in England in the early nineteenth century, some slightly earlier. Mr Coleman had a superb barometer by B. Roncheti of Manchester, c. 1790, and Goodison records no fewer that twenty-three signatures of Ronchetis, Ronchettis, Ronkettis or Ronkettis. Mr Coleman often has in stock barometers by the Italians Amadio & Son; P. Nolfi of Taunton; L. Petroni of Carlisle; J. Somalvico of High Holborn, London; and A. Molinari of Halesworth.

Mr Coleman gave me a set of rough-and-ready rules for distinguishing between earlier and later barometers. He emphasized, however, that the rules were by no means infallible, and that there were exceptions to all of them: *Cistern covers* (the cistern is the container of the mercury): hemispherical ones are in general earlier than flattish ones. Thomas Blunt (d. 1822) of Cornhill, London, favoured egg-shaped covers. Blunt is listed by Goodison as an instrument maker of some distinction; he designed some of the features of the 'New Barometer' of the Portuguese scientist J. H. de Magellan (1779) and became Mathematical Instrument Maker to His Majesty the King. *A shallow thermometer case* tends to be earlier (and is, incidentally, more agreeable to look at) than a deep-fronted one. *The vertical part of the barometer just below the 'pediment'*: the shorter it is, the earlier. A lot can be told from *the style of engraving* of the maker's name: elegant Georgian gives place to 'squiggly' Victorian Gothic. *Gradations around the dial*: the bigger the gaps between them, the earlier. Fine gradations are late. *Weather markings*: the earlier ones are set horizontally, the later ones around the circumference of the banjo type. *A central handle for the 'fixed hand'* is earlier than one placed under the dial. *Crossbanding* and *bowfronted thermometers* are both desirable, in spite of the fact that there may be no specific indication of date.

Mr Coleman's pet belief is that if one part of a barometer is good, all the other parts will be also – unlike the curate's egg.

The great Art Deco revival

In the past ten years, Art Deco – the decorative style of the 1920s and 1930s – has become established as a collector's quarry. 'The Old Rush', said one American headline over an account of the 'nostalgia' craze; 'Everyone's re-doing it', said another.

In New York a magazine was launched called *Liberty: the Nostalgia Magazine*, which contained an article of 1924 by Rudolph Valentino on 'How to have a sexy body' and a 1934 article, 'Did Edison speak to the dead?' More seriously, two major exhibitions of Deco have been staged: at Finch College, New York, and at the Minneapolis Institute of Arts; and later Ileana Sonnabend, the Paris and New York dealer, held a show of 1920s' and 1930s' silver by Jean Puiforcat, perhaps the greatest of Deco designers.

In England, interest in the film *The Boy Friend* gave impetus to the revival. New shops have opened such as L'Odéon Deco, 56 Fulham High Street, London SW1, specializing in the style; Editions Graphiques, 3 Clifford Street, London W1 has also gone in for it in a big way. Some English collectors even cross the Channel to patronize the new Paris Art Deco shops such as Dépot, 15 rue St Denis, which held a fine show of French glass 'De Gallé à Marinot', and the Galérie du Luxembourg at No. 98 in the same street, which has had an exhibition of paintings by Tamara de Lempicka, the most aggressively Deco of painters who chose conventional canvas as their vehicle. Even museums have shown an unusual awareness of the vogue; the Brighton Museum, for example, honoured Clarice Cliff with an exhibition of her 1920s' and 1930s' pottery in January 1972. A copy of the *Saturday Book* from the early 1970s was largely devoted to Art Deco subjects, with a *trompe l'oeil* jacket and box by Martin Battersby, who paints almost as well as he writes.

The biggest breakthrough of all has been in the usually rather conservative world of the large auction houses. Sotheby's now regularly hold sales of Art Deco at their Sotheby Belgravia branch, and at

Phillips' auction rooms a Chiparus bronze and ivory figure of a dancer, identical to one I was offered for £8 at a theatre hire depot in 1964, fetched almost £200 in 1972 and £5,200 when resold at Sotheby's Belgravia in November 1976.

The Hôtel Drouot in Paris held one of the most important sales ever of Art Deco in November 1972. It was of furniture of the 1920s formerly in the collection of Jacques Doucet. Doucet was a famous couturier in the years before the First World War. His fashion house is mentioned by Proust. At that time, couturiers were not quite acceptable in the highest society. The story is told of a *grand seigneur* who heard that Doucet was anxious to come and see his collections. 'By all means,' he said, 'but naturally you will hardly expect me to invite you into the the presence of my wife or her friends, whom you are used to seeing half-naked in your shop.'

Doucet had begun by creating a splendid collection of eighteenth-century furniture and other examples of the eighteenth-century decorative arts. But in 1912, quite unexpectedly, he sold the lot and decided instead to collect the decorative art of his own times. The pieces that he then acquired, and with which he furnished model salons, were all of the highest quality. They were among the last of the unique pieces made on commission with such expensive materials as shagreen, ivory, crystal, crocodile, lacquer and exotic woods; by the 1930s the emphasis was more on functionalism and mass production . . . and then came the war.

Half of this collection had previously gone to the Musée des Arts Décoratifs. The sale of this other half at the Hotel Drouot contained masterpieces from the *ateliers* of such designers as Paul Iribe, Pierre Legrain, Clément Rousseau, André Groult, Marcel Coard, and the cubist sculptor Gustave Miklos, and a lacquer screen by Eileen Gray, who studied at the Slade School of Art.

The catalogue of the sale was prepared by a syndicate of three experts, Jean Soustiel, Jean-Pierre Camard and Lynne Thornton. Lynne, an English girl who had worked at Sotheby's for ten years, started the Art Nouveau and Art Deco department there in 1967. Soustiel and Camard must be the only two Frenchmen to have visited Manchester, Birmingham and Liverpool to see the Pre-Raphaelites, and Bethnal Green and Walthamstow for William Morris, in addition to knowing all about Christopher Dresser, Doulton, the Martin brothers and Leighton House. These three pooled their reference libraries, which consisted of some 15,000 books plus catalogues, articles, photographs and illustrations. The whole venture was a particularly encouraging example of the kind of co-operation that might become more usual now Britain has joined the Common Market.

The Doucet sale illustrated very clearly the influence of Japanese and negro art on Art Deco. Doucet was amongst those who pioneered the collection of negro art; a wooden mask, probably the one referred to by Appollinaire in an article of 1918, was included in the sale. The Japanese influence could be detected in the tasselled drawer handles, exotic lacquering and general simplicity of line; while African influence was apparent in such works as 'table basse et ronde d'inspiration africaine' and 'siège massif de style nègre', both by Legrain. Anyone who still thinks that Art Deco only means plastic ashtrays and chrome electric fires should obtain a copy of the Doucet catalogue and spend a few days memorizing the pieces.

A French Art Deco pottery figure of a negro drummer – a symbol of an age dedicated to the rediscovery of primitive passions

49

Travellers' tales

Old travel books attract two main groups of collectors: those who are interested in the countries, and those interested in the travellers. The former include Australians and professors and leaders of newly independent African states who want to know what their lands were like in pioneer times, or during the bad old days of white domination.

Those who collect travellers rather than travels are fascinated by the succession of grand eccentrics; the men who could only find heart's ease in trackless deserts: Sir Richard Burton with his emancipated attitude to sex; the intrepid Victorian ladies who floated across crocodile-infested waters, parasols aloft, and hacked their way through the jungle in crinolines (usually, it must be admitted, ensconced in bamboo palanquins, accompanied by many servants and with phials of quinine at the ready).

It is a subject for any collector: prices range from over £500 for *A Personal Narrative of a pilgrimage to Al-Madinah and Mecca by Sir Richard Burton* to as little as £1 at the Farringdon Road book barrows (near Farringdon Underground station, London EC1) for lesser-known but often equally engrossing books with such condescending titles as *In Dwarf Land and Cannibal Country* (travels in Central Africa by A. B. Lloyd) or *The Land of the Pigtail* (by Mrs Mary Bryson of Tientsin, with chapter headings like 'The Land of Topsy-Turvy', 'Through Chinese Spectacles' and 'The Little People of the Flowery Land'.

I have collected Victorian travel books in a desultory way for what they reveal of British imperial attitudes. What amazes us about the Victorian past – even that part of it which is still less than a century old, the 1880s and 1890s – is how much it differs from our own day; just as what sometimes surprises us about the ancient past is its similarity to today: the advanced plumbing of Crete (every ancient convenience), the psychological insights of Suetonius and Ovid.

The popular idea of the Victorians is of a breed governed by repression: the female form constricted by whalebone corsets; piano legs in prudish frills; an atmosphere of hypocrisy and lowering religion. But send an Englishman abroad, with 'savages' to boss, set him up far from the conventions of drawing-room society, and the real Victorian shows himself. It is not always an edifying sight. This is an extract from Michael H. Mason's *Deserts Idle*, published in the 1920s, showing that the type persisted well beyond Victoria's reign (as many of the characters in Somerset Maugham's short stories also suggest):

> Then a new voice arose, a loud and persistent roar lifted in abuse of Hussein and of myself also, describing us both in terms unrepeatable. Any white man is a fool who allows any nigger to revile him openly. This man, the largest and most drunken in the village, presumed to disperse my messenger and to defy my authority. I was feeling very feverish and bad-tempered, so I stalked him between the little huts. Coming upon him, as he roared and stamped in an open space, I stretched him upon the ground, dragged him to the fire and, with the Kiboko, sobered him completely. In the morning he was most penitent, and as his jaw was broken, I spent half a day in setting it and making him comfortable.

Incidentally, that book has one of the best covers I have ever seen: a frieze of four gilt bearers stamped into the blue of the binding, with packs on their heads, loin-cloths, and golden ripples eddying outwards from their ankles; a brilliant piece of design, unfortunately anonymous. In fact, the book contains a feast of bonus pleasures; well, if you do not find them pleasures, you are not the person to be collecting old travel books. There are splendid illustrations and appen-

Cover shows Japanese influence
on English book design
of the 1880s and 1890s

dices on: (i) Rift valleys and volcanoes; (ii) Comparative vocabularies of native languages collected by the author in Central Africa; and (iii) Hints as to equipment. You learn, for example, that 'the consonants *kh* sound like a man clearing his throat to spit'; that the Luganda for clean is 'kirungikitubuvo'; that one should carry no tinned goods 'except, perhaps, a few pots of jam or marmalade'; that 'tea is essential' and 'curry powder and Worcester sauce are useful for hiding the taste of bad meat'; that 'hippo or zebra fat is good for boots; bacon fat rots them', and that you should not carry 'any such rubbish as powdered eggs, made-up farinaceous foods, bottled peaches, or eye-dropper baths'.

The book is dedicated 'To the little girl who waited for me, and to my father who has suffered more from anxiety, during my years of wandering, than ever I have from physical adversities'. Another irresistible trimming is the epigraph, from *Othello*, whose hero spoke:

> . . . of antres vast and deserts idle . . .
> And of the Cannibals that each other eat,
> The Anthropophagi, and men whose heads
> Do grow beneath their shoulders.

The amateur collector would be wise to consult two books issued by the publishers Routledge and Kegan Paul: *Three Victorian Travellers* (1964) by Thomas J. Assad, and *Victorian Lady Travellers* (1965) by Dorothy Middleton. Assad's book deals with three of the greatest Victorians, Richard Francis Burton, Wilfrid Scawen Blunt and Charles Montagu Doughty. Dorothy Middleton's 'globe trotteresses' are Isabella Bird Bishop, Marianne North, Fanny Bullock Workman, May French Sheldon, Annie Taylor, Kate Marsden and Mary Kingsley. The bibliography records some of the stirring titles of these and other ladies' travel accounts: *A Lady's Life in the Rocky Mountains* (Bird, 1879); *To Lake Tanganyika in a Bath Chair* (Annie Hore, 1886); *On Sledge and Horseback to Outcast Siberian Lepers* (Marsden, 1893); *Through Finland in Carts* (Mrs Alec Tweedie, 1898); *Sketches Awheel in fin-de-siècle Iberia* (Workman, 1897).

At the bookshop of Henry Sotheran, 2 Sackville Street, London W1, I found a first edition of John Hanning Speke's *Journal of the Discovery of the Source of the Nile* (1863). Speke blew his brains out after Burton, who was bitterly jealous of his achievement, had suggested that he was suffering from delusions. I also saw there the two volumes of a first edition of H. M. Stanley's *In Darkest Africa* (1890), damp-stained and with some foxing (which would now cost approximately £60); a record of a journey through Tibet in 1897 by A. Henry

Savage Landor, *In The Forbidden Land* – two volumes magnificently bound and with sinister lettering of spiky gold. The journey was, as they say, not without incident. One illustration shows 'the executioner bringing the sword down to my neck'. The text of some of these books conveys the flavour of the period better than any modern pasticheur could hope to do. Mrs Gill's *Six Months in Ascension: an Unscientific Account of a Scientific Expedition* (1878) contains this delightful passage:

> 'Croquet ground!' I repeated as a thought of Nebuchadnezzar and his way of living crossed my mind. 'Can we eat grass?' But I might have spared myself the question. Here was no soft, inviting turf for noiseless balls to glide over, no pretty green carpet to deck with puzzling white hoops . . . Oh no! The croquet ground behind Commodore's Cottage meant a level piece of glaring white concrete.

Or sample this, from F. W. F. Fletcher's *Sport on the Nilgiris and in Wynaad* (1911): 'It has never been my lot to see a tiger actually seize a bullock, though on several occasions I have spent hours with the cattle when I knew a tiger was in the vicinity, in the hope of witnessing the sight'.

At the Rosslyn Hill bookshop, Hampstead (about halfway up the hill to Hampstead from Belsize Park Underground station), I have bought two books mainly for their illustrations. H. W. Bates's *The Naturalist on the River Amazon* (1879) has a hilarious frontispiece captioned 'Mobbed by curled-crested toucans'. It shows Bates himself, with side whiskers, staring spectacles and a straw hat, in a horror-film situation. The frontispiece of *Across Asia on a Bicycle* by T. G. Allen and W. L. Sachtleben (1895) depicts the two pedalling heroes, and is entitled 'Through western China in light marching order'. They modestly claim in their preface: 'Never, since the days of Marco Polo, had a European traveller succeeded in crossing the Chinese empire from the West to Peking'. Two other books which I have browsed through at this same bookshop are worthy of mention. The first, which carried the ponderous title *A Thousand Miles of Miracle in China: A Personal Record of God's Delivering Power from the Hands of the Imperial Boxers of Shan-Si*, was written by The Revd. Archibald Glover, M.A. (Oxon) and is dated 1904. Or perhaps a collector would have liked to buy *Round the World in 1870* by A. D. Carlisle, B.A. Now, just over a century later, someone with time and money might like to retrace his route, and record the changes – a book on the lines of *Cobbett's Rural Rides Reridden*, for example. One warning, though: you may have a little trouble with the Chinese Embassy.

Paving the way with paperbacks

Over the past several years Dr Gregory Scott, a Kensington G.P., has collected over 600 first-edition Penguin paperbacks (from the first 1,000 Penguins issued up to the early 1950s) and over two-thirds of the first 200 Pelicans. The entire collection has cost him about £100 and he believes it could be sold for over £500 – a good example of how dross can be turned into gold by the collector's diligence, and an indication of the enhanced value that single works acquire when mustered in the aggregate of a collection.

Dr Scott lives in an old house in Kennington and has a taste for antique furniture. But not for his bookshelves the mellow gleam of gold-tooled bindings: there in proud array are ranged the orange of fiction, the green of detection, the dark blue of biography, the cerise of travel, the red of plays and the light blue of Pelicans.

As a pupil at Merchant Taylors' School, Crosby, Liverpool, Dr Scott went through the usual schoolboy phases of stamp- and coin-collecting. But one day in 1970, when training at Guy's Hospital, he went to Brighton with some friends. In one of the bookshops there he noticed a pile of old Penguins, including the Penguin Specials, which he is particularly eager to hunt down now. 'Everyone with me said: "What on earth do you want to buy those dirty old books for? They'll just fall to bits." And finally, foolishly, I left them.'

At that stage Dr Scott did not appreciate the range and variety of Penguin books. During the next few months, however, he often noticed them in bookshops and bought the odd one when he wanted to read a particular title. Then he came across some of the war issues. Penguin were especially lucky in the war period, because allocations of paper were made on the basis of how much individual publishers had used before the war, and as Penguins had been in the first enthusiastic spate of production they had used a lot and were therefore allocated a large quantity. Their quota not only permitted big printings of Penguins and Pelicans; it also made possible the launching of no fewer than four Penguin subsidiary series during the war years – a distinctly unpatriotic proceeding, some might feel, especially as one series, the luxurious King Penguins, contained titles as unintegral to the war effort as Redouté's *Roses* or James Laver's *Fashions and Fashion Plates 1800–1900* (though presumably a case could be made out for *Edible Fungi* in those days of food rationing).

Dr Scott began to realize that the very flimsiness of Penguin books was, from the collector's point of view, a positive merit. Because of their tendency to 'fall to bits', they were becoming rare; they were the sort of books that people threw out without a second thought. Dr Scott decided that if he was going to take an interest he had better get on with it. Apart from anything else, it was an interesting way of building up a library, a stock of books to browse through. 'Penguin's policy was always so varied; they didn't cater for one particular kind of reader.'

Before long, Dr Scott had added to his collection the first Penguin ever published (in July 1935) – a re-issue of André Maurois's biography of Shelley, *Ariel*, translated by Ella D'Arcy. He had also bought the first Pelican, Shaw's *The Intelligent Woman's Guide to Socialism and Capitalism*, issued in May 1937. Another desirable work is the 1,000th Penguin, *One of Our Submarines*, by Edward Young, issued in July 1954.

When he first began collecting, Dr Scott was 'not as ardent' about Pelicans as Penguins. He had the feeling that as they were factual books they would be out of date. In some cases this is of course true, but such works as Roger Fry's *Vision and Design* (1937) or Clive Bell's *Civilization* (1938) have as much (or as little) value as they ever had. Freud's *Totem and Taboo* was published in Pelican in 1938; and, as Dr Scott points out, 'the 1930s were the heyday of the Freudian movement'.

This is, indeed, one of the chief appeals of collecting paperbacks: because they were intended for a mass audience they reveal the *zeitgeist*. Class-consciousness, jingoism and the paternalistic 'Take it from here' attitude of the educating classes are all evident in the early paperbacks. Margery Spring Rice's *Working Class Wives* appeared in 1937; Sydney M. Laird's *Venereal Disease in Britain* was published in 1943 (with the somewhat unfortunate advertisement on the back cover: 'Ministry of Health says: Coughs and Sneezes Spread Diseases; trap the germs in your handkerchief').

The advertising on the back of wartime issues is very dated. On the back of *Nazis in Norway* (1943) is an advertisement for Mars Bars:

'Mary is earning her M.B. Collecting salvage, digging and saving for Victory are efforts by the youngsters that deserve encouragement. Mars (for Merit) Bars.' The advertisement on the back cover of H. G. Stokes's *Signalling and Map-Reading for the Home Guard* (1941) reads: 'There'll always be an England where Huntley and Palmer's Biscuits will always be pre-eminent.' Or there is the poignant appeal on the back of Jack London's *The Iron Heel* (1944): 'When you find Horlicks difficult to get, please remember that many have special need of it.'

The 'blurbs' about authors also make for nostalgic reading. In 1953, when Henry Green's *Loving* was first Penguin-ized, his identity was still being kept a dark secret: 'Henry Green is a pseudonym concealing a double identity – that of a successful engineering industrialist and that of a novelist – unique in contemporary literature.' Agatha Christie describes herself skittishly on the back of *The Sittaford Mystery* (1948): 'As for my tastes, I enjoy my food, hate the taste of any kind of alcohol, have tried and tried to like smoking but can't manage it. I adore flowers, am crazy about the sea, love the theatre but am bored to death by the talkies . . . loathe wireless and all loud noises.'

Agatha Christie was strongly associated with the development of Penguins as a friend of the firm's founder, Sir Allen Lane. It was while waiting for a train after a country weekend spent with her in 1934 that Lane was struck by the tawdriness of the books on the station bookstall and conceived the idea of 'good, well produced literature at a modest price'.

All who intend to collect Penguins should read *Allen Lane: A Personal Portrait* by Sir William Emrys Williams (Bodley Head, 1973). It must be the harshest book written by one friend about another since J. T. Smith settled the hash of the sculptor Nollekens, his former master. Of the founder of the great Penguin empire, Sir William writes: 'He read very little, either for personal or business motives, and he knew virtually nothing about literature, even about the writing of his own time . . . From the time he left school at the age of sixteen Allen did nothing to cultivate his mind or enlarge his knowledge.' Or again: 'This practice of involving others as scapegoats for his own lapses was attributable not only to moral cowardice but also to a decided streak of sadism in his nature.' With friends like that, who needs inedible fungi?

An earlier work by Sir William, *The Penguin Story*, written to celebrate the twenty-first birthday of the firm in 1956, is also indispensable to the Penguin collector. It is a lucid and entertaining account of the firm's development, with a complete catalogue at the end, showing the date each book was issued. Dr Scott refers constantly to this list, although he is anxious to avoid the mere obsession of 'making up the set'. Among the first editions he has recently acquired are E. F. Benson's *Dodo* (the 40th Penguin, 1936); Evelyn Waugh's *Vile Bodies* (the 136th, 1938); Robert Tressal's *The Ragged-Trousered Philanthropist* (the 251st, 1940); E. M. Forster's *Howard's End* (the 311th, 1941) and Christopher Isherwood's *Mr Norris Changes Trains* (the 321st, 1942) – the last of which contains the fictionalized account of that irrepressible old rogue Gerald Hamilton, of whom his *Times* obituary (18 June 1970) said: 'Not since Alice Liddell, perhaps, has there been a figure who enjoyed more *réclame* from being turned into fiction.'

Dr Scott does not intend to collect later printings of the books of which he has first editions: that way madness lies. But he would like to complete his collection of firsts, and to collect the other Penguin series. For most of his books he has paid about 5p or 10p, but today the price is often over 25p a copy. He is resigned to the fact that this account of his collection may push the price even higher – but, after all, he already has a huge collection, and – well – a Penguin in the hand is worth two in the bush.*

---

* If you wish to join the thriving Penguin Collector's Society, write to Mr D. J. Hall, 98 Hertford Street, Cambridge

Gathering Goss

One of the most prolific of English souvenir factories was W. H. Goss and Sons of Stoke on Trent. Between 1858 and 1940 this company produced thousands of wares for the souvenir market, of which the little heraldic pieces in 'ivory china' are the perfect modest collector's subject. There are huge numbers and limitless variations, and although a spectacular example can fetch as much as £45, far more can be picked up for £1–£2 on junk stalls. Goss china is the nearest ceramic equivalent to postage stamps, and as with stamps it is not necessarily the most beautiful examples that fetch most money, but the rarities and freak issues.

William Henry Goss, the founder of the firm, was born in London in 1833. He made a study of art and classical sculpture, and this enabled him to obtain a job with the Spode works at Stoke on Trent, which by 1847 were under the control of W. T. Copeland. Goss with his wife and three children moved to Stoke in 1857, where he was given a position as modeller and designer. Having mastered the technical side of the ceramics industry, he set up a works with a Mr Peake. Later he established his own manufactory in John Street, Stoke, where he remained until about 1870 when he moved to larger premises, known as the Falcon Works, off the London road.

People who have associated the name of Goss only with little armorial jugs and porcelain trinkets will be surprised by the range of adult-sized wares and even *tours de force* that the factory made. The frontispiece of the best book on the subject, *The Pictorial Encyclopaedia of Goss China** shows in colour a magnificent Moorish-Turkish-Persian style vase *c.* 1862. A richly ornamented work of prodigal virtuosity (measuring 20½ inches in height), it is equal in technique to anything produced by the Victorian Royal Worcester works, who went in for the same kind of pierced and patterned clever-dick stuff.

* By Diana Rees and Marjorie G. Cawley, and published by the Ceramic Book Company of Newport, Gwent (1970)

58

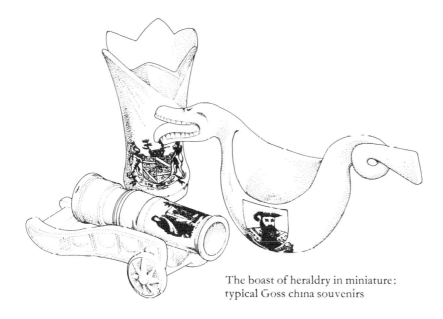

The boast of heraldry in miniature:
typical Goss china souvenirs

Goss also made lugubrious biblical-style terracotta flasks and ewers; lattice baskets in the lamentable manner favoured by the Irish Belleek factory; and, an arch-Victorian product, wafer-thin 'lithophanes' for use as lampshades, decorated with robust Titanias whose Swan and Edgar bodices glowed in the light of the oil lamp.

These products – being earlier and rarer – are more valuable than the heraldic faradiddles. They are the kind of artefact that makes pukka Gossologists bate their breath. Goss was strong on religious relics: his creations include a model of 'the font in which Shakespeare was baptized' and another of 'the font in which King Ethelbert was baptized by St Augustine in St Martin's Church, Canterbury' (complete with the arms of Canterbury). He also made a series of historic houses and cottages.

Then there are the more outlandish pieces. High on any list of fictile follies one would have to place the lifelike model of a Cornish pasty, whose verisimilitude is marred only, on certain examples, by the discreet addition of the Lostwithiel crest. Others in this line include the Rye cannon-ball; the Boulogne sedan chair; Fish basket (Channel Islands); Frid stol (sanctuary chair), Northumberland; the eponymous nose of Brasenose College, Oxford; and a model of a leek, solemnly inscribed 'Lord Harlech'.

One of his most popular models was 'Her Majesty's [Queen Victoria's] First Shoes'. As a contemporary news leaflet sententiously suggested: 'There is always something touching in looking at the shoe of a little child; for who can forecast the rough and often thorny paths the little pilgrim may have to tread!' The story of how Goss obtained the original shoe to model is one of the most lyrical *chansons de geste* of Gosslore. Queen Victoria's father, the Duke of Kent, went to live at Sidmouth in 1819 in order to benefit by the Devonshire climate. He gave a local shoemaker the order for Princess Victoria's first shoes. Instead of making only two, the cobbler made three, keeping one as a curiosity. The cobbler's daughter became the wife of Goss's porcelain agent at Sidmouth. Goss heard of this, borrowed the shoe and made an exact replica in porcelain. The shoe is four inches long, has a brown leather sole, white satin upper and is laced and tied in front with a bow of light blue silk ribbon. A binding of ribbon runs round the edge of the shoe and down the back to the heel. It would fetch about £20 today.

The value of a piece of Goss increases according to the aptness of the coat of arms to its object. For example, Queen Victoria's slipper is worth more with the Sidmouth arms than with those of Penarth. A Swiss cowbell is more desirable if inscribed 'Luzern' than 'Blackpool' or 'Southend'. A copy of the Melrose Cup, 'designed and made expressly for Wm Dick, Melrose', bearing the arms of Melrose Abbey is worth approximately £25; a piece almost identical but bearing the arms of Sandwich would sell for only £18. Anyone who wants to buy a present for Dr A. L. Rowse could look out for a Cornish pasty bearing the arms of All Souls' College, Oxford.

The Goss Collectors' Club was set up in the 1920s and has grown into an international league of about 500 members. To join you should write to The Secretary, Mrs. M. Latham, 3 Carr Hall Garden, Barrowford, Lancs.

A gem of an exhibition

It is odd how often two biographies of the same person appear at the same time, attracting those unkind reviews in which one is compared unfavourably with the other: Yukio Mishima and Charles Kingsley are recent examples. In antiques, too, there are moments when several people – scholars, dealers and collectors – seem to be moving, lemming-like, in the same direction. It is not just a matter of fashion, one imitating the other. It is something to do with the genius of a particular pocket of time (the Germans, I am sure, express that idea in one word): as if the time-fuses leading to it have all burnt out at the same moment.

By this process, there came a moment in the early 1960s when the time was ripe for a film about the trials of Oscar Wilde. Two companies made it simultaneously, and a *Punch* cartoon showed two men on a desert island, one of whom is saying to the other: 'When I get home, I'm going to make a film about the trials of Oscar Wilde.'

1972 was the year of nineteenth- and early twentieth-century jewellery. In June, Charlotte Gere's *European and American Jewellery, 1830–1914* (Heinemann) appeared, and in October Peter Hinks's *Nineteenth Century Jewellery* (Faber). The November 1975 issue of *The Connoisseur* was devoted to jewellery, with particular emphasis on nineteenth- and early twentieth-century makers: Tommaso and Luigi Saulini, the cameo carvers; the Giuliano family; and John Paul Cooper, a leading jeweller of the Arts and Crafts movement.

A Fine Art Society show in the same year was intelligently arranged in groups of jewellery which illustrated the many historical revivals that influenced Victorian and Edwardian craftsmen: the archaeological and historical revival, the Craft Revival and so on. (In the same way, future scholars may well exhibit artefacts of the 1960s and 1970s under Art Nouveau Revival, Art Deco Revival and Austerity/Binge Revival.) Mrs Gere, the leading expert on this subject, contributed a valuable introduction to the catalogue of the exhibition.

The 'long parade of ancient styles' from 1840 to 1880 began with A. W. N. Pugin and F. D. Froment Meurice; jewellery by both of them was shown at the Great Exhibition of 1851. A Gothic-style bracelet in the Fine Art Society show, made in 1857 by Hardman's, a Birmingham firm of ecclesiastical metal-workers, was supposed to have been based on a Pugin design. The most interesting example of direct historical cribbing in the show was a gold and coral cross by Carlo Doria, copied from a picture in the National Gallery attributed to Quentin Matsys. (Pictures and ancient ecclesiastical metalwork were, in general, popular sources.)

An enamelled and gem-set pendant, by Hancocks, *c.* 1855, was in the style known as 'Holbeinesque', supposedly derived from the jewellery designs by Holbein the Younger in the British Museum. A pendant by Carlo Giuliano, a ring by William Burges, and an enamelled morse by Alexander Fisher, all derived from mediaeval prototypes. Messrs. Waterhouse and West of Dublin made exact copies of Irish originals as part of the Celtic revival; and even works not directly copied might be said to have 'a touch of the Tara Brooch' about them.

Like the Celtic revival, the Hispano-Mauresque and Assyrian revivals were inspired by archaeological discoveries, including Layard's finds at Nineveh in the 1840s. The Roman goldsmith Fortunato Pio Castellani revived the ancient Etruscan art of granulation (described by Mrs Gere as 'surface decoration of goldwork carried out in minute beads of gold'), and the work of the Castellani family was much admired and imitated in England, notably by John Brogdon and Robert Phillips, who employed a number of Italian workmen, including, for some years, Carlo Doria, who may have made for him an Etruscan-style gold-fringe necklace (also exhibited in the show). The opening of Tutankhamun's tomb in 1922 brought about a new and powerful Egyptian revival.

John Paul Cooper (1869–1933) was undoubtedly the star of the show. The son of a Leicester hosier, he was a contemporary of Edward Gordon Craig at Bradfield College, where he began to read Ruskin. In 1889 he entered the office of J. D. Sedding, the architect (on whom Cooper wrote an essay, printed in a superb book issued in 1972, *Edwardian Architecture and its Origins*, edited by Alastair Service (Architectural Press)). He spent much of his time sketching and measuring churches for Sedding. After Sedding's death in 1891, Cooper worked for Henry Wilson, who had been Sedding's chief assistant. In 1892 he sent a gesso-decorated box to the Arts and Crafts Society exhibition at the New Gallery. From 1894 to 1932 he maintained an unbroken record of exhibiting with the Arts and Crafts Society. In the years following 1898, when he executed several architectural commissions, he seems to have devoted himself more and more exclusively to craft work: after the supervision of the building of his own house at Westerham in 1911, there is no further reference to architectural work in his diary.

What made the Cooper exhibits so interesting was that it was possible to compare them in each case with the original design books. For example, a cloak clasp of 1922, silver with chased and *repoussé* decoration of Cupid and Psyche, set with two chrysoprases, three garnets and a moonstone, was illustrated as No. 1067 in Cooper's stock book. It cost him £5 14s 2d to make and he sold it for £12. The price today would be approximately £250.

Here is a list of some of the other exhibits in the show (with an approximate indication of what they would now cost): a gold brooch made by Carlo Giuliano, c. 1880, with enamelled decoration set with lapis-lazuli (£1,000); a pendant by the same maker, about 1870, in gold with enamel, a sapphire, four emeralds and four pearls (£2,000); a silver and enamel brooch by Murrle, Bennett & Co, about 1905. (£60); a necklace and pendant delicately designed and made by Mr and Mrs Arthur Gaskin also about 1905, in silver and moonstones, probably for the Artificers' Guild (£150). Amongst the fine pieces not for sale was a silver necklet designed and made by Sir Alfred Gilbert (of 'Eros', Piccadilly, fame). He wound it into its contorted Art Nouveau form in twenty minutes flat for a friend of his daughter. She was on the point of departure for a ball and thought she needed some startling jewellery.

Recommended dealers include: the Fine Art Society (148 New Bond Street, London W1); Hancocks of 1 Burlington Gardens W1; Cameo Corner of 26 Museum Street, WC1; John Jesse of 164 Kensington Church Street, W8.

Silver brooch in the form of a proud peacock set with opals and mother-of-pearl. Designed by C. R. Ashbee and made by the Guild of Handicraft c. 1900

The shifting frontiers of the antique

Racing tipsters are allowed to plume themselves on their successful tips. In some newspapers, the Cassandra predictions of the political correspondents are torn out of Monday's issue and reproduced as a smug 'We told you so' when the catastrophe arrives on Friday. That excellent undergraduate paper, the *Cherwell*, was always on safe ground when it printed the headline 'Crisis looms in Union elections', for a week later there was invariably an ugly juvenile power struggle to bear it out. I think I can even indulge in a little quiet gloating myself. Early in 1973 I predicted that relics of the 1940s and '50s would soon be considered collectors' pieces. At Sotheby's Belgravia towards the end of that year a juke-box of 1952 vintage fetched £360. (The pre-sale estimate had been £100–£200.)

This 1952 juke-box, as characteristic of its time as the Dan Dare comic strip in *The Eagle*, was illustrated in Sotheby's catalogue under the brave heading 'The 1950s'. It was described in the catalogue as tenderly as if it had been a Ming bronze:

> The 'Chantal Meteor 200', a stylish 1952 juke-box designed by David Frey, has a circular revolving table which provides vertical support for one hundred records; beneath the hemispherical perspex dome, the indicator cards revolve with the records and are viewed through a television-shaped frame with chrome banding; the illuminated record selector spins within a chrome fender; the body is of black-and-white formica, chrome and wood, and tapers down to the bowed, triangular, aluminium-banded black base. Its two short, tapered legs measure 59 inches each; the words 'Chantal Meteor 200' are lettered in chrome (150 centimetres high); patent label: 'J. Foufounis patentee'; manufacturer's plaque: serial no. 2015. Chantal Ltd., Station Rd., Kingswood, Bristol.

Those short, tapered legs were the most canonically 1950s' feature of this Mekon's Delight. And did those feet in ancient time stand at the

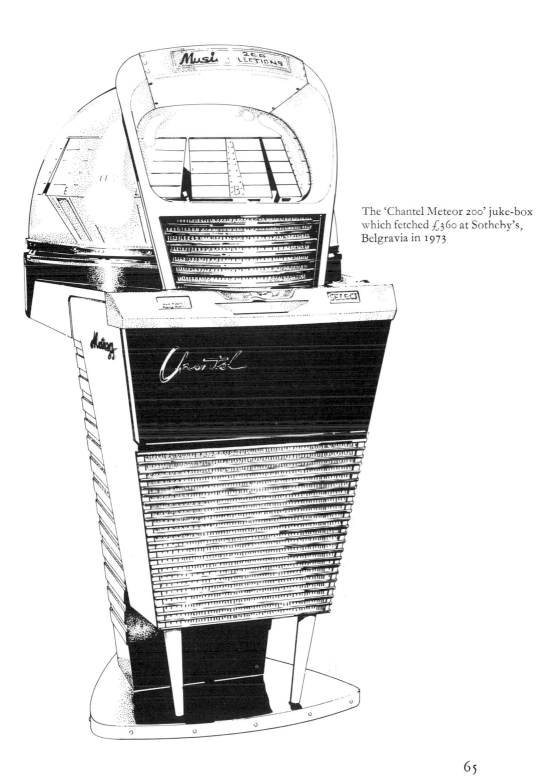

The 'Chantel Meteor 200' juke-box
which fetched £360 at Sothchy's,
Belgravia in 1973

Mecca, Walham Green? The juke-box was the kind of thing which would have been thrown out for scrap five years before. Now juke-boxes are sometimes to be seen as the centre- (and conversation) piece of a smart apartment, breathing the last enchantments of skiffle and the coffee-bar culture alongside the Chippendale, and planted firmly on the Axminster.

At the time of this preposterous development in Belgravia, the committee of the Grosvenor House Antiques Fair decided to throw open the fair to antiques and works of art up to 1930, abandoning the 1830 deadline which had obtained since the Fair began in the 1930s. The 1830 terminus was rapidly becoming ridiculous: first Victorian, Art Nouveau, then Art Deco and later even 1950s' 'antiques' came into favour and fetched commanding prices in the sale room. Most of us welcomed the decision of the Grosvenor House committee. The post-1830 section was held separately in the ballroom at Grosvenor House, at the same time as the main fair, and the same rigorous system of vetting was employed. The last thing the Grosvenor House committee wanted to attract was assorted 'kitsch' of the kind widely sold in the Portobello Road.*

There have been two further portents of the march of the antique. First, the Advertising Standards Authority published in 1973 a report on the 'instant antiques' industry – the extraordinary growth of such 'antiques of the future' as artefacts produced in limited editions in precious metal. It pointed out, for example, that the concept of the 'limited edition' is used far too loosely (the numbers issued are often grotesquely large, and are sometimes not known to the purchasers); secondly, gold or silver articles are advertised from time to time in a way which confuses the intrinsic value of the metal with the additional value which can be contributed by skilled craftsmanship; thirdly, many advertisements emphasize the investment value without making it clear how dependent future values must be on taste, world price levels and other factors. The authority therefore proposed that the number of articles in a 'limited edition' be stated in all promotional material; that all advertisements for articles of precious metal clearly specify the content and fineness of the metal used; and that all advertisements which make claims about the investment value of the articles for sale make it clear that there can be no guarantee of any future increase in value. Personally, I consider this last condition to be a little

* In 1976, in deference to the views of the more reactionary dealers, the Fair restored its pre-1830 deadline: a retrograde and short-sighted decision

harsh: that man is a fool indeed who imagines that there is a quick gain to be made from buying a commemorative medallion; and on this basis lollipop manufacturers would be obliged to print on the wrappers 'This confection may rot your teeth' – a measure, no doubt, which some dental Savonarolas would applaud.

Finally, one should take note of the growth of the admirable Commemorative Collectors' Society, which has now been in existence for five years with Sir Lincoln Hallinan as its chairman. This society deals with 'antiques of the future' (Princess Anne's wedding souvenirs, for example) and of the past, and has probably done more than any other organization to encourage the observation of proper standards in these wares. To join, write to the secretary, Mr Steven N. Jackson, at 25 Farndale Close (off Wilsthorpe Road), Long Eaton, near Nottingham.

Enduring ephemera

The last time I ever saw the late Charles Handley-Read, who with his wife Lavinia created that extraordinary collection of Victorian furniture and *objets d'art* which was shown at the Royal Academy six years ago, he said how much he hoped that someone would found a university department devoted to the study of paper ephemera. Charles, a hoarder of genius, would have made a good professor of the subject. If the department is ever set up, its members will have to give a lot of attention to advertisements. Since the eighteenth century nothing has given a better indication of popular preoccupations.

If one excepts the beautifully engraved eighteenth-century tradecards, with their rococo cartouches, advertisements are still amongst the cheapest artefacts of genuine historical interest that it is possible to collect – so cheap, in fact, that an enterprising school teacher could suggest the idea to his or her pupils as a holiday 'project'. If such a 'project' were organized, the children could be encouraged to collect both present-day and older advertisements, and to analyse what the ads tell us about the society of the time.

I have been looking recently, for example, at magazine advertisements of the 1940s and 1950s – the last age of extreme class-consciousness in Britain. An advertisement for Icilma Shampoo, of November, 1946, shows the head of an elegant woman. The caption reads: 'Softly curved chin, patrician nose . . . but she can't be beautiful without beautiful hair.' What copywriter today would attempt to sell his product by associating it with the word 'patrician?' Aged retainers were still in evidence, too, such as 'Old Hethers', the ingratiating, side-whiskered butler who recommended Robinson's Barley Water ('If you'll forgive my saying so.') An officer-type in a Rose's Lime Juice advertisement from *Lilliput* may be painting his own greenhouse but, never fear, the butler, Hawkins, is bringing him out a tray of Rose's Lime Juice. In the opinion of 'Vactric' vacuum cleaners, if you can afford to keep a maid or a charwoman, 'She will expect the best!'

Advertisement from *The Illustrated London News*,
27th October 1889

(Although the redoubtable expression of truculence on the face of the maid in question contrasts significantly with the servile deference an employer might have expected before the war.)

The birth of advertising agencies was at first viewed with general contempt: Grace Brothers of Bristol, who were amongst the earliest, crossly rejected the title, replying to a journalist's question with the words: 'Friend, we are not advertising agents; though we do give out our esteemed friend Fry's cocoa announcements.' An article in *Ainsworth's Magazine* for July, 1842 gave an analysis of the techniques used by publishers to promote book sales. The 'puff preliminary' – a rave review – was followed by the 'puff negative': 'It is not true that the talented author of *Fitz-Henry Fitz Hildebrand* disposed of the copyright of that charming work to the publisher for £1,000, nor is it a fact that the duel fought the day before yesterday at Wimbledon had any connexion with these witty volumes.' Then came the 'puff mysterious':

> It has been hinted that a certain noble duke . . . has been unable to conceal from himself that certain passages in the new novel bear reference to himself; and that some of them are calculated to cause a ruption with a beautiful and fascinating Contessa to whom he has been so long devoted and who had hitherto flattered herself that the details of her liaison with His Grace had been a profound secret. It would be well if a certain lordling who resides not a hundred miles from Grosvenor Square, and who also sat for his picture in this literary picture gallery, were to profit by the witty and caustic lessons of the author.

Advertisements often reveal that the Victorians, contrary to popular misconceptions, were perfectly prepared to call a spade a spade: the proprietors of Professor Browne's Celebrated Hair Cutting Saloons of 47 Fenchurch Street advertised with an honesty which might in other circumstances be described as bald, their 'celebrated Scurf Brushes'. But the most mind-boggling *tours de force* of copywriting came from Eno's Fruit Salts. Their mildest effort was to announce that Commander A. J. Loftus, His Siamese Majesty's Hydrographer, never went into the jungle without a tin. During four years of important survey expeditions in the Malay peninsula, Siam and Cambodia, he had recorded only one instance when a member of the party was attacked by fever – 'and that happened after our supply of FRUIT SALT ran out'. More impressive still were the fruit salt adventures of Joseph Thomson, F.R.G.S., among the Masai of Kenya:

> My voice not being astonishingly mellifluous it did duty capitally

for a wizard's. My preparations complete, the Brahim being ready
with a gun, I dropped the Salt into the mixture; simultaneously
the gun was fired and lo! up fizzed and sparkled the carbonic acid
. . . the chiefs with fear and trembling taste as it fizzes away.

There was apparently no limit to what could be said in praise of Eno's.
Under the headline 'How Kandahar Was Won', the proprietors quoted
from *Mess Stories*, by G. W. Vyse: 'During the Afghan War I verily
believe Kandahar was won by us all taking up large supplies of
ENO'S FRUIT SALT and so arrived fit to overthrow half a dozen
Ayub Khans.'

The prices I have paid for old advertisements range from £4 for a
sentimental calendar issued in 1904 by William Pook, Draper and
Coal Merchant, of Horley and Redhill, Surrey, to 5p for a weird postcard advertising Brooke's Monkey Brand Soap (the monkey heads
flit towards a cherub, with angel's wings attached to each – doubtless
obeying the principle that cleanliness is next to godliness), and 50 cents
in a New York junk shop for a 1920s' picture of a girl in spectacles,
which bore the caption: 'Milady dressed for sports looks her smartest
in All-Shelltex Shur-on spectacles.'

If I were to choose a modern exhibit for a collection of advertising
ephemera, I would opt for a brown plastic bottle which once landed
on my desk, its side ornamented with a gold question mark. Removing
the gold stopper, I released a long serpent of paper advertising a
'terrific new range of cosmetic products for men', which was to be
launched at a luncheon on board the M.V. Abercorn, berthed at
Charing Cross pier. A letter followed, adding: 'Incidentally, the
European Heavyweight Boxing Champion Joe Bugner is joining us
for our launch celebrations and I'm sure this will be a super occasion'.
Bottle and letter have been stowed away for eventual presentation to
the University of Meaningful Ephemera.

As a general introduction to the whole subject of advertising, E. S.
Turner's *The Shocking History of Advertising* (Penguin, 1968) could
hardly be bettered; but I would also specially recommend a more recent work, Diana and Geoffrey Hindley's *Advertising in Victorian
England, 1837–1901* (Wayland, 1972), which is entertainingly written
and illustrated with some of the most comic examples of Victorian
advertising, including the outlandish one which attempted to show
on a sketch-map how Lord Roberts's route, on his march to Kimber-
ley and Bloemfontein in the Boer War, spelt out the word 'Bovril'.
Bovril also advertised, after the declaration of Papal infallibility in
1870, 'The Two Infallible Powers: The Pope and Bovril.'

Victorian prints

We cannot come fresh to such a poem as *The Lady of Shalott*. It has been too much anthologized. It has been cannibalized by P. G. Wodehouse for funny quotes. Its drugging metre has been plundered by Sir John Betjeman for the comic effects of *Indoor Games Near Newbury*.

> Rich the makes of motor whirring,
> Past the pine-plantation purring,
> Come up, Hupmobile, Delage!

Single lines have been stolen as the titles for thrillers (*The mirror crack'd from side to side*). Others have acquired ridiculous modern *double entendres* ('The curse is come upon me, cried The Lady of Shalott'). Archaeologists have grubbed about for the remains of many-tower'd Camelot on Cadbury Hill.

But if we want to experience something of the poem's pristine potency for the Victorians, we can turn to Holman Hunt's painting *The Lady of Shalott* – in its way scarcely less of a masterpiece than Tennyson's poem. In the painting we see her just after the fateful look; penned in by the ornate rail of her loom, tangled in skeins of thread, her hair flaring in electric disarray. In the shattered mirror we catch sight, like her, of the helmet and plume of Sir Lancelot. The whole thing looks like the cabin of some fantastic Jules Verne spaceship, which has suddenly become depressurized, causing everything to hurtle about.

We know that Tennyson felt Hunt had taken unnecessary liberties with his text. In G. S. Layard's *Tennyson and his Pre-Raphaelite Illustrators* (1894), the poet is reported as having said 'My dear Hunt, I never said that the young woman's hair was flying all over the shop'. Hunt replied, 'No, but you never said it wasn't'. As Layard jocosely remarks, the fact that Tennyson does not mention the Lady of Shalott's hair 'would hardly preclude Mr Hunt from representing her other than bald.' And apparently Tennyson became wholly reconciled to the crimped and flying tresses. Layard also tells us that when he

first saw the great canvas in an unfinished state, the Lady was nude –
'and I could not but tell the artist that it seemed to me almost sacrilege
to drape so fair and exquisite a conception which taught the lesson at
one flash that modesty has no need of a cloak'.

Hunt's painting was sold at Christie's in June 1961, for 9,500
guineas. If it were to be offered at auction today, I suppose it would
fetch £30,000 or more, because of the vast increase of interest in the
Pre-Raphaelites. That puts it rather beyond the scope of most of us.
But there is an alternative, and a splendid one, in the print (after the
painting) by J. D. Miller. It is a brilliantly faithful reproduction of the
original; indeed, some might consider that the velvety tones of the
print's monochrome are preferable to the rather aggressively vivid
colours of the original.

In 1847 the Printsellers' Association was formed. It aimed to prevent the production of print proofs beyond an openly declared number. This number was to be notified to the association before the
issue of the first impression on a form which it provided. The first
meeting of the Association was held in the Old British Coffee Rooms,
Cockspur Street, London, on 5 February, 1847, and its first president
was Dominic Colnaghi, head of the firm of printsellers.

In its first year, seventy-five works were stamped, consisting of
15,322 proofs — an average of 204 proofs from each plate, including
artist's proofs, proofs before letters, and lettered proofs; the publishing value of these was £72,000. By 1892 the number of works declared
at the Association's office was 212, while 41,796 proofs were stamped,
giving an average of 197 proofs a plate at a total publishing value of
£214,016.

In that year the Association issued the first of its alphabetical lists of
engravings covering the period 1847 to 1891. These books are an in-
valuable record, and a must for anyone who aims to collect Victorian
prints on a large scale. A typical entry is for the print of *The Cricket
Match:* 'Painters: W. Drummond and C. J. Basébé; engraver or etcher:
H. Phillips; style: mezzotint; size: 35¼ ins. by 23⅜ ins.'

Then follow prices of the various kinds of proof, and the numbers
of each issued (175 artist's proofs at eight guineas, for example); and
finally, the name of the publishers, Gambart and Co. Gambart was a
roguish old dealer who lived in St. John's Wood and patronized such
artists as Alma-Tadema, who lived nearby. Most engravings were
executed by men with foreign names on whom little work has been
done: *A Sibyl* by Charles Waltner; *Flora* by Eugène Gaujean; *Spring* by
Abel Mignon; *Vespertina Quies* by Emile Boilvin; *The Mill* by Emile

73

Sulpis; *The Annunciation* and *The Mirror of Venus* by Felix Jazinksi.

Jazinski did etchings after Burne-Jones; his subtle gradations of colour test the eye more stringently than any number of chromatic King Cophetuas or rainbow skies. Then there are the prints by Whymper, father of the man who led the ill-fated Matterhorn expedition in 1865. Also worthy of note are the prints after the visionary painter John Martin: *Sadak in Search of the Waters of Oblivion* (executed by Alfred Martin, John's brother); *The Plains of Heaven* and *The Great Day of His Wrath* (by Charles Mottram), for example.

From the Christian fundamentalism of Martin one turns to the hymns to pagan materialism of Sir Lawrence Alma-Tadema and his friend Edward Poynter. I have seen a good print of Alma-Tadema's *Baths of Caracalla*. The engraved inscription records that the original was in the collection of Samuel H. Bronson of New Haven County in the United States. *Queen of Sheba's visit to King Solomon* by Poynter is the kind of work which might have inspired Rider Haggard or the director of a movie spectacular.

Prices for prints currently range from £50 to £180; those of works by Martin and Burne-Jones fetch the most, while Alma-Tadema and lesser artists – Blair Leighton and Valentine Walter Bromley, for example – are in the lower reaches.* Anyone with a collection of these need not be ashamed of asking people up to see his etchings.

* For a panoramic survey of the Victorian print trade I would recommend that you read *Gambart: Prince of the Victorian Art World* by Jeremy Maas (Barrie and Jenkins, 1975). One of the best dealers in prints is the Maas Gallery, 15a Clifford Street, London W1

Chiselled profiles

I often promise myself a holiday of total relaxation – lying on sun-soaked beaches while my body turns to mahogany and my mind to pulp. The fact is, however, that I cannot bear a completely unproductive holiday: I tire of the waves raving across the shingle and the surf-riders hallooing to each other from their boards, and am seized by the feeling that 'I must get up from the sea again'.

One year it was Devon and Cornwall. I spent the first two days basking on beaches like a Galapagos lizard. The third day found me traipsing, only semi-bronzed, round parish churches, where I began to make a note of interesting epitaphs. In the beautiful churchyard of Altarnun I found one to Digory Isbell (d. 1795) and his wife Elizabeth (d. 1805): 'They were the first who entertain'd the Methodist preachers in this County and lived and died in that Connexion but strictly adhered to the Duties of the Established Church.' The quality of the carving was outstanding, and I discovered that the tomb had been an early work of the sculptor Nevil Northey Burnard, the son of an Altarnun stonemason.

You can read a good account of him in *Cornish Characters and Strange Events* (John Lane, 1908) by The Revd. Sabine Baring-Gould (the author of that lugubrious hymn 'Now the day is over'). Burnard was a child prodigy. You can still see in Altarnun the fine head of Wesley which he carved at the age of sixteen above the old meeting house. Sir Charles Lemon of Fowey became his patron, and Burnard was later introduced to the Queen and Prince Consort.

He was allowed to cut a profile of the Prince of Wales, who was a boy at the time of the execution of the work. In Truro I saw the statue of Richard Lemon Lander which he cut on the latter's return from tracing the Niger River in 1830–31. Burnard later became a metropolitan curiosity, produced at London parties to entertain the company with his rustic sayings. The life must have proved too heady: he took to drink and died in poverty at Redruth in 1878.

Daniel Gumb was another Cornish sculptor who signed his carved epitaphs. I saw some of his work at Linkinthorne, Cornwall, where he was born at the turn of the eighteenth century. Gumb, another character described by Baring-Gould, was a great eccentric. He made himself a weird home under a stone near the Cheesewring. The roof served him as an observatory and he carved on it with a chisel 'a variety of diagrams, illustrative of the most difficult problems of Euclid'.

Travelling round parish churches is one of the best ways of initiating oneself into the study of sculpture. Snobs have often tried to define a gentleman – 'one who has a nanny'; 'one who uses a butter-knife even in private', and so on. But surely the most reliable historical distinction is between those whose tombstones are inside the church and those whose tombs are outside in the graveyard, to be buffeted into anonymity by wind and rain.

In a church in Dartmouth I came upon a monument to Roger Vavasour, dated 1695 and signed by Robert Weston. The quality of the sculpture was so impressive that when I got home I consulted Rupert Gunnis' *Dictionary of British Sculptors* (Odhams, 1953) to find out about Weston. Gunnis is not given to hyperbole, and when he says of certain Weston monuments, 'the figures have all the grace and movement of the Italian Renaissance, while the design anticipates the work of William Blake', we can be sure that Weston is no amateur. Colonel Maurice Grant, in his *Dictionary of Sculptors* (Rockcliff, 1953) says that in Weston, Gunnis 'may be said to have discovered, or rediscovered, a new English genius'.

What interested me most about Weston's monument to Vavasour were the figures of the child mourners. These reminded me strongly of the superbly modelled pottery statuettes of John Dwight's daughter Lydia, who died as a child in 1673. These statuettes, made in Fulham stoneware (Dwight was the founder of the Fulham factory), have sometimes been ascribed to Grinling Gibbons – temptingly but not convincingly.

We have no birth date for Weston, whose earliest known work is 1696, and his latest 1733; so it is just remotely possible that he modelled the Lydia Dwight figure in 1673; although, I must admit, not very likely, as he seems to have been a Devon man based in Exeter. Just a hunch for the students of Dwight to eliminate; but in any case, Weston should obviously be made the subject of a learned monograph, and I urge this task on any new graduate in art history.

I hope I have said enough to show how educational and stimulating church visits can be for the student of sculpture. He should own a copy of Gunnis; and he should certainly read the volumes dealing with sculpture in the Pelican History of Art, especially *Sculpture in Britain, 1530–1830*, by Margaret Whinney (Penguin, 1964), the leading expert on the subject (although I cannot quite forgive her for omitting Weston). For a more international conspectus, obtain *European Sculpture, Bernini to Rodin*, by David Bindman (Studio Vista, 1970), a concentrated and well-illustrated study.

By now you may have reached the point where you either want to begin a collection of sculpture, or at least have a few fine pieces about the house. For outdoor sculpture, I would recommend a visit to Crowther's in the North End Road, London SW6. For smaller indoor pieces, however, I suggest two of the most civilized shops in London: Mallett of Bourdon House, Davies Street, W1; and David Peel, 2 Carlos Place, off Mount Street, W1.

In the past, Mallett's stock has included a second-century A.D. Roman Venus from Syon House; a French madonna head, rather like Marlene Dietrich; two marble Roman babies, considerably repaired; an early English Apollo, fifteenth century, which Mallett's tracked down from a garden fête; an English white marble bust of a bewigged gentleman with protuberant eyes, and two late eighteenth-century bronze figures of Voltaire and Rousseau.

David Peel had in stock when I called an early nineteenth-century English head, 'La Zingarella', after an antique statue in the Louvre, perhaps a Diana; a 1530 Venetian bronze 'close to Pietro Lombardo – you could say this would be a more expensive article than the "Zingarella"'; a sardonic French bust, *c.* 1640–50, with a very baroque wig; the lion head from an early sixteenth-century porphyry fountain; a marble profile of Louis XIV from the circle of Coysevox; and a Flemish terracotta dated 1764 of two figures holding a full cornucopia. Their cup overfloweth; and among the fruits is a lizard – not the complacent Galapagos variety, but exactly like Bill the Lizard in *Alice*. David Peel commented, 'Lizards also turn up a lot in Augsburg silverwork and in ivories – on bases and so on'.

This was a cosmopolitan selection. But if you decide, as perhaps you sensibly should, to specialise in English sculpture, David Peel had in stock an early nineteenth-century bust of George III by Turnerelli. 'English' is stretching a point; for Peter Turnerelli (1774–1839) was the Dublin-born son of an Irish woman and of James Tognarelli, an Italian modeller. He made a famous bust of Grattan which Canova, on a visit to England, described as the best modern bust he had seen here. He was the first sculptor of busts (Gunnis says) to portray his sitters in contemporary dress instead of conventional classical costume. This bust showed George III at his most gaping and Hanoverian.

If you want to collect escaped church monuments, Mr Peel sells those too – at the time of my visit he was exhibiting a St Dominic holding a lily, in the temperate tradition of the northern Renaissance. It had been ransacked from an altar of *c.* 1500.

Hallmarks of success

Wynyard Wilkinson had his second book published when he was twenty-one: *Indian Colonial Silver* (Argent Press, 1971). It was an extremely scholarly and well-illustrated survey of European silversmiths in India from 1790 to 1860 and their marks. From research in the India Office Library, Mr Wilkinson was able not only to ascribe pieces to their makers in Calcutta, Madras and Bombay, but also to reascribe to silversmiths in India certain marks which had always been considered British. The book also clarified some marks previously ascribed to South Africa, and even eliminated one or two from Canada.

Wynyard Wilkinson comes of a colonial family. He was born in Nairobi where his father was a District Commissioner. His interest in silver began early. When he was only fourteen, and at Sevenoaks School, he made a catalogue of the Duke of Bedford's silver collection at Woburn. When he left Sevenoaks, he joined the staff of Coutts' Bank in the Strand, and worked there for two years. 'They really looked after me. It's a terribly good training. You meet a lot of people who will be useful to you afterwards; and you learn discipline – you *have* to be polite to people, however rude they are to you.' In his lunch hours, sometimes even during his elevenses, he would buy and sell silver at a sale room within two minutes' walk of the bank. This was Debenham Storr, where silver and jewellery sales were held each Monday. After he had been at the bank for two years, he was approached by 'someone I'd never heard of', the Queen Anne Press. The firm commissioned, and published when he was only nineteen, his first book, *A History of Hallmarks* (Queen Anne Press, 1971). 'They gave it away with Rothman's Hallmark cigarettes – you smoked ten packets and sent in the coupons. We got rid of over 82,000 of them.' He would like to see the book republished; he holds a half share in the copyright.

He had to leave the bank to write the book. With the money he

Teapot bearing the mark of Lattey Brothers & Co. of Calcutta (*c.* 1840s).
Height: 14 inches

made on it, he bought a half share in a stall at the Chelsea Antique Market. Later he moved shop to Grantully Castle, Aberfeldy, Perthshire, a building with Stuart associations, where he rented the entire ground floor. He operated under the name 'Silver Lyon', because Thomas Daniel, an eighteenth-century goldsmith trading in Foster Lane next to the Goldsmiths' Hall, worked under 'the sign of the silver lyon'.

I visited him during his Chelsea days to get an idea of the things he sold. He showed me a Glasgow silver lemon strainer, 1828, with two handles for suspending it over a large punch-bowl. It is of especial interest because the maker's mark WM AM ('as it were, William Macdonald and Andrew Macdonald') is not in Sir Charles Jackson's famous marks' book. He also had a powder funnel, apparently for face powder rather than gunpowder, London, *c.* 1660, by Christopher Shaw. Mr Wilkinson was amused by a description of an equally rare piece which appeared in the catalogue of one of the big London sale rooms: 'This item is almost unique on account of its rarity.' 'Absolutely meaningless,' said Mr Wilkinson. I noticed that he had not marked on the tickets the weight of any of the pieces. 'No, I refuse to treat pieces of silver like sacks of potatoes.'

One piece that must have weighed quite a lot was a quart mug, Edinburgh, 1788, by A. Grierson. I asked whether he had anything

80

in stock relating to the subject of his *Colonial Silver* book. I was shown a silver beaker, about 1830, with a cover 'to keep the flies off': it had been made by Gordon and Company of Madras. The cover was hand-beaten rather than spun. He also had several silver meat skewers, often bought today as paper knives. One of 1842, by Robert Garrard, had silver flights on the end, like those of an arrow. Mr Wilkinson explained that such pieces were sometimes given as archery prizes. By far his oddest exhibit was a silver toecap for gout sufferers to sew into a sock, by Charles Rawlins, London, 1824.

Although he has a crisp, alert manner and an on-the-*qui-vive* expression, Wynyard Wilkinson is not cockily precocious or bumptious, even if he does have a somewhat dangerous tendency to say things like: 'There are only four people in Britain who know about silver.' One of those four is Mrs G. E. P. How, who contributed an approving foreword to his book on Indian colonial silver. Mrs How, who deals in silver at Pickering Place, St James's, described one of the ways in which Mr Wilkinson's book has changed silver expertise.

> For many years the researches of those interested in late Scottish provincial marks have been bedevilled by pieces bearing a maker's mark and a thistle which appeared to be of late Scottish origin but which could never quite be fitted in. The most notable of these pseudo Scottish marks is that of the maker's mark JH accompanied by an anchor and thistle; in the past these marks have been ascribed to Greenock, but recently it has become obvious that they do not belong there and an Indian ascription has been tentatively advanced. Now Mr Wilkinson has been able positively to ascribe them and many others to Calcutta.

Mr Wilkinson is at work on a book which will cause similar consternation – about the silversmiths of the West Indies. Among other distinctions, he has been made a Fellow of the Society of Antiquaries of Scotland.

I am not the first to write a profile of Mr Wilkinson. When he was in India, *The Statesman*'s interviewer was amused that Mr Wilkinson was able to walk round Calcutta without a map, because of his India Office researches. The interviewer wrote: 'He managed to convince some collectors that their valuable Scottish silver collection was actually Calcutta silver. In minutes, the silver's value plummeted.'

Wynyard Wilkinson eventually moved his antique silver business to the grandeur of Duke Street, St James's. He was later forced to leave by a disastrous burglary; but, with his energy and scholarship and youth, he is likely to surface again in the antiques world.

Follies and fantasies

An exhibition of 'Follies and Fantasies' held some years ago at the Brighton Art Gallery and Museum made even the Royal Pavilion look restrained. Where else could one have seen under one roof Sir Edwin Landseer having his portrait painted by animals; telephone receivers in the form of lobsters; a cast of Lady Blessington's hand, and a silver bell push in the shape of a pig with a ruby snout? Only one thing could have made the exhibition better: if it had been the collection of one man, a parade of one man's subconscious. Apart from anonymous loans, the catalogue acknowledged 188 lenders of 623 exhibits.

The greatest collectors – such men as Horace Walpole and William Beckford – have been fantasists. Ministers to their own environment, they created their collections as something to escape into. Sometimes the collections took precedence over the outside world. As Macaulay sarcastically observed of Walpole: 'After the labours of the print-shop and the auction-room, he unbent his mind in the House of Commons. And having indulged in the recreation of making laws and voting millions he returned to more important pursuits, to researches after Queen Mary's comb, Wolsey's red hat, the pipe which Van Tromp smoked during his last sea-fight, and the spur which King William stuck into the flank of Sorrel.'

Strawberry Hill and Fonthill were palaces of fantasy. When the contents of Fonthill were about to be sold, William Hazlitt wrote: 'It is a desert of magnificence, a glittering waste of laborious idleness, a cathedral turned into a toy shop, an immense museum of all that is most curious and costly and at the same time most worthless, in the productions of art and nature. Mr Beckford has undoubtedly shown himself an industrious *bijoutier*, a prodigious virtuoso, an accomplished patron of unproductive labour, an enthusiastic collector of expensive trifles – the only proof of taste he has shown in the collection is his genius for getting rid of it.'

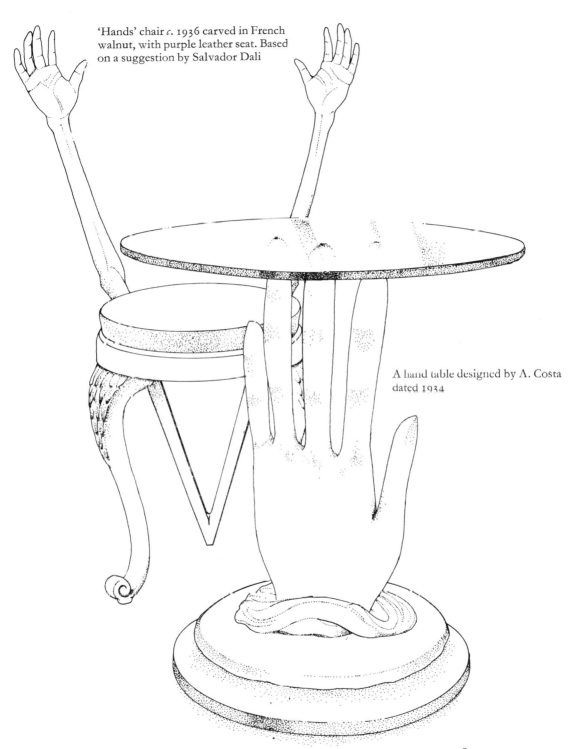

'Hands' chair *c.* 1936 carved in French walnut, with purple leather seat. Based on a suggestion by Salvador Dali

A hand table designed by A. Costa dated 1934

James Reeve, a portrait painter who when I visited him was living over Olympia Station in West London, is the only modern collector I know who has collected, not to fill elegant cabinets, or to form a series of anything, but simply because these were the things he wanted about him. And what things! There was a wooden baroque shrine with barley-sugar columns which came from an old colonel in Exeter. Like Reeve, he was a Roman Catholic convert, and when he died his Nonconformist housekeeper threw out all the papal trappings. A mummified monkey was given to Reeve by the uncle of Princess Elizabeth of Toro.

On the mantelpiece was a model of Crippen hanging; inside a drawer in the platform I saw a piece of the rope with which he was hanged. 'Believe it or not, that was given to me as a first prize at a children's party when I was six. It was the first object that fired my collection.' Reeve also owns a Victorian trade card printed 'William Marwood. Executioner. 6 Church Lane, Horncastle, Lincolnshire, England.' There were skulls galore, shells, corals, stuffed birds, an eighteenth-century artist's lay figure of boxwood, puppets, advertisements for giants and dwarfs, an egg perched on birds' legs, and an ivory snail, emerging with horrible liquescence from its helter-skelter shell. Everywhere branches, lianas and great kek stalks were creeping or hanging: you would think he needed a machete to get to bed.

How is such a collector formed, and where does he acquire the raw materials of fantasy? James Reeve was born in 1939. At six, he was sent to Pinewood School, and at once became a collector. 'Everyone collected there. The headmaster collected ties and tiepins. The maths mistress refused to throw away any of her empty talcum-powder tins. The Latin master, Nathaniel Wade, was a world authority on wild flowers. I collected pigeon feathers. We were given prizes for collecting. One boy collected cuttings from *Vogue*, which his mother sent to him, and he was an object of envy.'

Then to Rugby, which he loathed. 'One went on appalling long-distance runs until one's heart cracked. One had to retire to the churchyard to read.' There was not much collecting at Rugby, although 'everyone stole books from the library when they left. When I became a Roman Catholic, I sent mine back. A friend of mine removed a complete set of Lady Mary Wortley Montagu's letters.'

He thought highly of two of the staff – the headmaster, Sir Arthur Fforde ('later remarkable, as head of the BBC, for refusing to have a television set'): 'he always gave the impression that he hated the place as much as oneself'; and a Shakespearean scholar called Mr Tosswill, 'who worked on the rather undemocratic basis of selecting the cream of his pupils and making them into an elite club'.

Among his contemporaries he found only one kindred spirit, Anthony Short, who is now a film director. 'I remember one marvellous occasion, one of those field days when the whole school corps marched off to do battle with Stowe. We were supposed to shoot at them with blank cartridges, which are really extremely dangerous. If you got hit, you were out. Anthony and I had the happy idea of shooting ourselves: we eliminated ourselves for the whole afternoon and had a delirious time exploring the temples and grottoes of Stowe – a pleasant change from Rugby, where the main monument was to William Webb Ellis, the inventor of Rugby football.'

In 1958 he won a modern languages' scholarship to Magdalen College, Oxford. On arriving there, he was disconcerted to find that he had been allotted 'a mean little room over the main street', instead of in the eighteenth-century New Buildings, where someone he had particularly disliked at school had a lush suite of panelled rooms. After three months he left. His tutor thought enough of him to trail him down to Devon to try and persuade him to return, but without success.

In 1959, Reeve went to Italy. He had lodgings with two anachronistic sisters above the Piazza Antinari, Florence. One of them, who spent her days making whalebone corsets, would ask him every time he returned from England where the horses had watered. At this stage Reeve got to know Harold Acton, 'who was extraordinarily kind'.

To make ends meet, he hit on the idea of crystallizing chrysanthemums by dipping the petals in molten sugar. 'They became all the rage; they were decadent, smelt of autumn, and tasted of Channelle mushrooms.' An exhibition of his paintings was held at the British Institute. Plunging, as he easily does, into the macabre, he laid on a mock funeral for an English woman who had always wanted to witness her own obsequies. 'There was an empty coffin. Everyone came. She and I sat in a corner of the church opposite the one-time French embassy. Of course, when she finally died, wolf, wolf, nobody came.'

He was invited to a costume party at an American finishing school. 'I wore my death costume – made up by a little *modiste* in Florence, with dead flies stuck all over it. On the way there with my partner, Mary Jo Brant, my motor car gave out, and I had the awful business of pushing it into a garage, dressed as, and feeling like, death. When I was announced at the party, all the servants crossed themselves and fled. I was frightfully hungry. I had hired a skull as an accessory and during dinner I stuffed it with *canapés* to take away. When I was introduced to the headmistress, an absolute cornucopia of *entrées* fell out on the floor.'

In 1963 Reeve went to Spain, and stayed there for five years. On his arrival in Madrid, he went to the circus and met Don Eduardo, the impresario of the dwarfs. He was offered the job of hunting for dwarfs on behalf of the circus. 'I travelled the length and breadth of Castile, paying 4,000 pesetas (about £20 at that time) for a dwarf. In the minute villages one was received as the Second Coming. Even as late as the nineteenth century, as you probably know, dwarfs were left out on the Sierra to starve or be eaten by wolves.'

Reeve worked for a season at the Circo Pirce, designing costumes and sets for dwarf tableaux. 'My great coup was to discover Doña Alicia, a most beautiful dwarf, whose portrait I painted. She appeared as Marie Antoinette with a cardboard head which was ceremoniously lopped off with a dinky guillotine. My days with the circus ended abruptly: a Peruvian mystic fell in love with me. I introduced her to one of those white-faced, sexless clowns with a sequinned hat, and he tried to rape her. I had to leave.'

He rented a studio in the house of the widow of Alfonso XIII's court photographer. 'At one end of the room were all these painted stills of rooms in the palace. Alfonso couldn't take his mistress to the palace, so he had this brilliant idea of having them photographed against stills of the state rooms. The court photographer had illicitly kept copies of all the photographs. *Paris Match* would pay a fortune for them. I wish I had got hold of some.'

In Spain he collected things wherever he went. He was given relics by the sacristans of churches. In a monastery outside Segovia he acquired three skulls. 'In repairs to the refectory, several skeletons were found of visiting monks from a sister order, who had been killed by plague in the fifteenth century. The monks wrapped them up for me in greaseproof paper, just like Harrod's, and I took them away in my old jalopy.'

Reeve's main reason for leaving Italy and making a pilgrimage to Spain was to study Velázquez, as an antidote to 'the saccharine horror of Perugino'. Velázquez is still the painter he most admires. He attended the academy – 'the last school in Europe where they still practised the seventeenth-century anatomy-school methods of Vesalius. One studied portions of the body. It was valuable to feel the length of a tibia, or to hold an eyeball in one's hand.'

In 1968 he returned to England. 'I would hate to be an expatriate. After more than five years one becomes . . . odd.' A portrait painter who achieves good likenesses without slavish representationalism, Reeve has no lack of sitters. A cousin of the Literary Longfords, he has painted several of them; Lady Antonia in a high-backed chair, Lady Rachel in a raccoon coat, Mrs Judith Kazantzis lying on the floor. Recent sitters have included Lord John Cholmondeley, the Knight of Glin, and the late James Pope-Hennessy. The element of fantasy spills over into the backgrounds. With apprehension the subject peers round the canvas to see whether Reeve has painted in a monkey in a death embrace with a rattlesnake, a Hieronymus Bosch strawberry or a moulting albatross.

Where can the novice fantasist start his collection? Obviously it is the essence of such a collection that most of the *objets* should be *trouvés*, and that means foraging in junkshops for yourself. But James Reeve buys his sprays of coral, at about £1 each, from Sarogny Art Products, 11 Craneford Way, Twickenham. His shells come from The Shell Shop, Lyme Regis; but a good London source is Eaton's Shell Shop, 16 Manette Street, W1, where you can buy tun shells for between 30p and £1.50 each, a nautilus shell for about £3.50, an Aristotle's lantern for 15p, a Babylonian shell for 25p, a fan coral from about 20p to £3.50, a sea biscuit for £1.50, and a clam shell like a casket for 75p to £4.50.

The best London shop for such fantasy antiques as antler chandeliers or stuffed animals is Hirst Antiques, 59 Pembridge Mews, W11; it used to be a bakery, and the old ovens are still in the basement, making it more than ever like a primitive's vision of Hell. For a jaunt at the weekend, I recommend 'Not the Old Pharmacy' in the Surrey village of Albury (you can take in Albury Park, the stately home, too). This antique shop, run by a Dutch dealer who specialises in fossils, ancient glass and weird optical instruments, was originally called The Old Pharmacy. The Pharmaceutical Society wrote to say that it could not be called that, and in order to save the cost of repainting entirely, the shop was renamed 'Not the Old Pharmacy'. The shop is often open on Sunday mornings.

On the bottle

Everything seems to have societies and get-togethers devoted to its collection nowadays. There is, for example, an annual convention of the Chinese Snuff Bottle Society of America – and you can't get much smaller than snuff bottles. In America there are also serious collectors of different varieties of barbed wire. For all I know the addicts of this prickly form of nostalgia hold meetings in Wisconsin and issue a monthly bulletin called *Barbed Comments*. Postcard collecting is another growing mania, and postcard fairs are now held at regular intervals throughout the country.

One of the most flourishing societies for collectors of small antiques is the Wine Label Circle, founded in 1952. Wine labels – or 'bottle tickets', as the Victoria and Albert Museum sometimes calls them – are the little tags, usually of silver or enamel, which were made, mainly in the eighteenth century, to identify the contents of bottles or decanters. The best book on the subject, and an admirable one, remains Norman Penzer's work of 1947, *The Book of the Wine Label*. This was reprinted in 1974 and published under the auspices of the Wine Label Circle, with a foreword by André Simon.

No one could accuse Dr Penzer of lacking versatility. His other works include *Cotton in British West Africa, including Togoland and the Cameroons* (1920); *The Harem: an account of the institution as it existed in the Palace of the Turkish Sultans, with a history of the Grand Seraglio from its foundation to modern times* (1967); and *Paul Storr: Silversmith and Goldsmith 1771–1844* (Batsford, 2nd ed. 1971). From such a man one would expect a diverting and wide-ranging text, and one is not disappointed. Penzer rejects the idea that wine labels are 'just a Georgian triviality'. 'The humble bottle ticket,' he proclaims, 'is pregnant with interest – historical, sociological and aesthetic.'

The wine label was not a development of those seventeenth-century delft wine bottles which advertised their contents in blue glaze ('Sack' and so on) on their white bodies; it owed its existence to the Methuen

Treaty of 1703 and to the gradual appreciation and consumption of port wine in Britain. When it was discovered that such wines as port improved in the keeping, and that bottles were the better for having been laid down for several years, it became necessary to identify the contents, first by tags of parchment, later by bone rings and finally by silver bottle tickets. This was the birth of the wine label: its death came with the use of the printed wine label.

When did the bottle ticket first appear? No seventeenth-century examples are known. As Penzer says, 'The Civil War and Commonwealth hardly contributed to the development of table refinements.' Ale and sack were the only drinks in common use. The greater luxury of the Restoration – so familiar to collectors of English furniture – and the gradual appreciation of port in the first half of the eighteenth century (from about the accession of George I in 1714) made it necessary to distinguish the contents of different bottles, 'so dark and uninformative in themselves'.

In Hogarth's engravings of drinking scenes in 1731 and 1735 there is no sign of bottle tickets. But in *An Election Entertainment* of 1755 three bottles have hand-written parchment labels – gin, burgundy and champagne. And this was a popular scene: silver bottle tickets were already in use by the well-to-do. Amongst the earliest recorded silver labels are some marked 'ID', or possibly 'SD', of about 1743. Penzer thought they were by Isaac Duke of Wych Street, Drury Lane, entered in 1743, although he also considered the claims of Sandilands Drinkwater of the Hand and Coral, Gutter Lane, a silversmith who had two marks, the first of 1729–38, the other of 1739–56. Before the Marking Silver Act of 1790 (30 Geo III C31), hallmarking on wine labels was on a voluntary basis; but some labels were marked and Penzer gives a long list of known label-makers which has been added to and modified since 1947.

Enamel was another material frequently used. There is no collecting subject of which our knowledge has been so revolutionized in the past few years as enamels. As Arthur Negus ruefully said on a *Collector's World* television programme, 'We used to call all these things either Battersea or Bilston [South Staffordshire], but we now know that a lot of them were made in Birmingham, and we're not as sure as we used to be.'

I notice that the Victoria and Albert Museum labels a group on the walls of the Ceramics department 'Decanter labels ("bottle tickets"); Birmingham or Battersea about 1751–56', while another group is labelled 'South Staffordshire, about 1760–70'. We know that Battersea did make labels, for the Battersea sale of 1756 included 'a quantity of beautiful Enamels, colour'd and uncolour'd ... consisting of ... Bottle Tickets with Chains for all sorts of Liquors, and of different Subjects'. Other materials used less frequently were Sheffield plate, 'invented' by Thomas Boulsover in 1743, gold, pinchbeck, electroplate (from 1840), Britannia metal, nickel-silver, tin, bone, ivory, tortoiseshell and mother-of-pearl.

Reading the *Transactions* or *Proceedings* of a collectors' society – in this case the *Journal of the Wine Label Circle* – is rather like prying into someone's private diary. One reads of overdue subscriptions, of the proposal for a club tie allied with the perplexing question of what the women will wear instead, and of laggardliness in contributing articles; though the Wine Label Circle seems happily to be free of the ferocious disputes that rack certain other societies.

A lot has happened since Penzer's *Book of the Wine Label*. For example, an article by the Circle's president, Mr John Beecroft, in the *Journal* for June 1971 reveals that the maker identified by Penzer as Samuel Bradley was really Susanna Barker – a real victory for Women's Lib. The whole early history of the wine label has in fact been rewritten. The present view is that wine labels had their earliest beginnings in the decade 1729–39. When Penzer wrote his book, no label had yet come to light bearing the lion of the pre-1739 cycle; in more recent years over twenty-five have turned up. The earliest makers are now considered to be Sandilands Drinkwater, John Harvey and James Slater, and Mr Beecroft's opinion is that of these the earliest was possibly James Slater, whose early mark was a Roman 'IS'.

Another useful section in one of the Circle's journals was an article on pitfalls for the collector. These include labels that began life with the name of a fairly common drink, such as Madeira, but had this original name erased and replaced by one of the sought-after curious names such as Nig, Bottoms, Bounce or Zoobitty-match. Another example of these odd names is Shrub: Pamela Vandyke Price tells me that it is an anglicized version of the Arabic 'Sherb'.

As most casual buyers of wine labels will want to use them on decanters, I asked Miss Vandyke Price how long wines should be kept in a decanter. She replied that sweet wine will always stand up to aeration longer, although this applies mainly to fortified wines, and she offers the following advice.

Sherry: a Fino should be drunk within twenty-four hours; it begins to go off after two days and should never be kept more than five. *Sweet sherry*: this can be kept in a decanter ten days to a fortnight. Put the decanter in the least cold part of the refrigerator or, preferably, in a cool pantry. Never leave a decanter on the sideboard in a warm room. Everything depends on the amount of air to which the wine is exposed. If you put a bottle of wine in a magnum decanter the result will be disastrous. *Vintage port*: absolutely not more than twenty-four hours (other ports, ten days to a fortnight). *Brandy*: several weeks; not too warm, however, if you want to avoid evaporation. *Champagne:* champagne wine labels are a puzzle. It may be that, in the days when the term 'champagne' was used in a much broader sense, it applied to the still red and white wines of the area; on the other hand, there may have been a snobbishness about decanting champagne. One champagne shipper has a champagne decanter in its original cooler: the decanter lies on its side in something like a glass wine cradle.

Miss Vandyke Price added that decanters should be cleaned and thoroughly dried immediately after being emptied. She did not recommend the antique dealers' method of a twist of newspaper, but suggested a little Milton left overnight, with *very* careful rinsing afterwards.

For silver wine labels, good shops are Shrubsole of 43 Muscum Street, London WC1; Simon Kaye of 1b Albemarle Street, W1; S. J. Phillips of 139 New Bond Street and N. Bloom of 153 New Bond Street, W1. A good label can be bought for under £50, though you would have to pay far more for the fascinating label from the Beecroft collection by Benjamin Tait (Dublin, *c.* 1785) which depicts the first balloon ascent in Dublin from the Ranelagh Gardens in January 1785. I found some magnificent Battersea (?) enamel labels at M. Ekstein, 90 Jermyn Street, London W1, ranging in price from £175 to £500.

Should you wish to join the Wine Label Circle, the honorary secretary is The Revd. E. W. Whitworth, 4 High Street, Tisbury, near Salisbury, Wiltshire.

Two characteristic silver rococo wine labels

Trophies of war and austerity

After a 1920s' *canapé* by Marcel Coard fetched more than £13,000 in the Jacques Doucet sale in Paris in 1972, even those who are convinced only by prices ceased to scoff at Art Deco. Less than ten years ago, however, we were still hearing 'But I grew up with that stuff!' and 'I gave something just like that to the jumble sale only last week'.

It is tiresome, therefore, to find that the new collectors' subject, 'Austerity/Binge' – the decorative arts of the 1940s and 1950s – is being treated to the same unaffectionate derision now. I began studying this period of decorative arts in detail in 1968 and wrote a book on the subject in 1975 (Studio Vista). I feel, therefore, that I am now in a position to suggest some guidelines to those who are beginning a collection.

Why 'Austerity/Binge'? The period begins with wartime austerity and continues up to and including the 'You've never had it so good' era of the late fifties. For the Americans, however (who became so dominant an influence here in the fifties), this was much less a period of austerity, and when I asked an American dealer what they had called the period immediately after the war he replied, 'We called it the Binge'. This fresh-sounding yet period word seemed to me to typify the English 'regeneration' feeling of the 1951 junketings and beyond. I was amused to read in David Niven's *The Moon's a Balloon* that Montgomery posted just inside his Fifth Corps headquarters a large notice which read 'Are you 100% fit? Are you 100% efficient? Do you have 100% Binge?' Niven writes: 'We never discovered what he meant by "Binge" because nobody dared to ask him.'

The collector can begin with wartime relics, most of which naturally have little aesthetic appeal. Here are some of the things I have collected: a stamp designed by Fougasse to stick over the receiver rest of your telephone (or round the column of the 'candlestick' type) showing Hitler's head and inscribed 'Maybe he's listening too; careless talk costs lives'; a miniature chamberpot with Hitler's face inside, inscribed 'Flip your ashes on Old Nasty – Jerry No. 1 – The Violation of Poland'; the *British Boys' and Girls' Wartime Playbook* (colour your own barrage balloon); an air-raid warden's collapsible pencil-cum-torch; gas masks; prisoner-of-war envelopes; ration books; two books, *Allotmenteering in Wartime* by G. T. McKenna and *Eating without Heating* by W. E. Shewell-Cooper; a figure of Churchill by the Bovey Pottery; a pottery vase in the form of a hollow V for Victory, inscribed on the base 'Sample A.M. Jan. 1942'; a plastic American brooch forming the words 'Remember Pearl Harbor' (the 'Pearl' part is an artificial pearl); and (borrowed) a poster torn down in Cairo during the war, which advises soldiers to avoid prostitutes and VD with the immortal heading: 'There is no MUST about sexual intercourse'.

Because the period after the war was one of austerity, most of the things made then were not of high quality – plywood furniture, for example. But one thing it was possible to produce again with great quality was books. Some of the best English design went into *Contact*, a periodically issued book which was one of Lord Weidenfeld's early publications, with such men as F. H. K. Henrion and Vivian Ridler as the inspired art editors. You can also see from these books how class still obsessed people: one fashion article shows what the 'wage-girl', the 'salary-girl' and the 'capital girl' were wearing in 1948. Another publication that clearly reflects the interests of the time is the *Saturday Book*, founded in 1940 – an *omnium gatherum* which exhibits mass psychological tendencies because there was no constraint on the editor, and no political animus, to direct what he chose as articles and illustrations.

As with Art Deco, where certain motifs occur again and again (sun-rays, fountains, racing dogs, Aztec temples), Austerity/Binge has its distinctive pictorial themes; the mermaid is one, and the balloon another. I think it is not too far-fetched to suggest that in these motifs we see a process of 'amicization', of de-fanging and making friendly again the threatening symbols of war, in the way that an oyster turns a piece of grit into a pearl. Thus the mermaid is a lyrical symbol that the seas are free once more of the menace of submarine and torpedo; the colourful balloon is an amicizing version of the parachute. Heraldic motifs also come in, to make friendly the martial badges of war. And there are constant references to the circus, fairground, painted barges, gypsy caravans, Punch-and-Judy shows and other large-scale manifestations of English folk art which appealed to Englishmen returning from the war. Circus lettering – rather like Wild West

'Wanted' lettering in America – became popular in advertising and book design.

All very well, you may say, but where is the quality that will command high places on the modern market? Where are the equivalents of the Marcel Coard Art Deco *canapé*? Certainly the best American furniture, by such designers as Eames, will soon be worth a lot; but if I had to advise the 'investment'-minded collector I would tell him to go hotfoot to Italy and buy up as much as he can of the superb furniture made there in the late 1940s by such designers as Carlo Mollino, Enrico Rava, Paolo Buffa and Renzo Mongiardino. The influence of surrealism is strong in these works, as it is also in the equally desirable furniture of Paul Laszlo in the United States.

The Festival of Britain marks a division between two decades of decorative art, a caesura almost as decisive as that between the 1920s and 1930s. We may note in passing the circus and fairground aspects of the Festival: the Dome of Discovery like a big top, the Skylon, a kind of stylized helter-skelter; the Battersea Pleasure Gardens known soon enough as the Battersea Funfair.

The fifties were a time of increasing whimsy. The British got over the stultifying effects of the war; they held a Festival to signal their own recovery. They had a Coronation to cheer them up still further: more pageantry and heraldry. Gay Paree was open again, and its striped-awning cafés appeared on headscarves and skirts. The 'cocktail-cherry' style of table leg and chair leg came in, derived perhaps from models of molecular structure – a design cliché that reached its height in the Brussels Atomium. Flower arrangements *à la* Constance Spry were in. Emett and Hoffnung, with their whimsical conceits (Festival railway, vacuum-cleaner orchestra) became popular. So did vintage and veteran motors (*Genevieve*), penny-farthing bicycles, and cranky old machines of all kinds. The balloon was at its top altitude of popularity (*Round the World in 80 Days; The Red Balloon*). Flying saucers materialized everywhere. It was the longest Silly Season in history.

Collecting Austerity/Binge offers two possibilities: to buy cheaply things that will increase in value, and to make fascinating discoveries about a subject as yet hardly explored. This means, of course, that most of your buying will have to be done from junk shops and market stalls.

Left: Public house mirror with mermaid design, late 1940s

The point of old lace

In 1963, when I was editing the anonymous 'From a Collector' column in *The Times* to which various writers contributed, a Mrs Gabrielle Pond wrote to inform me that she was a lace collector. She asked whether I would consider commissioning someone to contribute an article on the subject; she could find no modern work of use to her. In my reply, I told her that I knew of no lace expert. Would she, as a collector, like to contribute an article? She did so; it was published; and five years later Mrs Pond also had published a short book entitled *An Introduction to Lace* (Garnstone Press, 2nd rev. ed., 1973), which is clear, entertaining and by far the best guide for the beginner collector.

Another book on lace appeared in the same year as the revised edition of Mrs Pond's guide: *Lace* by L. W. van der Meulen-Nulle (Merlin Press).* It is slightly larger than Mrs Pond's book, and its most appealing feature is the many photographs of Old Master portraits of gentlefolk wearing lace: the 'millstone' collar of Italian bobbin lace worn by Beatrix van Sypestyn (1593–1663); the cap, collar, cuffs and apron with bobbin lace worn by a little girl portrayed by D. D. Santvoort (1610–1680); the coiffure and dress of black blonde bobbin lace worn by Queen Maria Luisa of Spain in Goya's portrait – and so on. It is a cliché of art historians that the painting of lace by certain Old Masters is so exquisitely accurate that the lace could be woven again from the painted pattern.

In 1964 I advised collectors interested in investment to buy old posters; and in thirteen years prices for some of them have increased a hundredfold. In Phillips's sales, which have been held regularly since 1973, you can still buy interesting examples of lace for between

---

* Other books on the subject useful for the collector are *Lace* by Virginia Churchill Bath (Studio Vista, 1974), which provides close-ups, in photographs and sketches, of different kinds of lace and a great deal of technical information and *Victorian Lace* by Patricia Wardle (Herbert Jenkins, 1968)

One of a pair of cuffs designed by Lewis F. Day.
Honiton lace c. 1900

£10 and £15, which makes it the ideal subject for the non-millionaire beginner. But prices for the better pieces have already taken off. A flounce of nineteenth-century Brussels lace 6¾ yards by 17½ inches, fetched £120 in 1975 (now approximately £250), and a pair of unusually wide lappets (bonnet strings) of early eighteenth-century *Reseau Venise* lace (49 inches), sold for £240 (now £300). In a sale of March 1975, a late nineteenth-century lace-maker's glass lamp, 6½ inches high, sold at Phillips for £75 (now £150). To encourage the small-budget collector it should, however, be mentioned that in the same sale the following lot fetched only £10 (now £20): a triangular shawl of Chantilly; a similar flounce; a good length of Youghal lace of unusual design; a fragment of seventeenth-century Venetian point; an early shawl collar of Maltese; sundry bobbin appliqué edgings; and a strip of beetle wing embroidery on black net. Certainly, these examples would make very useful 'study pieces'.

There are two main types of lace: bobbin lace and needlepoint. To produce bobbin lace, one must plait and weave threads wound on to bobbins: the lace is made on a firm pillow to which a pricked-out pattern is tacked, and each twist of the bobbins is held in place by a pin. The pattern is formed by more compact weaving than that used in making the mesh. Incidentally, the bobbins themselves are collected now. The best known bobbin laces include *Point d' Angleterre* (1650–1750), which probably originated in England and was imitated in

Flanders for the English market; the fine lace of **Honiton**, Devon (where lace is still made) in which the sprigs and motifs were worked separately and then joined; *Valenciennes*, the boldly patterned narrow edging of which was often used on baby clothes; *Binche*, a Flemish bobbin lace based on an elaborate mesh background; *Mechlin* (Malines), which is very fine and soft to the touch, and was usually made with intricate hexagonal mesh and often used as a border for Indian muslins in the early nineteenth-century; *Brussels*, of texture similar to Mechlin but often, as with Honiton, made in separate sprays; and *Coralline*, a Venetian lace with a design reminiscent of branching coral.

Needlepoint, like bobbin lace, is made upon a pillow, but it is worked with a needle and thread in buttonhole stitch. Its principal varieties are *Reticella*, the earliest type of needlepoint, a close geometric form with a serrated edge; *Point de Venise*, the most famous needlepoint lace, composed of flowers built up with raised edges (Mrs Pond describes the effect as 'almost like carved ivory'); *Point d'Alençon* and *Point d'Argentan*, made in France from about 1650 but also at Burano in Venice with a light and gauzy appearance achieved by loose buttonholing; *Point de Gaze*, a Brussels lace in which flowers are often built up from layers of superimposed petals; and *Hollie Point*, an English lace of close texture made from the MiddleAges until the mid-eighteenth century, and originally used for such religious occasions as weddings and christenings – hence the name 'holy point'. There are also laces which combine bobbin and needlepoint techniques, such as the Belgian *Duchesse* or the tape lace made in Italy.

Beginners would be well advised to attempt to build up a sample collection of small pieces of every type. I refer them to Mrs Pond's book for the further refinements of lacemaking – appliqué (including Carrickmacross, *c.* 1850); cutwork; tambour (including the Isle of Wight variety favoured by Queen Victoria); crochet ('the only lace of distinction in this category was made in Ireland'), and black lace, which includes the beautiful Chantilly, and the silk bobbin lace with bold flowered design and delicate mesh ground known as *Blonde*.

The collector should also acquire a general knowledge of the history of lace making and weaving: the profusion and wonderfully skilled workmanship of lace in the seventeenth century; the founding of lace schools in France by Louis XIV about 1665, under the tuition of Venetian experts, which challenged the supremacy in lace-making of Italy and Flanders; the high prices of lace in the eighteenth century, with consequent smuggling; the ruin of the industry by the French

Revolution which outlawed the kinds of extravagant dress which were embellished with such aristocratic trimmings. The Revolution almost made lace-making extinct: early in the nineteenth century, when Napoleon I ordered an elaborate *layette* for the infant King of Rome, there was great difficulty in finding enough surviving lace-makers to carry out the royal command. Finally the age of machine-lace arrived, and then the final death blow of the Great War and the changes it brought in fashion and daily life. Mrs Pond ruefully records: 'Almost any pieces made in the last fifty years will not compare with the lace made in previous centuries.'

In 1968, Mrs Pond could write: 'During the many centuries that it was made until the beginning of this century, antique lace was highly appreciated both in terms of beauty and money. Now nearly seventy years later, it has no market at all.' This no longer holds true, and all the signs are that old lace – without the arsenic – is going to be very good 'box office' indeed.

Buildings on the bookshelf

What can you collect if your principal interest is architecture? The man who craves many mansions, like the man with a passion for mighty Wurlitzers, may be able to afford one; for the rest of us the answer is architects' drawings and books of architectural designs.

I recently talked to five dealers who specialize in this kind of thing (though all of them deal in other kinds of art books too). One of the better known dealers in architectural books and prints in London is Ben Weinreb who has a large shop next to the British Museum (93 Great Russell Street, WC1). He informed me that the main buyers of architectural books are American universities and libraries and that this was so in the nineteenth century, too, when American architects were drawing heavily on the past in their promiscuously eclectic buildings.

There is, however, a growing interest in the subject in England, which is largely attributable to our great architectural writers – Professor Sir Niklaus Pevsner ('no one ventures ten miles from home at the weekend without the relevant Pevsner Penguin in the car,' Weinreb commented), Sir John Summerson (who lives above Sir John Soane's Museum in London) and, of course, Sir John Betjeman.

The essential reference book for any beginner in architectural book-collecting is *A Biographical Dictionary of British Architects*, by H. M. Colvin (John Murray, 1954). Sir John Summerson's Pelican history, *Architecture in Britain, 1530–1830* (Penguin, 1969), is another basic reference book. If one were to dream up the nucleus of an ideal collection of books of architects' drawings and designs, one would unfortunately have to rule out the first architectural book in English, John Shute's *The first and chief groundes of architecture* (1536), as only three copies are known to exist, and none has come on the market. But the second book, Serlio's *The first book of architecture* (1611), can be bought for approximately £2,500. The *Vitruvius Britannicus*, seven volumes in all, which portrays the English country house from the restoration to the time of Henry Holland (and costs between £500 and £1,000 depending on whether you can obtain the first five or all seven tomes) is considered a *sine qua non*. Other suggestions for an ideal collection might include Inigo Jones's designs, published by William Kent in 1727, *Parentalia* (1750) by Christopher Wren's son Christopher: the Leoni edition of *Palladio* (1715–16); James Gibb's *Book of Architecture* (1739); *The Works of Architecture* of Robert and James Adam (three volumes, 1773–86); and perhaps something by Soane, Repton and Loudon – the latter a champion of the picturesque and the man whom some judge to be the founder of suburbia.

Weinreb's catalogues of the 1960s – on the picturesque, Gothic, the Society of Dilettanti and so on – have themselves become collectors' pieces, to the extent that he finds himself in the invidious position of having to buy them back. His former partner, Paul Breman, has issued an index of them, which must surely be the first contemporary index of a dealer's catalogues. If you intend to collect architectural books, this is one of the basic reference works. Breman now deals on his own from 1 Rosslyn Hill, London NW3.

Breman's own catalogues are less grandiose than the old Weinreb ones; but they show a similar talent for isolating a subject and illustrating it with relevant books. For example, one of his catalogues is entitled *Cottage Architecture of the Early Nineteenth Century*. This includes William Barber's *Farm Buildings; or Rural Economy* (designs for cottages, farmhouses, etc.), the first book of Irish rural architecture, which appeared in 1802 and owed much to Henry Holland; Charles Augustus Busby's *Series of Designs for Villas and Country Houses* (1808); and John Buonarotti Papworth's *Rural Residences* (1818), described by Breman as 'perhaps the most wholly delightful of all the cottage books', with twenty-seven coloured aquatint plates.

One of the items in a more recent catalogue by Breman, *English Architecture, 1598–1838*, is a lithograph prospect of Henry Holland's East India House in Leadenhall Street, London. The print, which dates from approximately 1820, shows the façade that Holland designed in 1798 to hide an existing building. Dorothy Stroud, in her excellent book on Holland, *Henry Holland* (Country Life, 1966), writes 'The Centre of his new façade was dominated by a hexastyle Ionic portico supporting a pediment in which was placed a sculpture of John Bacon, representing George III defending commerce in the East.

Paul Grinke, who deals privately from his London flat (38 Devonshire Place, W1) by appointment only, also worked for Ben Weinreb at one time and helped to compile some of the Weinreb catalogues. He once showed me a second edition of Papworth's *Rural Residences* (1832). Plate XI depicted 'A Vicarage House in correspondence with the architecture of the neighbouring church' – a very Oxford movement idea. I also examined *Observations on Hospitals for the Cure of Insanity*, written in 1809 by Robert Reid (an Edinburgh architect) and Andrew Duncan (professor of medical jurisprudence in Edinburgh University). 'This is generally classed as a medical book,' commented Grinke, 'but it is just as fair to call it an architectural book, especially as it has a fine engraving of a lunatic asylum at the end'. At one point in the book, Reid ominously observes: 'It may be fairly calculated that among forty patients, two or three of each sex will be in such an outrageous state as to render it necessary to have recourse to the strictest coercion.' Grinke also stocks original drawings. I examined the plans of Ardgowan House, Renfrewshire, which were drawn up for Sir John Shaw Stewart by J. C. Cairncross in 1797 and Francis Johnston's 1806 drawing of the end of the proprietor's room in the Bank of Ireland – which was modelled on Soane's design for the governor's room in the Bank of England, 1804–5. An amusing item with which he would not part was Sir William Chamber's design of 'A bath for Lord Middleton', the pedimented temple of which was to be the third Viscount Middleton's bathhouse overlooking the lake at Peper Harrow, Surrey (*c.* 1762–63).

I warmly recommend one dealer outside London, Sir William Duck of The Cupola, Balmont Road, Hastings, Sussex. The Cupola is an 1835 Italianate mini-palazzo based on the Tower of Winds, Athens. More like a pagoda than anything else, it looks across town and sea, and was designed and originally owned by Joseph Kay, surveyor to the Foundling and Greenwich Hospitals. In the tower hangs an oriental censer fitted with red glass and an electric light. 'It makes it look like a rather superior brothel – and I'm afraid we did have one letter addressed to 'The Copula',' commented Sir William. From the top of the tower my host, a William Morris figure with wild red hair, points out the thicket where Holman Hunt painted *The Strayed Sheep*, a church built by Coventry Patmore, another church where Titus Oates's father was vicar, and yet another in which Rossetti was married.

'I am a Goth,' says Sir William. He probably has the largest collection in England of books on the Gothic. His catalogues are written with tremendous ebullience. Of *Villa and Cottage Architecture* (1968), he writes: 'Almost all the splendid plates are of extremely ambitious and absolutely monstrous Carborundum Gothic affairs displaying a frenzy of polychrome and zig-zag brick and stonework; vicious chamferings; warring planes that leave the eye bruised and bleeding; prickly iron finials . . . vile entrance porches; and chimney pots that can only have belched solid black lumps of hexagonal smoke.' How long before Paul Breman catalogues the catalogues of Sir William Duck?

Finally, there is Marlborough Rare Books, 35 Old Bond Street, London W1, which amongst a rich stock, once boasted what must surely have been the most wonderfully outlandish of all architectural books. This is Charles François Ribart's *Architecture Singulière: L'Ele-phant Triomphal* (Paris, 1798). The author planned to build in the Champs-Elysées a house in the form of an elephant, three storeys high, including a ballroom. It was to be equipped with air-conditioning and furniture that folded into the walls. The drainage system obviously gave Ribart his most exquisite joy. Now, *there* is a project for a millionaire who wants to add to the gaiety of nations.

Among the kitsch and curiosities of New York

I first wrote about the New York antiques shops in 1971, when the American people were going through the phase of demanding 'organic' foods and reviling phosphates and enzymes. That mood had a parallel in the back-to-American-crafts collecting, which rejected the pompous mannerism of cabriole legs and ball-and-claw feet.

Six years have wreaked a big change. The new collector is younger and more knowledgeable than his 1971 counterpart. New York dealers today estimate the average age of their clients at 25–35 years old as opposed to the 40–60 age group in 1971. Most of them also agree that the private collector has been increasingly replacing the interior decorator, and is more interested in a piece as an individual aesthetic object than as a representation of a period or style. One of the larger establishments suggested that in 1971, eighty per cent of their clients were interior designers; now sixty per cent of their clientele are private collectors. The new collector, it seems, buys for quality rather than to indulge a mood.

In 1971 I examined early American folk art at what was then The Peaceable Kingdom, 390 Bleeker Street, Greenwich Village. It included primitive 'mocha' or spongeware pottery (mostly nineteenth-century); old samplers; patchwork quilts; rag dolls; and bird decoys, on which there is a learned book, *American Bird Decoys*, by William J. Mackay, Jr. (Dutton, 1965). The bird models, realistically carved from wood, included terns, owls, loons, herons, two extinct species (the Passenger Pigeon and Labrador Duck), and the almost extinct Eskimo Curlew (not to be confused with the Eskimo Curfew or Eskimo Knell). Folk art is usually anonymous, but Mr Mackay was able to identify many makers, to the extent that one illustration is captioned: 'This tiny green-winged teal decoy, its body carved from a cypress tree and its head of cedar, shows the unmistakable skill of either Lee or Lem Dudley, the twin brother decoy makers of Knott Island, North Carolina.'

A primitive American oil painting I saw and liked at The Peaceable Kingdom depicted an encampment scene along the Potomac from the war of 1812. The scene, with its women camp followers in Empire dresses, almost mimic soldiers in their gaudy frogged uniforms, and little steep-roofed tents like card houses, had a refreshingly lyrical character.

The 390 Bleeker Street site is now an antiques store called Pat Sales. This shop carries much the same kind of pieces as the Peaceable Kingdom: 'mocha' pottery, old samplers, and patchwork quilts. These items can be purchased for between $85–$585, with the top price representing a bride's quilt, c. 1840, from Massachusetts. It is a white-on-white medallion motif, exquisitely executed and in perfect condition. Bird models similar to the ones available at the Peaceable Kingdom can be purchased for about 20 per cent more than the $65–$150 price of 1971. Pat Sales has a wide variety of paintings in both the academic and primitive styles. Prices range from $900 to $2,500. Most notable was a *Portrait of Master Hibber*, painted by the Philadelphia artist Robert Street in 1849. Street combined a lush and primitive landscape at sundown with a rather academic but expressive figure dressed in a formal maroon velvet jacket. It was priced at $2,200.

The former owner of the Peaceable Kingdom, George Schoellkopf, now has a shop at 1065 Madison Avenue under his name. He no longer carries spongeware pottery, rag dolls and samplers, but recently had a nice collection of rare bird decoys and quilts. Other recent stock includes a tiger-maple drop-leaf tea table c. 1760 from Massachusetts. It is an extremely small and delicate piece with ball-and-claw feet, priced at $20,000. A painting by James Bard, c. 1850, of the side-paddle wheeler *The Commonwealth* which travelled up and down the Long Island Sound, was also on offer recently at $22,000.

The other American fad of 1971, the nostalgia craze so grindingly anatomized by *Time*, *Newsweek* and *Life*, was also reflected in collecting trends at that time. A paperback, *Curios and Collectables: A Price Guide to the New Antiques* (Dafran), edited by Ralph DeVicenzo, dealt with such items as Mickey Mouse watches, comic books, matchbox cars and Ku-Klux-Klan relics. A Mickey Mouse watch of 1935 in mint condition with the original box is worth approximately $300. A Betty Boop watch of the same year is worth between $400 and $500. Other interesting items mentioned in the book include Ku Klux Klaniana: the 1916 photograph of Imperial Wizard Colonel William J. Simmons, founder of the Klan; a Klan marching banner; and a snake-skin bullwhip, inscribed 'K.K.K.' on the handle.

One of the best shops for the more appealing souvenirs from the near past is in The Village – the antiques-infested triangle of Bleecker, Hudson and Christopher streets. In the window of Second Childhood, 283 Bleecker Street, amongst a fascinating assortment of old toys, I caught sight of a nubile rubber Olive Oyle doll. 'It's rubber – most of your rubber's all dried out now', the proprietor explained. I also examined there a Mickey Mouse movie-jecktor (including six rolls of film) which is now worth approximately $50; a 1930s' wind-up aeroplane ($10); a Hopalong Cassidy watch (which can cost between $6 and $100, depending upon condition); the first Mickey Mouse radio of 1932, made by Emerson (an item which is becoming increasingly rare and might cost between $300 and $400); and a 1950 Shirley Temple doll – enough to make the most ardent nostalgic quail. Owners of these kinds of antiques include Dustin Hoffman, whose Christmas present from his wife one year was an 1860 dentist's chair with a clown as the dentist. The spring mechanism in the toy activated a hammer under the chair, creating a suitably horrendous din.

In 1971 there were excellent Art Deco shops in Hudson and Christopher Streets. Second-Hand Rose at 549 Hudson was choc-à-bloc with chrome furniture, 1920s' French billboards, and steamship Gothic furniture – such as collapsible verandah chairs which might have come from a Charles Addams mansion. One dealer (Ruby-Shoes Day at No. 521 Hudson Street) specialised in 'movie-star stuff', much of which came from the MGM Studios sales of 1970. Glamorous costumes from the 1930s, which made even Ossie Clark's look like wan pastiche, were labelled after the stars who had worn them: Greer Garson, Katherine Grayson, Liz Taylor and Jeannette MacDonald. I was even tempted to try on a striped Mickey Rooney blazer for a size thirty-four chest.

The only one of these stores which now remains on Hudson Street is Second-Hand Rose at No. 549. Second-Hand Rose has gone through a number of transitions in the past six years. In spite of the fact that it stocks the same kind of merchandise, its emphasis has shifted to the 1940s and 1950s. It has recently had in stock a large selection of bamboo, rattan, and wicker furniture dating from the 1920s–1950s, all of which have been refinished in original period fabrics. A 3-piece set costs approximately $900. A 1950s' bamboo chaise longue is $525. The most pronounced change is the large selection of period wallpaper and fabrics. Many of these wallpapers were hand-screened on newsprint or waxed paper; they cost $20–$45 for a double roll. The wide variety of designs include palms, ferns

A relic of Hollywood's golden age: Jeanette
Macdonald's costume from *Maytime*

and flamingoes from the '30s and '40s in varied shades and colours; and cowboys, Second World War battle scenes, locomotives and space ships from the 1950s.

The most extraordinary shop in The Village in 1971 was The Duck and Dolphin in Bleecker Street, which should have been called the Dachsund and the Chihuahua, for it was furnished, wall to wall, floor to ceiling, with dogs. The dogs were made in all materials, from carrara marble to plastic: dignities and impudences in all sizes. When the shop was closed, it was guarded by a (live) Alsatian and a Great Dane. The Duck and Dolphin is now a barber's shop; the original owners now sell from their house in Pennsylvania.

Away from all this kitschery, the market in grander antiques was still flourishing in 1971. Madison Avenue had (and still has) some of the best shops. In the shop of Alan G. Malloy I saw a fine marble bust of Caligula (looking like the then fashionable draft-dodger with his moustache, sideburns and clean chin) which was later sold to the Getty Museum in California. Scarabs were well represented. In the Royal Athena Galleries, 1,000 Madison, I especially liked three Roman figures of gladiators from Anatolia (second century A.D.).

Some of the furniture in Florian Papp Ltd (No. 962) was almost stagily English – it reminded me of the use of Lincoln's Inn Fields as a backdrop for the film of *Tom Jones*: four-poster beds; a yew-wood veneer Queen Anne gaming table; a magistrate's chair, mid-eighteenth-century, inlaid with the symbols of justice; and a very squire-archal drinking table with swivelling decanter stands inset for swinging port between the gentlemen. It was all rather as if Bertie Wooster and Jeeves, like their creator, had made their home in New York State and brought over the ancestral furniture. Florian Papp have maintained a high degree of quality over the past six years. They stated that fine antiques have doubled in value while moderate pieces have gone up 50–75 per cent. They recently had in stock a horseshoe hunt table similar to the one described in 1971 (could it be the *same* one?) for $7,500, a George I walnut burl chest with brushing slide, for $8,500, and Chippendale library steps, with rabbitted and dovetailed joints that folded into a table, for $2,600.

Lilian Nassau, 220 East 57th Street was and is the Art Nouveau and Art Deco queen of New York. She sells the beautiful glass lamps of Louis Comfort Tiffany – an American product; and the sleek Art Deco furniture of Emile-Jacques Ruhlmann. (I once met Barbra Streisand there, who was at that time furnishing her new apartment entirely in Art Deco.) Her recent stock has included a rare and beautiful Art Nouveau enamelled copper vase of Calla-lilies by Louis C. Tiffany. She estimates that Nouveau furniture has risen in value by more than 100 per cent since 1971, with Lalique decorative pieces and Art Nouveau jewellery up by substantially more. The prices of Art Deco pieces have, however, remained steady – possibly because they were priced so high from the start.

The Antiques Center at 415 East 53rd Street, by the East River, which I recommended in 1971, still has some first-rate English pottery, notably Wedgwood, and French 1920s' drawings and books so fine that Paris dealers travel over to purchase their stock. In 1971, I paid a call on Vicki Glasgow, who had an entire shop of musical boxes, including an actual musical chair which played *The Marseillaise* when you sat on it. Vicki has now moved out of the city to 147 East Post Road, White Plains, N.Y. She has a wider range of musical boxes than in '71, and also issues a catalogue. Her stock has recently included a rare turn-of-the-century Regina Disc, that gives you a tune and a piece of gum for the price of a nickel.

For a completely different experience in American antiques' collecting, I drove with a New York dealer in 1971 the fifty miles to Englishtown, New Jersey, where there was, and still is, a fleamarket to end all fleamarkets. We started at 4 a.m. on a Saturday morning. Hundreds of cheapjack dealers travel there, sleeping overnight in their trucks. The keenest New York dealers wake them up with flashlights in the early hours of the morning. It reminded me of some brutal form of fishing, the fish lured to the surface with dazzling lights. In the winter they light fires and burn furniture. There is much at Englishtown that burning could not harm: not many objects are priced at more than three dollars. You can inspect there some of the artefacts which Americans collect: glass insulators from telegraph poles, peanut signs and group photographs (in 1971 a recent vogue – the price rises according to the number of heads in a photograph). I bought six 1940s' neckties at twenty cents each; one sports a design of gushing oil wells, and looks very tycoonish. My prize purchase was a 1913 advertisement for Campbell's soups – a reproduction which anticipated Andy Warhol's by more than half a century. I met Warhol two days later and gave it to him – but he was not as crestfallen at being pipped to the post as I had hoped. I thought we might have done a swap; after all, his soup can reproductions are not genuine antiques . . .

Partial to an American past

The first thing any antiques collector who anticipates visiting Los Angeles should do is to obtain an excellent book on the city by an Englishman, Reyner Banham: *Los Angeles, the Architecture of Four Ecologies* (Harper and Row, 1971; Penguin Books, 1976). Its David Hockney cover painting embodies the three things most characteristic of the city: blue sky, palm trees, private swimming pools. Los Angeles looked, indeed, like a gallery of scenes by Hockney when I arrived there in 1973: the temperature was in the '70s, purple ice plants were growing outside Fred Astaire's house in San Ysidro Drive, and neo-baroque grilles covered the goldfish pools in the gardens of the rich (to keep the raccoons at bay.)

With a kind *cicerone*, the sculptress Pascal, prepared to give limitless time and make introductions, I was able to visit some of those para-disal gardens and the homes of their owners, such as that of Mervyn LeRoy, who directed *Little Caesar* and *Quo Vadis?*, produced *The Wizard of Oz*, and has a fine collection of paintings, including the best Van Dongen portrait I have ever seen.

I also had the ideal guide to the antiques shops of California: Milo Scott Bergeson, who then kept an antiques establishment called The Dolphin near the Stanford University medical centre. (The Dolphin, which is now in San Francisco, is generally thought to be the best of the smaller antique shops in that city.) He flew out from San Francisco to introduce me to the antiques of L. A. and, later in the week, guided me around the shops of San Francisco.

The Angelenos were very partial to the past just then – and by that I do not simply mean nostalgia for the glories of a dying Hollywood, although that was evident enough. A big campaign to preserve historic houses was raging across America and the word 'historic' en-compassed, amongst other things, the somewhat unfortunately named 'sod houses' of Ord, Nebraska. A Sod House Society had been founded, open only to those who had 'lived in a sod house, worshipped in a sod church, taught in a sod school, or worked in a sod structure'. Della Harrison of Norfolk, Nebraska, had written a poem about these pioneer homes:

> Humble little old sod shanty!
> Yet it was like a shrine to me,
> Better than the great mansions,
> For it was home you see.

On a grander scale are the Spanish mission buildings of the eighteenth century; Victorian houses of Charles Addams' type, and Art Deco palaces. Anyone whose interest in antiquity goes beyond antiques that can be put on a shelf, should consult *Architecture in Southern California* by David Gebhard and Robert Winter (Peregrine Smith, Inc., 1977).

The antique shops of Los Angeles are mainly concentrated in three streets: Melrose Avenue, Robertson Boulevard and La Cienega Boulevard. The general standard of these shops is lower than that of San Francisco, and there are certainly few of London or New York quality. Many Californian dealers have a disconcerting habit of mixing antique with reproduction furniture. However honourable the intention, this is bound to confuse the inexperienced collector – especially when one considers such goods as the popular nineteenth-century Bentwood furniture by the Thonet brothers, which was extensively copied later.

The Sir Godrick Custom Cabinet Shop, of 2163 West Washington Boulevard, offered a collection of fifty-eight nice silver watches. This shop also contained a good selection of late nineteenth-century dolls (one cost $180) and a number of model locomotives. Now Sir Godrick handles only restorations. In 1973, F. P. Austin, 915 North La Cienega, might have sold you a Georgian mahogany master's chair in Chippendale style, with the original seat leather, for $3,600; he still carries the same kind of merchandise, and prices have remained constant.

Margot Flatau, of 721 North La Cienega, specialized in turn-of-the-century posters (she knew all the leading poster dealers in London and Paris.) Her stock at that time included a splendid Chéret *avant la lettre*. She also had a *trompe l'œil* painting of French revolutionary *assignats*, which I thought cheap at $120. With the exception of Mucha's and Lautrec's works, whose prices have gone up 'over 50 per cent', she feels prices have remained stable since 1973. In Baldacchino, 919 North La Cienega, I found a delightful equestrian lay figure of about 1810 – the ideal gift for a Munnings or Frederic Remington of the future. Baldacchino continue to carry the same quality and type of merchandise. In Antique Mart, 809 La Cienega, I was tempted by a transfer-printed English cream-ware teapot showing 'Minerva protecting Telemachus'; but, lacking a lid, it was scarcely a bargain, by English standards, at $195.

Yvette Liardet, of 646 North Robertson Boulevard, charged me $1.50 to enter the upstairs galleries. This was to discourage browsers: the money was refunded if you made a purchase. (A mean scheme, in my opinion.) Outside, an ominous notice read: 'Wanted: good cabinet makers.' I noticed a wooden rattle at $36, charmingly labelled 'French noise-maker'. I made a French noise and left (without paying the $1.50). I understand that the shop no longer charges this fee for admission.

The young proprietor of Jeffers-Harriman, 724 North La Cienega, who imported almost all his stock from England, told me: 'I have a Bachelor's in speech pathology, a Bachelor's in psychology and a Master's in audiology. I became an antiques dealer because I hate bureaucracy. Here I don't have to do what people say, and if I don't like someone, I can say "you get your ass outa here".' Currently in stock were a butter churn at $90, which he predicted would be turned into a table, a hinged butter mould at $10 and a clock, badly stripped, but with a fine brass face engraved 'Everard Billington, Markett Harborou' at $180. The gallery now carries only seventeenth- and eighteenth-century furniture, with emphasis on the William and Mary and Queen Anne styles. Much of his stock is still imported from England. For Art Nouveau and Art Deco I recommend Tiberio, of 458 Robertson Boulevard; the assistant knelt when I presented my card. In the summer of 1976, Tiberio opened a second shop in 'a classier neighbourhood', 238 North Cañon. They still carry a wide variety of Art Nouveau and Art Deco pieces, and claim that fine Nouveau has risen at least one thousand per cent in value.

By far the best antique shop I visited in the L. A. area in 1973 was Carl (now Richard) Yeakel's at Laguna Beach, where the surf-riders were bicycling away from the sea in the evening haze, their boards over their shoulders. Mr Yeakel (pronounced yake-el) had stock to rival any in London or New York. There was a European gallery, and another devoted to marine objects. For $235 you could have bought a canary-coloured mug, late eighteenth-century English, printed: 'My son, if sinners entice thee, consent thou not lest disgrace come up on thee'; and for $6,600, a handsome James I refectory table. In one window, I caught sight of a collection of falcon hoods in a glass case. The shop is now run by Carl's adopted son (hence the change of name).

I also attended an auction at Sotheby Parke Bernet, Los Angeles. It was a fairly run-of-the-mill sale of pictures. The most interesting incident in the whole sale was when a dull self-portrait by Raimondo de Madrazo y Garreta (1841–1920) made as much as $6,000 (for the simple reason, I imagine, that it had belonged to an American cousin of Sir Winston Churchill). The most attractive painting in the sale, a Tissot of two girls seated in a boat watching a heron, went for $32,000. There is a flea-market next the auction room, and uncharitable Angelenos remark that they cannot tell one from t'other.

The best of the larger antiques shops in San Francisco is Merryvale of 3640 Buchanan Street (which is housed in the showrooms of the SF Gas Light Co. 1893, one of the city's prized pre-earthquake houses), with a stock as impressive as Yeakel's. It is ironic that the gas company building survived, for it was the splitting of the gas mains by the earthquake which caused the unquenchable fires in 1906. I saw there an English walnut and mulberry escritoire at $5,800; a Turner pottery jug showing Falstaff in the basket at $295, and a Swansea mug portraying 'Lord Hill' at $550. A visit to the loo is a *must*: the basin is in the form of an elephant's head, its trunk forming the S bend.

The other antiques' hunting-grounds of San Francisco are Sansome Street, Jackson Square and Union Street. S. Arbes and Company, 700 and 701 Sansome Street, which sold excellent furniture in 1973, and where I examined a portrait of *Lady Seaton, Wife of H. M. Minister of Sweden,* boldly attributed to Raeburn, at $2,175, now specializes in English, French and Italian furniture, paintings and tapestries. James Waste, at 463 Jackson Street, was selling a symphonion with thirty-one discs for $1,675; a model traction engine for $650, and a mug printed with the insignia of the Ancient Order of Druids for $60. They now place more of an emphasis on seventeenth- and eighteenth-century pieces, and import all their goods through their agent in England. A sinister exhibit was to be found for $36 in James Henry Walker's shop at 710 Sansome Street: a green glass bottle painted with the words 'tinct. nucis vom. poison'. A good cover picture for an Agatha Christie novel?

Californian dealers have an odd habit of describing more or less anything before 1800, short of a mastodon bone, as 'Queen Anne' (in one case, Queen Ann). Do they know how short her reign was? 'Georgian' is always safer. A piece which might have been genuine Queen Anne was what Louis D. Fenton, of 432 Jackson Street, described as a 'pretty little secretary', and sold for $18,000 before we arrived. His shop also featured an interesting George II Sheffield oil

Eighteenth-century American decorated domestic ware protests
against Parliament's punitive colonial taxes

lamp of neo-classical form for $450. They have since moved towards
George I and Louis XV furniture; but also stock a wide variety of
oriental goods, such as a Ming dynasty Buddha and a Chinese opium
bed. Persian carpets are also well represented.

The drive from San Francisco to Sandy Bergeson's shop, The
Dolphin, then at 605 Cambridge Avenue, Menlo Park, California, was
magical. Highway 280 runs beside the Hatchhatchy reservoir, its
banks burgeoning with mountain lilac and Californian lupins (although the Californian poppies were not out when I made the trip).
The stock at that time, which was first-rate, included a William-and-
Mary knee-hole desk with gilt *chinoiserie* at $14,000, and a marvellous
walnut card table of similar date at $7,500. All prices were clearly
marked (as they were in almost all the establishments I visited.) The
shop is now located at 408 Jackson Street, San Francisco. He deals in
seventeenth- and eighteenth-century American, English and French
furniture, silver and porcelain.

In general, the age of the collector in California is greater than that
of his counterpart in New York. With the exception of Tiberio's,
which claims to attract the custom of rock groups, the age-range is
approximately from the late 30s to the mid-60s. Almost all the shops
claim to have upgraded their merchandise since 1973 and the dealers
agree that prices have levelled off – except those for Art Nouveau and
Art Deco pieces. Many dealers now find European prices prohibitive,
and buy only in the United States.

Twenty rules for dealers

A connoisseur of antiques soon becomes a connoisseur of antique dealers. I have visited hundreds, both here and abroad. My most alarming experience (there are witnesses to vouch for this) was of being pursued down a street in Amsterdam by a berserk dealer who had removed a teapot from his window which I had then declined to buy. I also recall an occasion when an Oxford dealer, after an inter-necine haggle over the price of a Georgian card case, gave it to me 'for trying hard, mate'.

Over the years I have mentally made a set of rules which I would try to follow if I were setting up an antique shop. I have never yet found a shop that obeyed all of them. Here are twenty of the most important; in the long run, all of them are in the dealer's interest – as well as his customers'.

1 When choosing a shop, the essential things to look for are window – and parking – space. Without the latter, what you put in the former may fail to attract a wide public.

2 Do not call your shop something twee like 'The Delightful Muddle'. (There are already four 'Delightful Muddles' and the woman who invented the name is said to be fuming). 'J. Smith Antiques' is more professional.

3 Label and price each piece clearly. The best way to do this is to buy a small printing press and print the tickets (the press can also be used for your letterhead, unless you are fussy and insist on an engraved one). The legend engraved in reverse on a Georgian cornelian fob-seal, for example, should be printed out plainly: a customer with the initials C.D. may be tempted to buy the seal if he is told that this is what the (unreadable) reversed Gothic characters read. In this case, impressions in sealing wax could also be displayed.

4 Avoid such labels as 'Very unique copper gruel basin – lovely for flowers.'

5 Eliminate price tickets which read '£EGV', etc. Most dealers can

break your code anyway; for the rest, clear price labels suggest integrity – although I accept that ten to twenty per cent should be added on to indulge the inveterate haggler.

6 Do not put 'Not for Sale' notices on your best pieces. These will madden collectors and convince the police that your shop is really only a cover for opium peddling. If you must put these pieces on show, 'Reserved' is less inflammatory.

7 Give a written guarantee of authenticity with each object (the form can also be printed on your machine) describing, as far as possible, age, date, maker, place of origin, pedigree, etc. Return money without argument if the piece is proved a fake, a cunning repair job, or anything other than you said.

8 Do not pounce with a 'Can I help you?' Customers who need your help will ask for it. The time to get worried is when they start helping themselves.

9 Never say things to customers like 'Try not to touch'.

10 Do not follow them around like a suspicious police dog. Small, valuable pieces such as jewellery should be kept in locked glass cases.

11 Before delivering a long, only partially accurate *spiel* on a given antique, make sure your customer is not (a) an expert from the Victoria and Albert Museum; (b) her Majesty's Inspector of Taxes. When still in short trousers I was already being told things by antique dealers which I knew to be flagrant bamboozlement; this might be called teaching your grandson to suck eggs.

12 It is a mistake to ask a mink-swaddled duchess 'Are you trade?'

13 Have nothing to do with any 'rings'. You can beat the ring by outbidding them, or by buying elsewhere than at auctions.

14 Do not put just one object in the window, like an orchid on velvet. You are not out to win a Constance Spry competition. The public abhors a vacuum.

15 When a piece is damaged or repaired and a customer asks its price, point out the damage to him before he does to you. This is honesty; and it also spikes his main gun in haggling. The phrase 'a tiny hair crack' is usually tendentious. Make sure your wares are what they're cracked up to be.

16 Begin by aiming for small profits and a quick turnover. People will get to know that your prices are low and you will build up a regular clientele, which can gradually be schooled to accept higher prices.

17 Specialise in something, even if you are a general dealer, and read books and articles on your speciality.

When not serving customers, you can be swotting up from bound volumes of *The Connoisseur*, *The Antique Collector* and other periodicals. I never cease to marvel at the complacent ignorance of many antique dealers. They are not only like wine dealers who do not know the difference between claret and Burgundy; they do not know the difference between claret and stout, plonk and vintage port.

18 Keep a record of customers' names, addresses and wants in a book. Then keep them posted. Read through the book occasionally to remind yourself that Mr X collects Wedgwood cream-ware, Mrs Y wants Bristol glass, Miss Z yearns for fertility corn dollies.

19 If there is room, display trays of objects outside on a trestle: 'All at 25p'; 'All at 50p'. These are groundbait, and are a useful disposal unit for damaged or lidless pieces which make good study items for beginners – especially young collectors. (Always be charming and informative to young collectors, however little money they have. The banks have learnt, and so must you, that these are the customers of the future and that now is the time to hook them.)

20 When browsers leave without buying anything, do not mutter 'We're not a museum, you know'. It may be painfully obvious.

Victorian spelter vases. Of all materials spelter, a zinc
alloy, is the one dealers are least eager to buy

No comment, please

What irks antique dealers most about collectors and other buyers and sellers? The following are the comments with which you are least likely to ingratiate yourself:

1 'Yeah, I can see the little lion, but where does it say sterling?'

2 'It is definitely old. It belonged to my grandmother and she was eighty-four when she died.'

3 'If only there was a pair of them, I'd have them like a shot.'

4 'I only really wanted one.'

5 'It's a lovely ring, but are the stones old? How can you tell they are *real* diamonds?'

6 'I thought Queen Anne furniture had to be made of walnut.'

7 'Well, there were eight of them, but we gave the other four to the children when they got married – two for each, you know.'

8 'I did have some other things but I sold them to such a nice **man** from Brighton.'

9 'Worcester, is it? Did they do that pattern in a nice lilac? Blue just wouldn't look right in the drawing room.'

10 '£48? Could you tell me how much that is in real money?'

11 'Have you got an old movement that would fit this clock?'

12 'Can you get this stopper out for me? By the way, it's the wrong one. You wouldn't have one that matched the decanter, by any chance?'

13 'A man came to the door and offered me £150 for it. So I said to myself, it it's worth that to you, it must be worth more to me.'

14 'Chinese bronze, is it? I've polished that every week for years, and it never would come up like the other lamps.'

15 'I'm sorry, I can't sell you that, I promised it to the doctor. He was so good to auntie, you see.'

16 'We're doing a Colour Supplement feature on Decorative Antiques for the Home. Would you be awfully sweet and just let us borrow these seven pieces? We'd only keep them a few days. We'd love to

credit you, but space is very limited just now.'

17 'I wonder if you'd be interested in my Victorian brass desk set in part exchange?'

18 'Dad took the rivets out and re-did it with plastic wood.'

19 (The assumption here is that antique dealers are out-of-work actors). 'Didn't I see you in *The Mikado* at Lowestoft?'

20 'You've been just wonderful showing us all these beautiful things. So interesting. We'll be back.'

The grander dealers in some cases resent the condescending attitude of the art-historical and museum world. One dealer in oriental art told me: 'You get some young chap newly down from reading oriental languages at university. There aren't many jobs he's qualified for; but, although he doesn't happen to be particularly interested in oriental or any other art, he can and does get a job in the oriental art department of a major national museum. And immediately he is an "expert", and people will come into my gallery and tell me, "Oh, Mr Snooks says it's so-and-so", when I've been twenty years in the business and have seen more oriental works of art than he's had hot dinners. What is more, some of them never acquire any real feeling for art – although they know how to read signatures.'

I was discussing these ideas the other day with an American art historian on sabbatical leave from Princeton; and he put the excellent question (which ought to be set in university general papers): 'Which is more of help to the other, the art historian, or the art dealer?'. The dealers allege that without their continued raking over of the art market, new works would not come to light for the art historians to pronounce upon. The most obvious recent instance of this is the discovery of a Raphael by the American dealer, Ira Spanierman, which was later the subject of a law-suit brought by its previous owner.

The art historians reply that without their painstaking research into archives and patient analysis of detail, the dealers would be unable to classify the things they sell; and their definitive argument is: 'If you had a disputed Raphael, would you rather have a certificate from the greatest museum expert in Europe authenticating it, or one from the greatest dealer in Europe?'

Rock revival

I recently acquired a set of dentures, villainously sharp and the colour of old Madeira – 'a perfect match', as my secretary said. The price was £30 plus V.A.T. They formerly belonged, I am assured, to an ichthyosaurus, 150 million years ago, and were found in the demure Austenesque resort of Lyme Regis. They gave me the idea of writing about the oldest antiques which one can collect – minerals and fossils, some of which have a respectable vintage of 500 million years.

I was accompanied on my trip through geological time by a book entitled *The Collector's Encyclopedia of Rocks and Minerals*, edited by A. F. L. Deeson (David and Charles, 1973). It contained fascinating photographs and biographies of such minerals as Adamellite ('igneous rock of the granite clan'), Aenigmatite, Amazonite, Apache Tears ('gemstone variety of obsidian'), Asparagus Stone, Babingtonite ('easily fuses to black magnetic globule'), Bigwoodite, Boghead Coal, Cat's eye, Celadonite, Coquina – and so on down to Zircon, Zunyite and Zussmanite ('perfect cleavage in one direction'). Rock of ages, cleft for you and me.

A leading dealer – Mr Brian Lloyd, who sells minerals and fossils from the fourth floor of 14 Pall Mall, London W1 – informed me that up to about 1900 there was a large demand for minerals amongst collectors. 'Then for some unknown reason it stopped. The revival came with two big collectors – Sir Arthur Russell and Arthur Kingsbury – both of whose collections are now in the Natural History Museum.' Sir Arthur Russell, who began his collection at the age of eight (in 1886) with some crystals from a Cornish tin mine, travelled throughout Britain adding specimens to his collection, which eventually numbered some 14,000 mineral specimens. He bought the collections of Phillip Rashleigh (1728–1811) and John Ruskin, and died in 1964.

Mr Lloyd added that a craze for mineral collecting began in America about twenty years ago: 'Practically every town has its "rock shop", with a lot of emphasis on cutting and polishing' (which Mr Lloyd, as a purist admirer of minerals, rather deplores). In his opinion, the British rock revival began about ten years ago.

You can begin your collection very cheaply – colourful crystal specimens can be bought for as little as £2. But the average range of wares in such a shop as Mr Lloyd's might be represented by the following larger pieces, each costing between £100 and £200: a section of petrified wood from Arizona, cut and polished; a cluster of sorrel-red vanadinite crystals on matrix (rock base) from Mibladen, Morocco; Smithsonite from the Kelly mine, Magdalena County, New Mexico (this has the green-blue colour of certain brands of expensive soap, which gives a curious plastic effect like those souvenir portraits which show Mark Phillips at one angle and Princess Anne at another); and a pink, spongelike sample of rhodocrosite from Baia Sprie, Romania. One of the mineral samples I liked best was of variscite with crandallite from Fairfield, Utah – it looked like a seventeenth-century plan of French fortifications, with pale markings against a green background. Mr Lloyd also sells such relevant old books as Philip Rashleigh's *Specimens of British Minerals*, *1797–1802*. 'There were so many eighteenth-century books on flowers and birds, so few on minerals', Mr Lloyd commented.

While stock for the London dealers is supplied by a wide variety of international geology dealers, the chance of the man in the street (well, in the Lake District, anyway) picking up examples of minerals suitable for sale are quite remote. You can find specimens, but the ones you discover will not be marketable. The good ones have to come from the mines, and by the time they have reached the surface, on the miners' dump, they tend to be damaged; although small specimens obviously stand a better chance of surviving. Mr Lloyd commented: 'After butterflies, minerals are the most easily damaged collector's subject of all. By comparison, you can knock a porcelain collection about.'

Another point to remember is that minerals from mines no longer worked are likely to be dearer than those from mines still operating. For example, green fluorite from the Heights Mine, Co. Durham, long since closed down, is much more expensive (though no more beautiful) than blue fluorite from La Collada Mines, Asturias, Spain, which are still being operated.

Pukka geologists and local museums who want to create a representative collection will profit by a visit to the extraordinary warehouse of Gregory, Bottley at 30 Old Church Street, Chelsea. It must

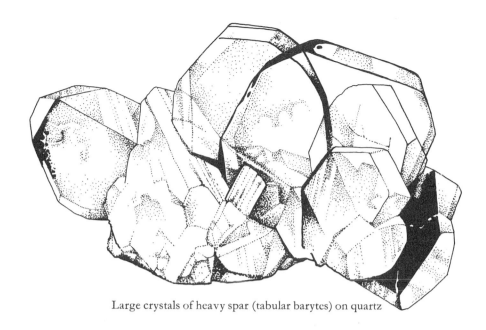

Large crystals of heavy spar (tabular barytes) on quartz

be the most perfect surviving example of a Victorian business interior in the whole of London. The visitor makes his way through a narrow corridor littered with boulders and up a staircase into the showroom, where viridian green Dioptes from south-west Africa, quartz and precious opal glisten and glow in old-fashioned showcases.

The business was established in London about 1850 in Russell Street, Covent Garden, by James R. Gregory, an enthusiastic collector of precious stones and meteorites. In 1875 the business moved to Charlotte Street; later to Kelso Place, South Kensington, and to its present address in 1926. In 1931 the business was taken over by Mr and Mrs E. P. Bottley, who introduced micro-section cutting, grinding and polishing on a large scale and designed the Petrological Microscopes, the Single Stage Goniometer and the Bottley White Pulverizer, to name but a few boons to mankind.

In 1949 the Vernon Edward models of prehistoric animals were added to the collections and after Edward's death A. L. Pocock, who also designed for Fabergé, made further models. I was delighted to find at Gregory, Bottley a model of the ichthyosaurus, so I could see exactly how my cherished new jawbone fitted in; Gregory, Bottley also had for sale an ichthyosaurus vertebra, large as a bachelor's tin of baked beans . . .

Other good books on this fascinating subject include *The World's Finest Minerals and Crystals* by Peter Bancroft (Thames and Hudson, 1973) and *Rocks and Minerals* by E. P. Bottley (Octopus Books, 1972).

Magazines of history

One collectors' quarry which has not yet been fully exploited by dealers or cottoned on to by collectors is old magazines. Few antiquarian booksellers issue catalogues of them, and in countrywide auctions great batches are sold off for derisory sums.

The richest seam for the collector is undoubtedly the sumptuous illustrated examples of the 1890s and the Edwardian period – the *Strand*, the *Pall Mall*, the *Windsor*, *Pearson's* and the like. These were magazines for the whole family, who often had as strong an interest in 'Society' as in society at large. The interest was not merely snobbish: the aristocracy still had considerable power at this time, and such articles as 'Who Owns London: The Capital Belongs to a Handful of Peers' have a genuine historical interest.

As a sample of the sort of material that can be expected, the contents of one volume of an Edwardian run of *Harmsworth Magazine* included: 'The Czarina's Dancers: How Poor Russian Ladies Dance Their Way to Fortune'; 'Cycling Through the Air'; 'A Marvellous Airship Described'; 'Adventures of a Snake-Catcher'; 'Who Owns London?'; 'Lord Battersea at Home'; 'Some English Lady Artists' and 'Our King's Pigeons: How the King Won the Pigeon Derby.'

Some of the subjects chosen by the editor of *Harmsworth* would still furnish good articles for, say, *The Sunday Times Magazine*: one issue, for example, contained an article on school magazines, which included interviews with the juvenile editors.*

The magazines of that period could call on the talents of a galaxy of good writers to contribute to even a light-hearted causerie – let alone anything more serious. When Tennyson died the *Idler* magazine, edited by Jerome K. Jerome, solicited opinions as to who would be the next Laureate. Oscar Wilde characteristically replied: 'Mr Swinburne is already the Poet Laureate of England. The fact that his

* *The Sunday Times* recently published such a feature

124

appointment to this high post has not been degraded by official confirmation renders his position all the more unassailable. He whom all poets love is the Laureate Poet always.' While to the same symposium Bernard Shaw contributed the caustic view that 'Mr Swinburne is a born Poet Laureate: he has always been worshipping somebody; and he would soon get used to the substitution of the Prince of Wales for Victor Hugo.'

The standard of fiction in the magazines was also high. My grandmother well remembered the excitement with which she would await the arrival of the latest Sherlock Holmes' instalment in the *Strand*; and my run of *Harmsworth* contains the serialization of E. Nesbit's *The Railway Children*. The *Wide World Magazine* was launched in 1898 with the proud motto: 'Truth is Stranger than Fiction'; it purported to publish true adventures, but it was soon exposed that 'How I Was Buried Alive' by Baron Corvo (the future author of *Hadrian the Seventh*) was an invention, and that the preposterous Antipodean adventures of Louis de Rougemont were a *tour de force* of mendacity. Both accounts stand up very well as fiction.

The other great appeal of the old magazines is their line illustrations; in the days before photography had really superseded drawing, the 'black-and-white men' – Phil May, Seymour Lucas, John Hassall, Townsend, Beardsley, Sullivan and Pegram – were still dominant. The average quality of illustration in such magazines as the *Strand* is extraordinary, but it is even higher in the special arts-oriented magazines of the 1890s – *The Quarto*, *The Butterfly* and *The Evergreen*, for example. One of the finest artists contributing to magazines of this stamp was Wilde's friend Charles Ricketts. There is an affectionate account of him in the autobiography of a former director of the National Gallery, Sir Charles Holmes – *Self and Partner (Mostly Self)* (Constable, 1936). Laurence Housman was another leading illustrator in the same William Morris/Beardsley tradition.

There are many different ways of collecting magazines. You might decide to go for the first serialization of great novels; or you could trace the work of a single artist through many magazines – Sidney Sime, for example, a sinister draughtsman who contributed to *Pick-Me-Up* in the 1890s and also to *The Unicorn*, *The Idler*, *Eureka*, *The Butterfly*, *The Pall Mall Magazine* and the *Magazine of Art*. A third course might be to collect articles on a single theme – such as transport, fashion or education.

When I wrote about collecting old magazines in *The Times*, I was rather depressed to receive letters saying 'I have a copy of the *Strand*

Magazine for July 1893. Can you please tell me what it is worth?' The whole point of my article had been to suggest an item that could still be collected at minimal cost.

In spite of the fact that old magazines command fairly modest prices, there are two groups which are becoming increasingly popular with collectors: art magazines, and children's comics. Such art magazines as *The Connoisseur* or the *Burlington Magazine* are sought after (mainly in long runs) as extended reference works, while earlier art magazines – the *Art Journal* (or *Art-Union*, as it was called when first established), for example, which was founded by the cantankerous S. C. Hall (believed to be the original of Dickens's Pecksniff) – are bought for their wood-engraved illustrations, some of which help to identify paintings that would otherwise be hard to attribute.

Which was the first art magazine? By this I mean, not a magazine containing writings on art *inter alia*, but one wholly devoted to art criticism or history. In a footnote to his recent *Rediscoveries in Art* (Phaidon Press, 1973) Francis Haskell writes: 'The earliest [art journal] of which I know is *Miscellaneen artistischen Inhalts*, edited by Johann Georg Meusel, which appeared at six-monthly intervals at Erfurt, the first volume being published in 1779.' The end of the eighteenth century may sound a surprisingly late date for the founding of the first art magazine; but this reflects the curiously late stage at which art began to be treated as something distinct from civilization at large. Left-wing culture historians never cease to deplore this divorce: first, because a Michelangelo and the decoration embroidered on a pair of jeans are to them equally significant expressions of the societies they represent; second, because at the stage art was split off as something discrete, it was the province of exclusive coteries of connoisseurs and wealthy patrons, and not of arts' councils.

For the English collector, English art magazines are obviously the most convenient prey. Michael Collins, who wrote on 'English art magazines before 1901' in the March, 1976 issue of *The Connoisseur*, mentioned a few prototype art magazines such as the *Academic Correspondence* published by Prince Hoare, Honorary Secretary of the Royal Academy for foreign correspondence, in 1804. But he believes the first successful art magazine in England was the *Annals of the Fine Arts*, begun in 1816, which had an anti-academic slant fostered by Keats's friend, the painter B. R. Haydon. The magazine, which was not illustrated but contained essays, reviews and topical reports, was not exclusively devoted to the visual arts: Keats's *Ode to a Nightingale* and *Ode to a Grecian Urn* were first published in the fourth issue.

The *Annals* were short-lived, and in 1838 Charles Landseer expressed regret that there was no magazine to represent the arts. In 1839 his plea was answered, by the founding of the *Art-Union*. From a first edition of 750, the magazine grew to an average monthly circulation of 3,000. Its finest hour was covering the Great Exhibition of 1851. It continued until 1912, and included articles by writers of the quality of Arthur Symons, G. B. Shaw, Gleeson White, Edmund Gosse and W. M. Rossetti.

Obviously the *Art Journal* would be an essential ingredient in any collection of English art magazines. The collection might also include *The Journal of Design and Manufacturers* started by Henry Cole in 1849, which concerned itself with the reform of practical design; the Pre-Raphaelite magazine *The Germ*, founded in 1850 with a Holman Hunt etching as the cover; and the various 'decadent' magazines of the 1890s – *The Savoy, The Dial, The Quest, The Evergreen, The Elf* and, of course, *The Yellow Book* with its Beardsley illustrations. If you felt like expanding the collection into foreign magazines, you could begin with those of the French Romantic movement, such as the French *l'Artiste*, or with the great German *art nouveau* periodicals, *Pan* and *Die Jugend* (1895 and 1896 respectively).

I got some idea of the prices for runs of old art magazines from Ben Weinreb, the book dealer of 93 Great Russell Street, near the British Museum. For Nos 1–56 of *The Studio* (lacking a few issues) he was asking £385; for single volumes of the same magazine – the great design periodical founded in the 1890s – he asked £8. He had in stock the *Art-Union/Journal* complete from 1847 to 1902, bound in quarter red morocco, for £825. The first magazine in the world wholly devoted to architecture, J. C. Loudon's *Architectural Magazine*, he was offering in the set of five bound volumes, 1834–38, at £250. This magazine was reprinted *in toto* in 1973; he also had the reprint (originally priced at £110) at £35 a set. The Dutch magazine *Wendingen*, in a set of 12 volumes 1918–31, cost £1,000, but he also had many single parts at £7. He had the *Architectural Review*, the premier architectural magazine in the world, from its beginning in 1896 until 1967, bound, for £4,250; or from the beginning to 1975, unbound, at £3,250.

Harold Landry, who deals from his home at 19 Tanza Road, London NW3, also specializes in old magazines, mainly artistic and literary. In general, his holdings of old art periodicals are outstanding. Paul Breman of 1 Rosslyn Hill, London NW3 also frequently has art magazines; as he is a Dutchman, one is not surprised to find *Wendingen* on his shelves. One of the largest collections of old magazines in Europe is held by William Dawson and Sons Ltd, Cannon House, Folkestone, Kent.

Ben Weinreb told me that the idea of collecting magazines was first suggested in *New Paths in Book-Collecting*, a symposium edited by the late John Carter in the 1930s. Weinreb added: 'The point of collecting magazines is that, more than anything else, they show ideas in growth.'

Children's comics are collected for another reason. The standards and ethical systems they enjoin – the concepts of 'pluck', 'honour', of not 'sneaking' – are now in the class of bygones. The hooded secret societies of schoolgirls in the *School Friend* of only twenty-five years ago, who hissed at each other, 'Could it be Miriam, that unpopular prefect?' and shut the school sneak in the potting shed, seem as dated as wig-stands or cooking-spits today. The Open University, which is already interviewing doddering old servants on tape recorders to find the answers to such pregnant social questions as 'Did servants distance members of the servant-owning family from each other?' will find the answers to many other social inquiries within these flimsy pages: the 'rags' once confiscated by irate teachers may now be doled out by professors as historical documents for relentless analysis.

Puzzle pots and mystery pieces

The phrase 'puzzle pots' usually means those appalling instruments of bucolic entertainment: jugs and mugs which appear to be pierced with holes, and which deluge you with ale if you do not know the trick of how to drink from them. But it might also have another meaning: pottery bearing inscriptions and pictures whose original significance is now lost.

It would be difficult to form a collection of such pieces: for a start, they are rare, and inevitably the collection would be depleted as the puzzles were solved. Yet encountering one of these enigmas is part of the fun of collecting. Solving such puzzles was the basis of the old television programme, 'Animal, Vegetable, Mineral', in which arcane objects were passed from hand to hand among the panellists and pronounced on by such experts as Sir Mortimer Wheeler and Dr Glyn Daniel, sometimes with ribald speculation. When collectors get together for a drink, the mutual admiration and envy of each other's cabinets is soon done; but the puzzles remain, the beginnings of labyrinthine debates and sometimes of fierce arguments. Like fakes, they can bring battle honours to the expert and scars to the unwary.

Here are a few tantalizing examples of mystery pieces whose secrets are still undisclosed. I am indebted to Mr John May, dealer in commemorative pottery at 40 Kensington Church Street, London W8, for bringing the first two to my attention.

The first puzzle is on a decorative plate which was almost certainly potted and painted (in underglaze blue) in Liverpool and bears the inscription 'Capt. Quibel M.P. 1788'. The plate is absolutely 'right' for the date of the inscription. But who was Captain Quibel – or Quibble? Quibel is not recorded as a sitting member of the House of Commons during that session in any possible spelling of the name; neither does he appear to have fought successfully or otherwise any by-election at the relevant date; nor was he a sitting member of the Irish parliament.

The only notorious by-election in 1788 was one at Colchester, fought by George Tierney, lost but then won on a reversal in committee. It is possible that the plate was produced for the next year's election – when Tierney faced the same opponent – as a piece decrying Tierney as a 'quibbler'. But there is no record at the Colchester library and record office of any such slogan having been used in either of the campaigns. Alternatively, Quibel may have been a sea captain and the 'M.P.' tag an obscure local joke. The plate is painted, not printed, and could therefore have been a 'one-off' piece.

The second puzzle concerns 'The Bishop of Heliopolis'. This transfer of a christening scene, sometimes with and sometimes without the inscription, appears on a wide range of plates and other wares produced, judging by the pottery, some time in the 1840–50 period. The transfers are always in black, and are sometimes 'clobbered' (overpainted) in red, yellow, blue and green. As well as the caption 'The Bishop of Heliopolis', there is a print of Windsor Castle on the reverse of one jug, and the inscription 'Royal Christening' on the base. The print also appears on a child's plate, in the series of 'great events of the reign' which also includes the coronation print, the marriage print, Windsor Castle, the anti-Corn Law prints and Father Matthew and the temperance pledge (which may have been made for the Great Exhibition of 1851).

Heliopolis, now a residential suburb of Cairo, was the Greek name for one of the most ancient of Egyptian cities, the Biblical On, seat of the worship of the sun god Ra. Would it be possible to discover a Bishop of Heliopolis in the Church of England, or in the Greek or Roman Catholic churches? Hieing me to the British Museum catalogue, I found three bishops listed: Heliopolis: Anthimos, Bishop of. *See* Anthimos (Komnenos, etc). Heliopolis: Stephen Alexander, Bishop of. *See* Wuerdtwein. Heliopolis: and Theira, Gennadios, Metropolitan of. *See* Arampatzoglou. Wuerdtwein had published books in the 1780s and Arampatzoglou in the 1930s, which seemed to rule them out. But Anthimos, successively Bishop of Heliopolis and the Cyclades, published some verse in 1837 – the year of Victoria's accession – so he might be a possible. The Heliopolis pieces were produced in large numbers, and not for a sophisticated clientele. It seems, then, that less than 150 years ago the name of the Bishop of Heliopolis was current coinage, so well known that no explanation was necessary. In spite of this, no one has been able to find a clue to his identity.

Then there is the 'ghost' jug. This has a curious history. It belongs to a man who bought it in a junk shop without knowing what it was

The 'Bishop of Heliopolis' plate and the ghost jug

and then wrote to *Country Life* 'Readers' Enquiries' to ask. They published his letter and said that the design on the jug depicted Lafayette mourning at the tomb of Washington; but this seems unlikely. The jug cannot have been made before 1850, judging by the pottery, and was probably not made much after 1880. It clearly shows a ghost looking at the tomb in which, presumably, his body is interred – again, presumably, at the place of death. It could be Napoleon (perhaps made at the time when his body was shipped back to France – 1840, so not all that likely), or Captain Cook, made when the Cook Memorial was set up in 1874. The jug is seven inches high, and painted in a particularly virulent shade of mauve.

Finally, there is the 'Placemen' problem discussed by Anthony Ray in his book *English Delftware Pottery in the Robert Hall Warren Collection* (Faber, 1968). The Warren Collection, in the Ashmolean Museum, Oxford, contains some English delft plates which raise a problem to which no satisfactory solution has yet been proposed. They represent two versions of the same engraving, not yet traced, depicting 'Justice' trampling on 'Evil', who holds in one hand a torch and in the other a scroll inscribed 'The Petitions', 'The Pollinn' or 'Placemen'. It seems as if 'Justice' is preventing 'Evil' from setting fire to the scroll.

These plates have often been associated with the popular support for John Wilkes, the profligate political reformer; that would date them about 1768–70, the time of Wilkes's petitions. But the border of one of the plates is typical of 1740, and this is more likely to be their date. It is probable that the plates refer to the early eighteenth-century agitation against the political corruption that managed elections and filled Parliament with 'placemen' (political yes-men) elected by influence, and pensioners whose emoluments were dependent on their complaisance. It is estimated that in George II's first Parliament there were 257 placemen.

Mr Ray mentions the bills against placemen introduced by Samuel Sandys in 1730, 1734, and 1740. All were thrown out by Walpole; but oddly enough, when the 'Place Bill' of 1743 was passed after Walpole's death (1742) and some of the placemen were ejected, Sandys voted against the Bill. It is probable that the plates date from this time; but until the original engraving and its context can be traced we shall not be sure.

The art of motoring

When Mr James Barron invited me to come and see his collection of antiques relating to the motor car, which have been the subject of an exhibition at the Bethnal Green Museum, I expected an array of ancient sprockets, venerable big ends, axles lying on velvet cushions, and fascia boards inlaid with walrus ivory. What is more, I expected Mr Barron to be an R.A.F. type with handlebar moustaches, a wizard-prang voice and oily overalls. I was quite wrong.

Mr Barron is a quietly spoken, un-R.A.F.-ish film maker and a celebrated marksman who has represented Great Britain in inter-national competitions. His collection, begun over twenty years ago, was not formed because he is passionately interested in motor cars – he only very occasionally goes to a race – but because it was a subject commemorated in many different media: posters, engravings, litho-graphs, paintings, ceramics, bronzes. There are not many spare parts of cars in the Barron collection, although he does own Sir Malcolm Campbell's crash helmet, made by Herbert Johnson (formerly of Bond Street), who created in the 1960s those jazzy crash hats which were painted with psychedelic squiggles. Collecting art and antiques relating to the motor car has enabled Mr Barron to trace the develop-ment of several art forms – especially the poster, of which he has about two dozen museum-quality examples ranging from the early period of the pictorial poster (the 1890s) to the present day.

The incunabula of the automobile are represented by a seventeenth-century Dutch engraving of land yachts, and what he believes to be the best existing collection of prints of self-propelled steam carriages of 1827–40. It includes those designed by Hancock (who wrote a book about his twelve years' experience of the steam carriage), and a splendid engraving by C. Hunt after W. Summers.

Mr Barron has made two collections by artists who specialized in painting cars. One is René Vincent, who designed catalogues and posters for Peugeot and Berliet in the early 1900s and became a de-

133

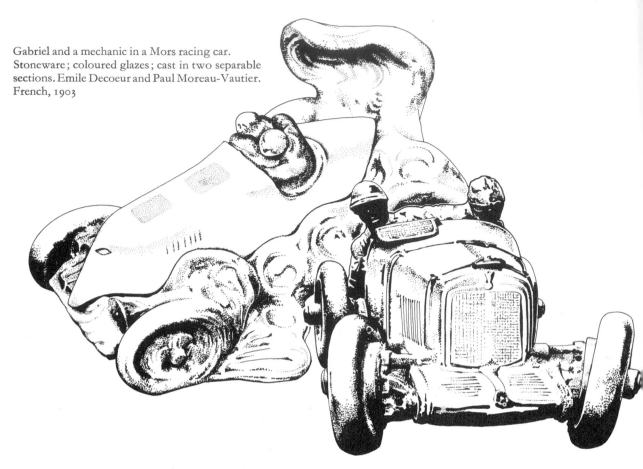

Gabriel and a mechanic in a Mors racing car.
Stoneware; coloured glazes; cast in two separable
sections. Emile Decoeur and Paul Moreau-Vautier.
French, 1903

The F. Gordon-Crosby racing car which was presented to
S. C. H. Davis. Inscription: 'To Sammy from his
colleagues. Premier award in his greatest trial.'
Bronze on marble base. English, 1931

lightful Art Deco artist. The most impressive specimen of his work
in the collection is the maquette for a Michelin catalogue, with fold-
back flaps which reveal the amusing contents of each stylish motor;
in one, we recognize that the fashionable women's heads which can
be glimpsed through the window belong to marble busts which are
being inspected inside by a connoisseur; in another, a swell is having
his shoes cleaned; in a third, a member of a sultan's harem is receiving
amorous attentions from a lusty slave. Mr Barron has never found the
final printed version of this catalogue and one wonders whether
Michelin rejected the design as a mite too risqué.

The other specialist artist is F. Gordon-Crosby, who joined the
staff of *Autocar* in 1907 after training as an engineer with Vauxhall

134

Motors and Daimler, and who remained with the magazine until his death in 1943. Gordon-Crosby did a series of 'Car-icatures' of such drivers as 'B. Bira', Lord Howe, A. W. K. van der Becke and G. E. T. Eyston; he also created a series of racing scenes entitled 'Meteors of the Road'.

Mr Barron is trying to form a representative collection of Gordon-Crosby's originals. He owns, for example, a painting of the White House crash at Le Mans, 1927, which shows S. C. H. Davis driving the winning Bentley. This work hung in the Cork Street showrooms of Bentley before the Second World War, and was used as an advertisement for Bentley Motors. Gordon-Crosby added to it the painted caption 'Carrying On'. Mr Barron also owns a bronze by Gordon-Crosby which was presented to one of his colleagues on *Autocar*, 'Sammy' Davis, when the latter entered hospital in 1931 after a serious crash.

Mr Barron remarked with understandable indignation upon the lack of attention that Gordon-Crosby's oils and gouaches have received. 'The trouble is, nearly all of them belong to *Autocar*. Previously they were all stored in a basement and the few overalled assistants around never had time to go down and dig them out. Now a few of them have seen the light of day. But Gordon-Crosby remains virtually unknown except to a small circle of enthusiasts.'

Mr Barron owns one painting by a man with claims to be the earliest of the specialist motor artists, Guy Lipscombe, who worked for *The Motor*, the principal rival of *Autocar*. Very little of his work has survived.

Turning to his poster collection, Mr Barron remarked that 1920s' and 1930s' examples are harder to come by than the early motor posters of the 1890s. The collecting of posters, which had been a flourishing fashion in the 1890s, had become *démodé* after the Great War. One of his best early examples shows a woman driving a De Dion Bouton, while the Comte de Dion's black chauffeur, sitting beside her, takes a rest. The intended moral, I assume, was that even a woman could handle the simple controls; but it reminded me of Harry Graham's *Ruthless Rhyme* of 1899:

> I collided with some 'trippers'
> In my swift De Dion Bouton;
> Squashed them out as flat as kippers,
> Left them *aussi mort que mouton*
> What a nuisance 'trippers' are!
> I must now repaint the car.

Mr Barron's earliest ceramic piece is a *faïence* motor of the 1890s. He also owns a pottery car by Dalpeyrat and one of Gabriel in the Mors racing car, finely modelled by P. Moreau-Vautier for Emile Decoeur. He paid £100 for this eleven years ago and was once offered £400 by an English dealer; a French dealer, also in pursuit of it, has hinted that he would probably give more. Mr Barron illustrated his method of collecting when he showed me a bronze modelled by Moreau-Vautier. It commemorates Blériot's crossing the Channel: the Spirit of Earth is attempting to restrain an airman charging off on a Pegasus. 'It has nothing to do with motor cars, but once I had the name Moreau-Vautier in my mind, I was looking out for other things by him', Mr Barron explained.

The collection includes a large number of car mascots. Two are by John Hassall – a policeman (known as 'robert mascot') and an airman which cost two guineas when purchased and would probably fetch £10 each today; others include an 'Ole Bill' mascot by Bruce Bairnsfather (originally one guinea, and now worth approximately £30); glass ones by Lalique (his 'Spirit of the Wind' mascot fetched £250 at Sotheby's three years' ago) which cost him only £25 and a glass *Art Nègre* style example. Mr Barron poured cold water on the old myth that Lalique eagle mascots were commissioned by Hitler for his marshals' Mercedes cars, although he thought that some of the Nazi leaders may have used them for this purpose.

Another important section of the Barron collection (lithographs by E. Montaut and Gamy) documents the early mechanical achievements of the turn of the century: motor racing, speed boating, airships, aeroplanes and motor cycles. A number of Montaut's lithographs were auctioned at Christie's a few years ago and fetched between £40 and £50 each; but Mr Barron has recently seen some framed examples in a Fulham gallery at £130 apiece. Approximately 100 different subjects are known, and the editions of each lithograph ran to about eighty prints. Only two of these subjects are British: a Bristol biplane flying over the Avon Gorge, and a Brands Hatch scene. Mr Barron advises that such rare examples should not be exposed to sunlight; cloth flaps hang over his specimens in true British Museum fashion.

The Barron collection also contains four fine silver snuff bottles in the form of long-coated motorists (Cheshire hallmark, 1903); a Louis Wain drawing of cats with an old car; silver watch cases with *repoussé* decoration of motors (in one of which Théry wins the Gordon Bennett race of 1905); and models, some made for promotional purposes, of cars which broke the world speed record.

Is your family album valuable?

One no longer has to argue about the artistic value of good photographs; and although no one has yet bid £2m for a daguerreotype, the interest in nineteenth-century photographs as a collector's subject has grown so much that the larger auction houses can no longer afford to ignore it.

Parke-Bernet in America have held a number of important sales which have been devoted solely to old photographs and photographic equipment. The sale of Will Weissberg's collection there in May 1967 included 700 American daguerreotypes of the Civil War. In February 1970, a group of 129 daguerreotypes taken by William Constable of Brighton between 1842 and 1853, fetched $2,400. These works (particular favourites of Constable) were accompanied by a manuscript journal written by Susanna Grece, the photographer's niece and assistant. The journal contains a record of family life, and notes important visitors to the studio – who included Prince Albert and the Baroness Lehzen (the latter 'a most agreeable woman, not bigger in dimensions than myself'.) A half-plate daguerreotype camera and portable tripod fetched $2,600 in the same sale; a book of George N. Barnard's photographic views of Sherman's campaign was sold for $5,400.

In 1970, the (almost) complete papers of Mrs Craik (author of *John Halifax, Gentleman*) turned up in Australia. One of Mrs Craik's scrapbooks contained an unexpected bonus: ten calotype photographs by David Octavius Hill, including one of William Etty from which the latter painted his self-portrait which is now at the National Portrait Gallery. Hill (1802–70) was a Scottish painter. Wishing to commemorate the disruption of the Church of Scotland in 1843 by a huge canvas which would represent the 474 ministers and lay persons present at the signing of the Deed of Demission, he turned to photography for his likenesses. He was assisted by the chemist, Robert Adamson. The ten examples, all inscribed by Hill with the names of the subjects, were sold at Sotheby's to a private collector in Chicago for £520.

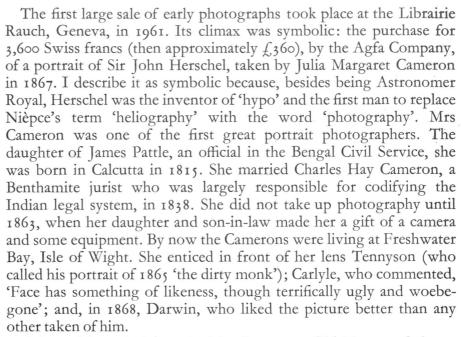

A Daguerreotype camera *c.* 1840

The first large sale of early photographs took place at the Librairie Rauch, Geneva, in 1961. Its climax was symbolic: the purchase for 3,600 Swiss francs (then approximately £360), by the Agfa Company, of a portrait of Sir John Herschel, taken by Julia Margaret Cameron in 1867. I describe it as symbolic because, besides being Astronomer Royal, Herschel was the inventor of 'hypo' and the first man to replace Nièpce's term 'heliography' with the word 'photography'. Mrs Cameron was one of the first great portrait photographers. The daughter of James Pattle, an official in the Bengal Civil Service, she was born in Calcutta in 1815. She married Charles Hay Cameron, a Benthamite jurist who was largely responsible for codifying the Indian legal system, in 1838. She did not take up photography until 1863, when her daughter and son-in-law made her a gift of a camera and some equipment. By now the Camerons were living at Freshwater Bay, Isle of Wight. She enticed in front of her lens Tennyson (who called his portrait of 1865 'the dirty monk'); Carlyle, who commented, 'Face has something of likeness, though terrifically ugly and woebegone'; and, in 1868, Darwin, who liked the picture better than any other taken of him.

Other celebrated pictures by Mrs Cameron – Old Masters of photography – include the ethereal profile of Mrs Leslie Stephen, so like that of her daughter, Virginia Woolf; the anthropoid dome of Darwin, and the fanatic turbaned head of William Palgrave, the explorer. The present market value of an identified Cameron photograph is from £100 to £150.

The man who taught Julia Margaret Cameron to take photographs was David Wilkie Wynfield, a member of the 'St John's Wood Clique', the group of artists which included W. F. Yeames, painter of *And when did you last see your father?* Mrs Cameron commented: 'To his beautiful photography I owe *all* my attempts and all my successes.' In 1963, I read in a memoir of Yeames by M. H. Stephen Smith which appeared in 1927, that the painter had presented a collection of Wynfield's photographs to the Royal Academy library. The Academy had the ticket recording the gift, but the photographs could not be found. Through the kindness of the then librarian, Mr Sidney Hutchison, I was permitted to make a search in the library with his assistant, Miss Parker, one Saturday morning. Finally, in an architect's table, we unearthed a green leather box, stamped in gold: 'Photographs by David Wilkie Wynfield.' It was locked, and none of the Academy keys fitted it. The librarian was telephoned and gave permission for the box to be prised open with a chisel. Short of peeling the cerements off a mummy, I am unlikely again to experience such an archaeological thrill as I did when we uncovered those photographs. Sepia brown, they nearly all represented Academy artists in fancy dress.

Caches of this kind are rare, and few come on to the market. Tristram Powell (organizer of a J. M. Cameron exhibition at Leighton House, Kensington, in 1971) has two pieces of advice for those beginning a collection. First, pester the curator of your local museum to know whether there are any photographs in the vaults. Secondly, if there is an old-established photographer in your town, ask him if he has any old albums or plates.

The beginner should learn to identify the different photographic processes which succeeded each other after the 'official invention of photography' in 1839: daguerreotype, calotype, glass-plate, wet collodion, ambrotype, dry-plate, and so on. The best simple guide to these is contained in an appendix to Helmut and Alison Gernsheim's *Masterpieces of Victorian Photography* (London, 1951). The many books by Gernsheim, some written in collaboration with his late wife, which include *The History of Photography* (Thames and Hudson, 1965), are all worth reading whether or not you intend to collect. Mr Gernsheim is himself a photographer, and his great collection of photographic history is now at the University of Texas. His biography of Mrs Cameron was published by the Fountain Press, London, in 1948. He has also written books on Lewis Carroll as photographer, Roger Fenton, the photographer of the Crimean war, and Daguerre. I also recommend Aaron Scharf's *Art and Photography* (Allen Lane, 1968) which illustrates the ways in which painting and photography have interacted in the past hundred or so years. Gordon Winter's *A Country Camera*, a delightful anthology of English country scenes of the nineteenth century, has been reissued (David and Charles, 1976).

The best places to look for old photographs in London are the auction rooms of Sotheby's Belgravia, and Christie's South Kensington. Your own family album may be an easy point of departure for your collection: but do not expect to sell such recent examples at Sotheby's. 'We don't want to be deluged with photographs of 1920s' bathing belles', commented the Sotheby's representative who catalogued the Craik papers and Hill photographs.' *C'est magnifique, mais ce n'est pas Daguerre* . . .

Going for a gong

I am always thinking up plots for best-selling novels which I shall never write. One of these is called *The Tubies*, and spotlights the habits of a new kind of homicidal hoodlum. They go round in gangs and push innocent commuters under Underground trains. To write this bestseller, one would have to work for a period as an Underground train driver, and I haven't the time. But I commend the idea to Anthony Burgess. 'The distant rumble of a tube train. The rails sing at Mornington Crescent as the 8.53 hurtles towards its berth and Mr Alfred Smith to his death . . .' Sure to be filmed as *From Rush Hour with Hate*.

Then there is my television play *For Valour*, about a cinema commissionaire who proudly wears, outside the local Classic, the V.C. ribbon he is entitled to for gallantry in the First World War. We see him stop skinheads tormenting a hippie. His old commanding officer pops round with his wife for the weekend film, and greets Fred cordially.

Fred sees on television that a V.C. has fetched £2,000 at Sotheby's. This is his chance to give his tubercular wife Valerie that much needed holiday, etc. But should he sell his glory? (Flashbacks to his wartime exploits.) Pensive in the shabby armchair, he wrestles with his soul . . . His married daughter nags him to sell. ('It's only a bit of old bronze'.) His wife repines. Victor, having overcome his scruples, puts the medal into Sotheby's. As the bidding mounts, scenes from the war again supervene. 'Do I hear five hundred?' asks the urbane auctioneer. (The camera moves over 500 Passchendaele crosses.) The final crash of the gavel is like a mortar shell. It brings him back to a beaming room, flash-bulbs, and the news that his V.C. has fetched a record sum of £4,000.

His wife is wanly radiant and an evening paper carries the headline: 'For Valerie!' For the last scene, we are outside the Classic again. Fred salutes as his commanding officer again approaches, but the disgusted Brigadier cuts him dead. The camera swings upwards to where an Art Deco board bills the current oldie: *Carrington V.C.*

The record price for a V.C. is in fact £7,125, which was paid at Sotheby's in 1975; according to Mr E. C. Joslin of Spink's, the celebrated dealers in orders, decorations and medals, the value of a V.C. is, on average, between £3,000 and £7,000 Many good medals can, however, be bought for under £10. There is, of course, nearly always an interesting story to a V.C. The value depends very much on how many were given to a regiment, and in a particular campaign as a whole.

How do you collect medals? The best general introduction for the beginner is probably *Collecting Medals and Decorations* by Alec A. Purves (Hamlyn, 1972). Mr Purves sensibly suggests that the novice will want to start by collecting generally. As with the philatelist, he will then be able to decide after a period of fairly indiscriminate collecting what interests him most. It will be useful for him to learn such technicalities as how to test a medal for base metal with concentrated nitric acid, and how to check the diameter with callipers if he suspects that the edge has been re-named.

This naming of medals is perhaps the chief fascination of the subject. Before the Second World War, most medals bore round their edges the names of their recipients. For example, I bought some time ago from Spink's the Ashanti War Medal of 1874 because of my interest in that year. It is a splendid affair. Struck in silver, it displays the Queen's head on one side and a dramatic scene of British soldiers beating up the savages on the other (which reminded me of Pollaiuolo's famous battle drawing). It was designed by Sir Edward Poynter, who became President of the Royal Academy. The edge of the one I bought was stamped: 'G. Popplestone. Shipwt. H.M.S. Simoom. 73–74.' Popplestone is an unusual name. When I last looked, there was only one listed in the London telephone directory, and I made a mental note to write and ask him whether my shipwright was an ancestor. There might even be a photograph of him wearing the medal. I have also asked a researcher to obtain for me a copy of Popplestone's service record from the Public Records Office.

Mr Peter Coad of Bristol, a well informed collector, has adopted similar practices to enable him to track down a number of the recipients of his fine medals. When I visited him recently, he showed me a pair of medals which he thinks are worth approximately £30 the pair: the Egypt Medal of 1880–89 with bars for Tel-el-Kebir, Suakin, 1884, El-Teb-Tamaai, The Nile 1884–85 and Kirbekan; and the Khedive's

Star which was awarded to all troops. Mr Coad could not understand why the surname of the recipient had been changed on the medal and wanted to confirm that it was authentic. Once he had obtained the man's record from the Public Records Office the reason became obvious: during the Egyptian Campaign he had officially changed his name.

Mr Coad also owns an unusual pair of medals awarded to Asst. Surgeon J. McKinnell: the Baltic Medal of 1854–55, and the Indian Mutiny Medal of 1857–58 – in other words, a curious combination of naval and military awards. The records revealed that McKinnell had resigned from the navy of his own accord because of ill health. He had asked to return but had been refused – it was thought that the health hazards were too great. Without, therefore, telling the army of his previous naval service, he joined the Black Watch and subsequently took part in the Indian Mutiny. Mr Coad estimates that this pair is worth approximately £70. I asked Mr Coad how he had begun collecting. A friend of his, a very varied collector, had been on the point of leaving for Malta, and had given Mr Coad the choice of several objects which he wanted to dispose of for nominal sums. ('We were far too good friends for him to give them to me.') Mr Coad had been attracted by a small frame of medals on the wall, and purchased it for £5. He was showing it to a Bristol antiques dealer when two medal collectors came over and told him what an exceptional group he had bought. The next day they visited him, bringing some examples from their own collection. Mr Coad was hooked.

He began by collecting military general service medals. After acquiring the rarest clasp – for the Battle of Benavente, 1809, when only ten bars were awarded – 'I suddenly looked at it hanging up over there and thought: "How boring!"' He then went through Major L. L. Gordon's book *British Battles and Medals* (the fourth edition, published by Spink's in 1971 was revised by Mr E. C. Joslin) to discover who had taken part in the widest range of campaigns. With the exceptions of the Royal Artillery and the Rifle Brigade, the 42nd/73rd Royal Highland Regiment (the Black Watch) seemed to offer the widest scope, combined with a fascinating regimental history.

Mr Coad not only collects Black Watch medals; he collects memoirs and histories associated with the Black Watch, and also owns an almost complete run of Army Lists from 1799 to 1968, including a number of the lists printed privately by Lieutenant-General H. G. Hart, which indicate when an officer was promoted to different ranks, and provide a *résumé* of his career. In collecting the medals of a given

An interesting group of medals to Qr. Mr. Sjt.
William Maxwell, 74th Foot (left to right):
Regimental Medal of Merit, 2nd Class, for
the Peninsular War, with six battle honours;
Military General Service, 1793–1814, with
7 bars; Army L. S. & G. S. (William IV type)

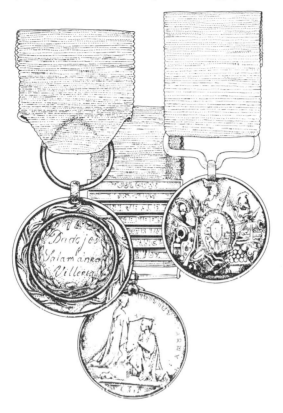

regiment, he suggests that you will find both regimental museums and
regimental magazines of great assistance.

Among the prizes of Mr Coad's Black Watch collection are a group
of three medals won by Sergeant J. Arnott, who served through the
Peninsular War and at Waterloo. (He was so proud of having been at
Quatre Bras that he had his own bar engraved for it.) Mr Coad thinks
that the three medals – the Military General Service Medal, 1793–1814,
the Waterloo (Quatre Bras) medal and a regimental medal for meri-
torious service – would be worth about £250. Sergeant Arnott was
wounded at Waterloo; as was Ensign G. D. Bridge of the 73rd Regiment (which became the 2nd Battalion, Black Watch), whose Waterloo

Medal Mr Coad also owns and values at £100. Arnott's wounds may well have been attended to by Assistant Surgeon D. M'Pherson, whose Waterloo medal Mr Coad estimates to be worth £80. He has discovered that M'Pherson died at Chatham in 1839, and intends to write to the Chatham local library to find out whether an obituary appeared in the local paper.

Recommended reading for the collector is the *Standard Catalogue of British Orders, Decorations and Medals* by Mr E. C. Joslin (Spink's, 3rd ed. 1976), in which many of the medals mentioned are illustrated and all are priced. The following London dealers are recommended: J. B. Hayward and Son, Piccadilly Arcade, W1; Spink & Son Ltd., King Street, SW1; Baldwin and Sons of 11 Adelphi Terrace, WC2; B. A. Seaby, 11 Margaret Street, W1; and, outside London, Charles Lusted of 96a Calverley Road, Tunbridge Wells, Kent; A. D. Hamilton and Co., 7 St Vincent Place, Glasgow G1, and Angus Antiques of 4 St Andrew's Street, Dundee.

Serious collectors should join the Orders and Medals Research Society (Membership Secretary: Mr N. I. Brooks, 33 Berkeley Avenue, Greenford, Middlesex) and the Military Historical Society, Centre Block, Duke of York's Headquarters, Chelsea, London SW3.

Mapping out the past

Only by telling a middle-class English girl that one detests Pooh Bear (as indeed I do) can one arouse such rabid, blind hostility as by telling a philatelist that one considers stamp-collecting a footling occupation (as indeed I do). When I was a schoolboy I went in for stamp-collecting and all that messing about with tweezers, hinges, watermark trays, and perforations – just as I did for breeding white mice and collecting frog's spawn in jars. But when I was a child, I thought as a child, spake as a child and collected as a child. I soon became disenchanted with the endless 'sets' bearing the basilisk profiles of monarchs and dictators. (Stamp designers have not, on the whole, been in the Pisanello class.)

I took the first faltering step towards specialist collecting when I read in a comic that it was a good idea to collect 'map stamps'. You would be amazed how many stamps are illustrated with the maps of the countries concerned. Eventually I tired of these miniature gummed charts, too, but my album of them survives and I was recently assured by a stamp dealer that the collection is almost as worthless now as when it was formed in the 1950s. 'In fact', he said, 'if it is of any sentimental value to you, I should hang on to it.' I wondered what sentiment could possibly attach to five titchy maps of the Falkland Islands. The only map stamp for which I had the least romantic regard was one of a place then known by the voluptuous name of Tanou-Touva, formerly part of Mongolia but annexed by Russia in 1944.

All the same, as a veteran map-stamp collector I was intrigued to learn in 1975 that the greatest of all stamp dealers, Stanley Gibbons, had decided to 'diversify' and open a shop in London to sell maps. I visited it while the stock was being set out to talk about map collecting with the manager.

The first question I put was one which any beginner would need to ask: How do you tell an early map from a late one? Paper is one clue: the early papers have a pleasing grainy texture, which is easily distinguished from the bland flawlessness of later papers. The method of printing is also revealing: the earliest maps were printed from wood blocks, a relief process; then came copper engraving, an intaglio process; lithographic printing, a surface or planographic method which came in during the nineteenth century; later still metal, plastic and paper plates superseded stone, and the image is now transferred photographically to the plate.

One of the biggest problems for the map collector is colour. Early maps were all printed in black and white. Colour printing was not introduced until the nineteenth century, but traditionally maps had been hand coloured at extra charge, and map colouring was a respected profession. Hodgkiss records that in seventeenth-century France the profession was so esteemed that Nicholas Bérey was granted the title '*Enlumineur de la reine*'. But how does one distinguish between early contemporary colouring and modern work – for there are still excellent map colourists at work? Like most aspects of collecting, it is a matter of experience.

Maps range in price from £5 for a nineteenth-century country map ('miniature country histories in their own right' is how Gibbons chose to describe them), to £22,500 for a full set of Blaeu's *Atlas* of 1654. (The Blaeu family of Amsterdam, a map-making dynasty, were the best known cartographers of their day, competing, not always amicably, with the rival house of Jansson.) Also in the high price range comes such a masterpiece as 'The Panorama of the Thames from London to Richmond, Exhibiting Every Object on Both Banks of the River' by Samuel Leigh, of 18 The Strand, *c.* 1800. This beautiful aquatinted panorama extends to 60 feet in length. Selecting a few maps in the middle price range, there are those of various British cities from the world atlas of cities by the Germans Georg Braun and Franz Hodelberg – Exeter at £120 (coloured), London at £275 (coloured), Edinburgh at £110 (uncoloured). They were published in 1590, and it is still puzzling scholars how the high vantage point was obtained.

A. G. Hodgkiss's *Discovering Antique Maps* (Shire Publications, 1975) is an admirable and well illustrated little book which gives clear hints for the beginner, and introduces him to the arcane terminology of the map collector: 'swash lettering,' for example, is the flourishing lettering often used to fill in unwanted space – as in 'PARTE OF SUFFOLKE' and 'PARTE OF ESSEX' on the Speed map of Cambridgeshire. And he lists the main early mapmakers, with brief comments on each.

An elaborately ornamented cartouche from the eastern
section of the map of Savoy by Joannes Jansson (1650)

Stanley Gibbons' map shop – Mapsellers of 37 Southampton Street,
London, is near to their stamp headquarters in the Strand, and it is
interesting to bear in mind that between 1500 and 1800 this area was
rich in mapsellers' shops: John Rocque, for example, land surveyor,
engraver, mapseller and typographer to the Prince of Wales, had a
map shop from 1751 to 1753 close to, if not on the site of, Gibbons'
premises. Other dealers in maps include: P. J. Radford, formerly of
Portsmouth but now in the sumptuous setting of Sheffield Park,
Sussex; Weinreb and Douwma of 93 Great Russell Street, London
WC1; Baynton Williams of 18, Lowndes Street, SW1; and Clive
Burden of Rickmansworth.

American billboard masters

Few English publishers today will commission a large art book without first securing, on the strength of a 'dummy', an American co-publisher to bear some of the cost. In one way the author benefits from this system: his royalties naturally increase with the American sales. But he is also likely to have to put up with a number of fairly pressing suggestions from the American publisher while writing the book. When I was writing my first book on posters, which appeared in 1969, the American publisher sent a forceful message that he hoped the book would contain *as much on American posters as on French ones* – apparently basing this injunction on the idea that his American readers were bursting to read about their own products, however inferior those might be to the European.

It seemed to me as absurd as to suggest that a book on jazz should contain as much on French jazz as on American. Everyone knows that the best poster designs, since the main beginnings of the pictorial poster in the 1870s, came from France, with Toulouse-Lautrec as the unchallenged prince of posterists. Still, American publishers being the tough, rimless-spectacled guys they are, I decided to investigate the range of American posters. I soon discovered to my surprise that there were many I wanted to illustrate, and that there was much to say about them. I also found that, even in America, very little had been written about the early American posters of the 1890s and 1900s since they were produced.

The best place in England to look at early American posters is Lords Gallery, 26 Wellington Road, London NW8, near St John's Wood Underground station. Mr Philip Granville, the proprietor of the gallery, recently held two concurrent exhibitions, one of American posters in the 1890s, the other of the works of Edward Penfield, one of the best poster artists of that time.

In chauvinistic revenge on my American publisher, I was able to show in my book that the American poster originated in England;

more specifically, in Brighton Grammar School, where in the late 1880s were three exact contemporaries all of whom would have an influence on the art world: Aubrey Beardsley, Charles Cochran (later Sir Charles), the impresario who staged Noël Coward's revues and brought Mistinguett, Sarah Bernhardt and Chaliapin to England, and George Frederick Scotson-Clark, a posterist who became art editor of *The Century* magazine in America and was also described as 'a second Sainte-Beuve' in recognition of his several books on cookery.

The American poster owes much to these three men. Beardsley's drawings were probably the most powerful influence on American poster art, certainly on the art of Will Bradley, an artist well represented at Lords Gallery. Cochran and Scotson-Clark were artistic missionaries who went to America as young men: Scotson-Clark designed posters there which introduced Americans to the new French-influenced style; Cochran was the first to chronicle the early development of the American pictorial poster in *The Poster* magazine of the 1890s.

In an article on 'Theatrical Posters in America' which he contributed to *The Poster* of July, 1898, Cochran wrote:

Seven years ago, when I first visited America, I was struck with the horrors that looked down upon one from the hoardings. The huge theatrical posters, although beautifully printed, were entirely lacking in taste as regards design and colour. The figures were tailors' dummies without life or movement, and the backgrounds were the old stereotyped German photographic reproductions of scenes from the play advertised. Things in the States are very different now, and with the exception of a few purveyors of cheap melodrama, the American impresario strives his utmost to secure original and tasteful designs from first-rate artists.

What had brought about the change? Partly Scotson-Clark's Beardsleyesque posters and his proselytizing on behalf of his former schoolfellow. Partly the Mucha posters that Sarah Bernhardt brought with her on her American tour; though the great actress was not amused to see a cruel parody of her cadaverous features staring down from a poster which proclaimed *Carter's River Bitters Will Make You Eat*.

But it was in 1894 that the poster craze really took hold of New York, when Eugene Tompkins heralded a revival of the play *The Black Crook* with a number of posters by the French artist Jules Chéret, whose posters had influenced Toulouse-Lautrec himself. To 1894 also belongs the first outstanding American poster by an American artist, Will Bradley's advertisement of Tom Hall's novel *When*

Hearts are Trumps. Bradley later wrote a memoir of his life, published by the New York Typophiles as *Will Bradley: His Chap Book* in 1955.

He was born in 1868, the son of the cartoonist of the *Daily Item*, the newspaper of Lynn, Massachusetts. His own first job earned him $3 a week, as a printer's devil with the *Iron Agitator*. He served a full apprenticeship in printing with various newspapers, and eventually set up his own printing works in Chicago, where the Tom Hall poster was printed. While the influence of Beardsley is nearly always evident in Bradley's work, there is never any question of sterile pastiche. Lords Gallery had examples of his work on sale when I visited.

Edward Penfield, born in Brooklyn in 1866, took his main influence from another source – the Japanese wood-block print, which was after all Beardsley's own inspiration. He was the most prolific American artist of the '90s. Between 1893 and 1899 he designed seventy-five posters for *Harper's* monthly issues, small in size, for putting up inside bookshops. Nearly all these posters show the *haut ton* of the day: elegant men in bowler hats and elastic-sided boots; women in frilled silk dresses and picture hats. Only once are working people represented, and that is in a poster for *People We Pass: Stories of Life among the Masses of New York City* by Julian Ralph. (Lords Gallery had this on sale at $180; prices for other Penfield posters ranged from $80 to $400.)

The Lords Gallery also had on display a number of posters by Ethel Reed, including one for the *Boston Illustrated* (signed, 1895) at $240. Miss Reed was another posterist strongly influenced by Beardsley. I knew that she had designed a fine poster for Richard Le Gallienne's *The Quest of the Golden Girl*. But Mr Granville surprised me by asking: 'Did you know she was Le Gallienne's mistress?'

I borrowed from the London Library Richard Whittington-Egan's and Geoffrey Smerdon's book about Le Gallienne, *The Quest of the Golden Boy* (Unicorn Press, 1960). They record how in February, 1897, Le Gallienne had a violent row with his future wife, Julie Norregard.

It is almost certain that it arose over a young American woman from Boston named Ethel Reed, a beautiful and talented artist who had contributed drawings to *The Yellow Book* ... Richard fell wildly in love with her, and Jimmy Welch, who knew all about his brother-in-law's passion for Ethel, spent an entire evening pacing up the platform of Witley railway station trying to persuade Richard to back out of the impending marriage with Julie before it was too late. It is also a fact that long afterwards when he was living in America and heard from a mutual acquaintance that Ethel had gone blind, Richard was terribly upset and wrote a very revealing poem to her which was included in his *New Poems*, published in 1910.

Quotations from Le Gallienne's letters in the book make it clear that the affair was pretty ardent. I also borrowed from the library Le Gallienne's own book *The Romantic '90s* (1926). Referring to the 'charming "teas"' of the publisher John Lane, he says: 'One met distinguished and beautiful women, dowagers, socialists, poets and artists – and among the latter I particularly recall the Rossetti-like head of Mrs Graham R. Thomson, the boyish, bird-like charm of 'E. Nesbit', the flower-like loveliness of Olive Custance – since Lady Alfred Douglas – and the noble silent beauty of Ethel Reed, whose early death robbed the world of a great decorative artist.'

For those who intend to collect American posters seriously, the essential reference work is *Das frühe Plakat in Europa und den USA* (vol. i, 1973, published by Gebr. Mann, Berlin). Also valuable is *American Posters of the 'Nineties*, based on an exhibition held in 1974 by the Boston Public Library, the Currier Gallery of Art and Dartmouth College (published 1974 by the Stinehour Press, Lunenburg, Vermont) and *Bradley*, a catalogue of an exhibition of his posters held at the Metropolitan Museum of Art, New York, in 1972. The only American poster gallery comparable with the Lords Gallery in London is the Reinhold-Brown Gallery, 26 East 78th Street, New York, whose proprietors, Susan Reinhold and Robert K. Brown, are among the most knowledgeable experts on old posters that I have met.

It looks good on paper

In writing about antique papier mâché, I speak as a papier mâché master craftsman of over twenty-five years' experience. One of my most disgusting memories is of tearing up newspaper and soaking the resulting grey confetti in a pail of water; the damp paper mess was then squeezed out, flour-and-water paste added, and the pulp smoothed over the face of a school-friend, with two drinking straws stuck up his nostrils to prevent asphyxiation. We were making a 'life mask'. This was one of the Things from that lethal book *1001 Things a Boy Can Do*, which also included instructions for heating gramophone records and bending them into flower pots.

Rudimentary though my methods may have been, they were a fairly accurate parody of the basic method of making papier mâché commercially. The earliest English papier mâché, however, which was used in the seventeenth century for applied decoration in architecture and cabinet-making, was not made of paper at all, but of plaster mixed with vegetable matter – straw, nettles and bark. This was known in the trade as 'fibrous slab', and the principal manufacturer was named Wilton, the father of Joseph Wilton the sculptor. In 1748 a paper dealer named Masefield had a 'papier mâché manufactory' in the Strand; in 1756 Robert Adam was using papier mâché instead of plaster; in 1758 Robert Dossie's book *The Handmaid of the Arts* outlined a method of making heat-resistant paperware; and in 1765 *The Complete Dictionary of Arts and Sciences*, published by The Revd. T. Crowther, also gave details of a paper-pulp process.

Papier mâché was an outcome of the 'japanning' (lacquering) trade, and is thus allied to the Pontypool tin-ware (which often looks remarkably similar to papier mâché of the same period), to which the same hard varnish was applied. By 1770 the manufacture of papier mâché was so established in Birmingham as to have become a separate trade. In 1772 Henry Clay revolutionized the industry by his invention of a new heat-resistant paperware that could be sawn like wood.

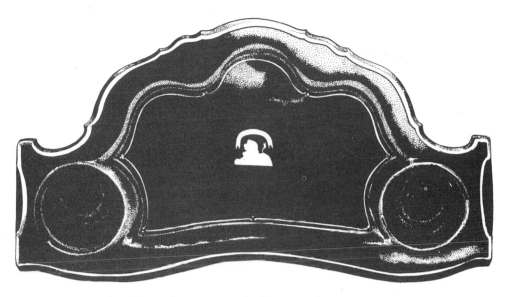

A papier mâché supper tray by Jennens and Bettridge *c.* 1850

Clay, one of the most important manufacturers, became High Sheriff
of Warwickshire in 1790 and moved from Birmingham to Covent
Garden, London in 1802, having made a fortune. Another famous
manufacturing firm, Jennens and Bettridge, took over the old Clay
business in 1816. They exhibited furniture at the Great Exhibition of
1851 and became 'Makers to the Queen'. The third name to look out
for in papier mâché is that of Spiers and Son of Oxford. They did not
make the papier mâché themselves, but bought blanks from Alsager
and Neville, some already partially decorated. Their ware is usually
very finely painted.

To see a lot of papier mâché in the flesh, and to benefit from the
tips of a specialist, I visited Mr Richard Grosvenor, who dealt in
papier mâché and little else at 4 Trebeck Street, Shepherd Market,
London W1. Mr Grosvenor, a cousin of Lady Leonora, gave her for
a wedding present when she married Lord Lichfield a papier mâché
card or cake stand which bore a view of the family seat of Eaton Hall,
Cheshire. He began dealing in papier mâché nine years ago.

Tables and trays were among the larger articles made of papier
mâché and stocked by Mr Grosvenor. In general, one would pay between £85 and £100 for a tray with gilding; more costly items which
I examined included: a mid-nineteenth-century tray with neo-rococo
decoration in profuse gilding (approximately £300); a set of three

trays by Jennens and Bettridge in Indian red lacquer at £275; a plain oval tray, black with gold trellis decoration (early nineteenth century), £150; and an oval tray decorated with a seascape of 'Nelson Breaking the Line' (mid-nineteenth century) which would cost approximately £200. The names of the different shapes of tray are 'straight edge', which refers to Clay's early trays with straight turned-up edges; 'Gothic', with gadrooned edges; 'Windsor', an oval tray with turned-over rounded edges; and 'Victorian', a shape exclusive to the firm of Walton, in Wolverhampton, another great centre of the papier mâché trade. I also examined a 'parlour maid's tray' – so named from its slightly concave front which made it easier to carry close to the body. The rare (and therefore more valuable) colours of lacquer are Indian red, apple green, ivory and red. Mother-of-pearl decoration is characteristic of the mid-nineteenth century and beyond, but not of the earlier pieces.

A table could cost as much as £1,000, but that would be an expensive piece in extremely fine condition; the average table is likely to cost between £80 and £200. Another costly item is a teapoy: from four lacquered canisters on a stand you would select different teas and blend them in glass bowls at the centre. The price for this would probably be £1,000. A fine pair of chairs with wooden frames but solid papier mâché backs might cost £100–£200 each. In the lower price range, one could buy a Jennens and Bettridge glove-box, decorated in mother-of-pearl and with its original leather hand-strap, or a *chinoiserie*-decorated 'writing slope' (portable writing desk), for £50–£75. Other smaller items which Mr Grosvenor often has in stock include letter-boxes, wine coasters, bellows, ink stands, snuffer trays and glove boxes.

Papier mâché is very hard-wearing – provided it is kept polished. The excellent standard work on the subject is *Papier mâché in Great Britain and America* by Jane Toller (Bell, 1962).

Fantasies from the curious and rare

Is there any case for altering antiques from their original state? Most museum men, dealers and collectors would reply with an outraged 'no'. The museum expert will recall with a shudder the old dear who brought along a fine Chinese bronze from which she had painstakingly removed the ancient greeny-brown patina with metal polish and a scrubbing brush. The book collector sighs for the drab original boards which Keats may have fingered when he received his first copies – replaced, on the order of some insensitive Victorian squire, by lush red morocco stamped with his crest in gold. The gutted spinet converted into a cocktail cabinet, the Ming vase drilled with a hole and fitted out as a table lamp, are nightmares to haunt the connoisseur.

In recent years, however, a young dealer called Anthony Redmile has demonstrated that conversion of antiques can mean something more than skulduggery with a fretsaw and gluepot in a back room. His conversions are as public as Billy Graham's. By designing and making extravagantly modern settings for his antiques, he has created a new kind of object, and almost a new style. Purists will no doubt find it abominable. Those with a more baroque taste, or a penchant for High Kitsch, will revel in his wild and opulent conceits; the narwal tusks on silver plinths; the huge Catherine wheels of Indian army swords; the ostrich-egg chandeliers; the preposterous confections of antlers, palm trees, silver artichokes, ammonites, lapis lazuli, nautilus shells and water buffalo skulls. They are objects to feed the fantasies of a Beckford or a Beardsley.

Anthony Redmile comes from the village of Redmile in what used to be Rutland. As a child he lived in the grounds of Belvoir Castle (pronounced 'Beaver', as in the limerick 'There was a young lady of Belvoir, Whose husband was wont to decelvoir'). The 'Gothick' style of the castle and the swags of militia on the walls were an early influence on him. Members of his family were in the antiques business in the Midlands – 'in fact, they had a monopoly there before the war.'

Redmile attended Nottingham Art School and St Martin's School of Art in London. He trained as a crafts designer. 'I went through Maples from A to Z; worked in all their factories – the woodwork factories, metalwork factories, casting factories in the West Country and in their studio. I had a traditional mechanical education.' Then a friend offered him a job restoring antique porcelain in a studio in Albany Street. He restored for Sotheby's and some of the London museums, and mended pieces from the Wernher collection of porcelain at Luton Hoo. He gave up the restoring trade for health reasons. 'One was inhaling dangerous fumes all day. I have a beard now because I blew myself up with a kiln I designed.'

He had already been dealing in antiques from his own restoring shop. Now he went over to selling antiques full-time. He soon realized that there was a big market, especially amongst interior decorators, for unusual antiques – the rare and curious, rather than the beautiful pieces. Some years ago he bought up the Old Kensington Pottery Works at Kensington Court, just opposite the Antiques Hypermarket. With the capital he had amassed in the restoring trade, he set up departments of metalwork, woodwork, ceramics and painting, and began to create mounts and settings fit for his bizarre wares. 'I only wanted to do large, important things. There were already too many craftsmen making small, bijou items.' Some of the objects were mounted on simple silver stands or plinths, and allowed to speak for themselves – for example, a mammoth tooth from Russia with a rich ivory patina fissured like mud in a drought. Others were set atop pyramids of campery, giant artichokes of 'German silver' (a nickel alloy – to use solid silver would be monstrously expensive). There was a large American market for these extravaganzas, which has since been rapidly overhauled by Continental enthusiasts. Mr Redmile also has London shops at 73 Pimlico Road and 36 Sloane Street, very modern in style: 'I think these elaborate antiques look best in a clinical setting.'

Here are a number of items typical of his stock: a chandelier of sixteen ostrich eggs mounted in German silver with ivory and lapis lazuli ornament which would cost approximately £1,500 ('I couldn't get ostrich eggs from Australia; these come from South Africa'); a Victorian wooden turtle in a silver box with a real blonde turtle shell as lid, the box set with malachite cabochons: length 1ft. 2in. (£80); an elephant's jawbone used as the base of a mirror and set with a seventeenth-century Persian vase ornamented with a modern mask in German silver: height 4ft. 6 in. (£200). Redmile likes to make things in pairs: 'In the antiques trade they used to say "What a pity you don't have the pair!"' I saw a pair of saw-fish swords (£150 each) on German silver bases; and a pair of Venetian carved monkeys holding ostrich-egg candelabra (£500 for the pair). There was also a gauntly impressive singleton: an Indian water-buffalo skull, polished and bleached, mounted on a German silver plinth: height 4ft. (£300). Redmile has even experimented with hinged human skulls for after-eight mints, 'but it put some people off'.

When I visited him he was working on a French château with Erté. The furniture was to be created exclusively from antlers – 'most of it is still walking about in Scotland.' He was also working on wall sconce designs sketched by Mrs Onassis. He owns a pet boa constrictor ('Harrods got a bit uptight; I was repeatedly buying hamsters and guinea pigs for it') and he made it a cage in a form which resembled a 12-feet-high chalice, with eight little onion towers inlaid with malachite, the whole set on a silver palm tree with a porphyry base.

Redmile has now begun signing his things. 'So often I see a photograph of some luxurious interior in one of the magazines with my pieces prominently displayed, and with no credit whatever.' He has set up his own lapidary; he used to send stones to Germany to have them polished. A few years ago, he paid a visit to Mexico where he ordered large consignments of agate eggs and abalone shells, for use in veneers. 'The Mexicans use abalone shells boringly,' he comments. 'Up to now the only pleasure the fish gave one was as abalone steak at Sally's Valhalla in San Francisco.' Another enjoyable pastime is that of selling mounted ammonites to America. 'The American customs wanted a certificate proving that the things were dated pre-1840. I think they were satisfied when an expert vouched that they were forty-five million years old.'

Redmile claims that his Amazing Marriage of old and new has enabled him to beat the recent slump in the antiques trade. 'The American recession altered the whole market. Many dealers think they can go on making a pretty penny just selling antiques as they always have done. But so many people know about antiques now, through the television programmes and collecting magazines, that the old rules do not apply. People even know today about the "fun" stuff which is needed by interior decorators. Only by providing a new product can one avoid the general decline in business.' What of his clients? Does he think of them as people with very bad taste or with a sense of humour? Redmile gazes pensively at a totem pole of polished monkey skulls. 'My customers have very chic taste indeed.' A major exhibition of his exotic creations ruffled the traditionalism of Harrods in October 1976.

I visited another of London's leading converters, Nita Miller of 42 Grosvenor Hill, W1. Mrs Miller converts vases and other objects into lamps. Not, I hasten to add, Ming ones; and, personally, I think her discreet adaptations of plain-coloured Chinese vases quite justifiable. Mrs Miller set up in business twenty-nine years ago when she was widowed four years after her marriage. She started in a flat in Knightsbridge, hiring three girls as assistants, all of whom are still with her. She has been at Grosvenor Hill since 1950. In all these years she has had no real competitor, she says. Much of her business is supplying embassies and palaces with lamps. When I called, a crate was just going off to Buraimi Oasis. She likes to think that: 'The last thing an ambassador sees before he goes to sleep is a Nita Miller lamp, and it is the first thing he sees on waking up and switching on the light in the morning.'

She was selling a *sang-de-boeuf* vase with lotus base (now approximately £120). But not all the lamps were Chinese vases. They included a Persian rosewater ewer of the eighteenth century (£145); an Egyptian turquoise-enamelled vase (approximately £250); a Scandinavian red glass vase (£45); a rose quartz goddess (£400); a Georgian copper urn (£150). The most expensive lamp in stock when I called was a Thai Buddha, with an attractive tinge of pink in its gilding (£750). Every lamp had a price ticket on it and each shade was listed in a price list. Mrs Miller is not keen on coloured shades: 'If you want light, you don't want colour. You'll never notice the shade if it's right.' Somewhere among the mangrove swamps tonight, a Second Secretary will not be noticing his shade as he switches out the light above the celadon vase . . .

Tom Thumb treats

Why should small antiques not be treated with as much respect, aesthetically, as larger ones? If one is talking of silver, the matter of intrinsic value has to be considered; but it is still sadly true that if a critic is presented with two pieces of sculpture in a material of negligible value such as stone, one twenty feet high and one two feet high, he is more likely to be impressed by the bigger.

The house of the average collector is decreasing in size, however, and there are signs that at last the miniature is coming into its own. Anyone who has walked through the miniature town of Madurodam in Holland and heard the unmightiest of Wurlitzers pumping out its squeaky melodies will be able to appreciate the charm of a single drawing-room cabinet acting as a pantechnicon, and not as a mere showcase for five or six pieces of porcelain or man-sized silver.

In 1972 an American collector's hoard of miniature silver realized £27,380 at Christie's. Most of the minuscule wares fetched approximately double the auctioneer's estimated prices. The two top prices were £1,700 for a set of four George I table-candlesticks and a snuffer-stand with snuffers, c. 1725, the snuffers by David Clayton; and £1,150 for a rare James II fire-grate, fire-dog, fender, shovel, fire tongs and trivet by George Manjoy, 1688 – the largest of all these pieces being only four inches high.

Both Clayton and Manjoy were silversmiths over whom there has been some controversy, and both were almost certainly specialists in miniature silver, seldom turning their hands to full-sized pieces. Miniature silver of the eighteenth century and earlier raises the same kind of question as early dolls' houses of the same period: were they made as specimens by craftsmen to show off their skills – or perhaps as travellers' samples; or were they intended as playthings for children? One hears much talk, for example, of so-called 'dolls' houses' made as architects' models, to show a prospective client the kind of house he might like to commission. Perhaps this did happen sometimes, but

159

my own inclination is to believe that most of the small houses and the majority of the miniature silver and furniture were made as toys. Swift wrote in *Gulliver's Travels* (1726) of 'a set of silver dishes and plates . . . not much bigger than what I have seen of the same kind in a London toyshop for the furniture of a baby house' (i.e. dolls' house).

A learned introduction to the Christie's catalogue of the collection mentioned above describes how the initials 'G.M.', found on certain items of miniature silver, have in the past been attributed to George Middleton; while a mark that appears on Britannia Standard silver, 'Ma', has been ascribed to Isaac Malyn. The records of makers' marks at Goldsmiths' Hall, London, however, reveal conclusively that 'Ma' was the mark of George Manjoy, who worked in London from the end of the reign of Charles II until the early eighteenth century; and it seems reasonable to conclude that the 'G.M.' mark on standard silver is his also. Unfortunately, documentary proof is lacking: the records which linked the names of goldsmiths with their marks prior to 1967 were all destroyed in a fire at Goldsmiths' Hall.

Similarly, there has in the past been a mis-ascription of the mark of the leading toy-maker of the reigns of George I and II. The mark has been attributed to Augustine Courtauld; but, as the Christie's expert pointed out, Courtauld was a Huguenot and always incorporated a fleur-de-lis in his mark; also, he is well known as a maker of full-sized objects. It seems more likely that Mr C. C. Oman is right in suggesting that this mark, which appears to be 'A.C.' when upside down, is in fact, 'D.C.' when read the right way up and belongs to David Clayton, being entered in the Goldsmiths' records in July, 1720.

The sale proved that miniature silver must be treated, commercially at least, with respect; but what of that other province of Lilliput, the miniature book? One of the principal dealers in such books is Mr Louis W. Bondy, whose shop is at 16 Little Russell Street, London WC1 (near the British Museum). In May–June 1964 Mr Bondy contributed an amusing but authoritative article on miniature volumes to the *Journal of the National Book League*. Miniature books, he wrote, are either loved or hated. He had hardly ever found anyone indifferent to them.

Those who love them, and there are hundreds of such collectors, love them passionately, with the sort of possessive and protective love that a man lavishes on a very dainty, beautiful woman or a small and over-sensitive child. Those who hate them never let an occasion go by without expressing their dislike and giving vent to their spite. They call miniature books stupid little toys, 'a-

160

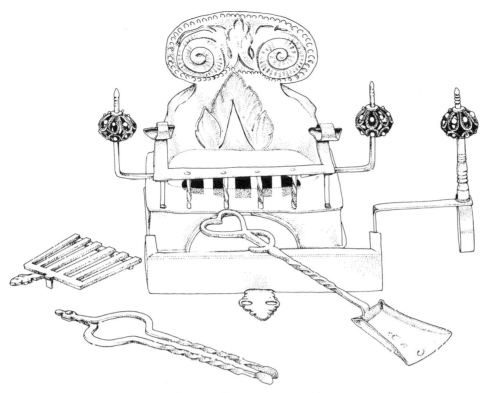

A rare James II fire grate, fire dog, fender,
shovel, fire-tongs and trivet. The largest
of these pieces is only four inches high

biblia', non-books and a waste of perfectly good craftsmanship.
One very small man, a great bibliophile in all other respects, flew
into an uncontrollable rage when face to face with a tiny book.
He considered it a parody of his own insignificant stature.

What is a miniature book? Apparently collectors commonly agree on
a maximum height of three inches. Mr Bondy, however, also insists
that the book must not be roughly bound and crudely printed, but
conceived as a whole on a tiny scale – exquisitely printed in small
type and bound in a binding tooled with delicacy in proportion to its
size. Like the Lord's Prayer on a cherry stone, it is a challenge to the
designer and craftsman. Literally small masterpieces have been produced by some of the great printers: Plantin of Antwerp, Jannon of
Sedan, the Foulis Press, Glasgow. Engravers, too, have made some
enchanting miniature volumes; for example, the *London Almanack*
which was produced for about two hundred years by the Company of
Stationers.

Naturally, children's books have been a favourite for miniature productions. Amongst the earliest were John Weever's rare *Agnus Dei* of 1601, the 'Water Poet' John Taylor's *Verbum Sempiternum* of 1693, and his *Book of Martyrs*, which appeared in a tiny two-volume edition dated London, 1616. Thomas Boreman's *Gigantick Histories*, published in London in 1740, are also much sought after. Miniature books have been used in clandestine propaganda, as by the anti-Nazi Underground in the Third Reich. For similar reasons, erotic literature has been presented in miniature; Mr Bondy instanced a limited edition of Piron's *Ode à Priape* and a tiny obscene ABC published *circa* 1850'.

Here are two samples from Mr Bondy's current catalogue (the most expensive and the cheapest items): *La Gracieuse*: a very rare set of ten miniature books (each measuring 42 × 32 mm) in a miniature bookcase, containing the fables of Fénelon, La Fontaine, Florian and Moreau. Price: approximately £300; 'The Gettysburg Address': one of 1,000 numbered copies, each page within gold lines, bound in red leather, seventeen pages long, measuring 42 × 32 mm. Price: £5.50.

Diogenes would have found a library of this kind very convenient in his barrel. These dolly delights and Tom Thumb treats are far too good to be left to the children.

Written in stone

I have always been fascinated by Egyptian hieroglyphs: the writing you see on the stone resembles a well-stocked aviary standing to attention; but it means 'The divine wife and great royal consort, Aahmes Nefertari, beloved of Amun-Ra, living eternally'; or 'the hereditary prince and overseer of the granaries of Amun'; or 'I reached a good old age with daily favours and an excellent head and pure hands.'

In 1972, six pieces of ancient Egyptian sculpture were sold at auction in London. They had all been dug up in the course of an amateur excavation of the Temple of Mut in Ahser by two Victorian maiden ladies, Miss Benson and Miss Gourlay, in the 1890s. The two described their adventure in a book published by John Murray in 1899 (entitled *The Temple of Mut in Ahser*). It makes amusing reading. They treated their many Arab workmen and boys like two determined Victorian schoolmarms – preventing theft, for example, by threatening to beat them. They gravely adjudged a quarrel between two boys, one of whom had kicked the other in the eye as they swam together in a lake, and dismissed an overseer who demanded higher wages for 'the indignity of working under a woman'. The men received two piastres (five old pence) a day, the boys one and a half piastres; but the ladies wished it to be known that 'a native can purchase from 80 to 100 eggs for one shilling.' They added this magnificent economic *non sequitur*: 'The immense eagerness to get work at the wages offered proves that the people are not ground down to the economic minimum.' The men were forced to work through the fast of Ramadan.

The cry of 'Antica!' would go up when the men uncovered the base of a figure (often found buried upside down), and there would be a feverish scrabbling to clear it of sand. Although the women had no idea how to conduct a scientific dig, they uncovered a number of superb specimens, some of which are now in the Cairo Museum. One of the most important pieces is a standing statue of Ser, priest of Amun; and this is also the most copiously inscribed item. In an appendix to Misses' Benson's and Gourlay's book, the inscriptions on this piece were transcribed, but not fully translated, by Percy E. Newberry. What exactly they said is still in dispute. Amongst other offices, Ser held those of Scribe of the Offerings of Amun in the Third Phyle, and Great Seer of the Southern On (classical Hermonthis – modern Armant). Ser's 'wife and mistress of his house, the sistrum-player of Amun' is called Nai-nub, a name read by Newberry as Sanai-nub. Engraved on the left upper arm is the figure and name of 'Mut the Great One, Mistress of Isheru', and on the right that of the 'Great Khonsu the Child, son of Amun', who is wearing the Junar horns and disc on his head and holds his finger to his mouth in the gesture of youth. The inscriptions on other sculptures found by Misses Benson and Gourlay – those, in particular, on a statue of Menthuemhet, Count of Thebes – are of great historical importance, providing our only Egyptian source for the two successive Assyrian invasions of Thebes by Assurbanipal.

The earliest form of writing was pictography, in which the pictures directly represented specific objects or, by the arrangement of objects in sequence, simple events. Later ideographic writing still used pictures, but they now represented not only the object, but ideas related to it. The next stage was a script based on words with phonetic as well as ideographic values, the best known of which are Egyptian hieroglyphs and Sumerian cuneiform. Both of these were syllabic in structure; the origin of alphabetical writing is, however, still uncertain, although it can probably be traced to a Caananite script which seems to have been the precursor of Greek and Hebrew.

Charles Ede Ltd, of 37 Brook Street, London W1 often stock antiques bearing ancient inscriptions. Wares which I have seen there include the base of a heart scarab in green schist dating from the New Kingdom – which cannot, therefore, be later than 1085 B.C. The finely incised inscription was that of Amun-mose, Keeper of the Pool of Amun. A limestone fragment with part of a single column of large hieroglyphs painted in black and red on an ochre background was also on sale; it came from the tomb of Sethos I (1318–1304 B.C.) in the Valley of the Kings at Thebes, and had been excavated by Belzoni in the early nineteenth century. Not all the hieroglyphs which I examined were on stone. You could have bought a fragment of linen bearing a five-line text and a standing figure worshipping the cow-goddess Meht-urt. Of three fragments of linen inscribed with extracts from The Book of the Dead, two cost less than £20 – a reasonable price for a talisman from the Ptolemaic period.

A bronze figurine of Osiris with inlaid eyes.
Saite period (663–525 B.C.)

For between £30 and £300 it is sometimes possible to find letters in cuneiform script – which look rather like dog biscuits. I have examined one at Ede's which was sent by members of an Assyrian trading colony resident in Anatolia. The clay tablets were nearly 4,000 years old; yet several of the letters might have been written today. One finds references to take-over bids, delivery delays because of civil unrest, and of creditors being dunned for payment. I have also seen a small tablet which recorded the receipt of one dead sheep by Ur-Nigingar (dated 2051 B.C., and perhaps an offering for the temple at Nippur) and a large tablet which proved to be a letter from Ilia and Laqipum to their senior partner (or, possibly, employer), Idi-Ishtar. The script informed him that by selling his stock of barley and calling in fifteen *minas* of copper owed by three other business associates, they had been able to buy up the firm of Arshiakh. Business remained poor, however, and they suggested that Idi-Ishtar send them more money so that his wife and children should not starve in his absence. Within this price range you could also purchase a brick inscribed in cuneiform with the name of Nebuchadnezzar, 'King of Babylon, supporter of the temple Esagila and of the temple Ezida'. (Nowadays the name is transliterated 'Nebuchadrezzar', but the king referred to is that mentioned in the *Book of Kings*). You might, on the other hand, prefer part of a brick from the ziggurat at Choba-Zanbil, on which the Tower of Babel was based.

I am afraid, however, that none of the stones to which I have referred would have sufficient artistic merit to appeal to the former Warden of All Souls, Oxford, John Sparrow, whose *Visible Words* (Cambridge University Press, 1969) is the best introduction to the aesthetic aspect of epigraphy.

165

Pictures to appreciate

There seems to be some idea abroad that paintings and drawings are for the Duveens and Rothschilds of this world, while the rest of us must content ourselves with 'applied arts', like pottery, or pretty trinkets for the cabinet. How often, for example, is a painting shown on television's *Going for a Song*? While Arthur Negus grunts his benediction over teapots and pistols, yew-wood tables and gout-stools, no one is asked to pass judgement on a Millais sketch or a Brangwyn water-colour.

From the Times-Sotheby Index and the sale-room columns, which rightly concentrate on the highest prices, it is possible to gain the impression that pictures are the exclusive preserve of the rich. In fact, genuinely interesting works can still be bought for under £50. That is the principle on which Abbott and Holder, of 73 Castelnau, Barnes, London SW13, have based their business. Mr Eric Holder said that he aims to sell to 'the working chap with wife and kids, who can afford £40'. A few years ago, he used to tell beginners 'never spend more than £20'. The rule holds good now if you alter the £20 to £50. His other piece of advice is to buy what you *like*. 'If you just follow the fashions, you will be paying fashionable prices.'

There is nothing quite like Abbott and Holder in the whole art world. Who else, for example, issues a monthly catalogue headed: 'Attributions . . . are fully guaranteed. Money back and a box of Black Magic chocolates should (unlikely) we be wrong'? The Abbott and Holder catalogues are among the minor literary treasures of our time. The catalogue descriptions are racy, quirkish and often very funny. When they describe an Adrian Allinson *Azalia in white vase* as a 'rich Hampstead-in-the-thirties oils', you know just what they mean. Is it possible to resist Frank Reynold's *A la Russe-Golfski* – 'a very colourful and funny water-colour of joy and despair over a missed put in Russian ballet terms'? Edmund J. Sullivan is rebuked for 'an unpleasant cruel streak' in two drawings, in which 'a devil with attendant skeleton works a guillotine and . . . skeletons and corpses dance at night in a field of guillotines.'

Louis Wain's *Foul!*, showing two footballing cats being halted by a referee cat, is a 'wizard water-colour for a cat-loving Chelsea supporter'. F. C. Underhill's *Norham Castle* is 'after Turner and pretty close too!' They describe a painting by William Strang, R.A. (1859–1921), as 'Head of a man, in legal robes and a black head cover, whose intelligent and kindly features persuade one that he is someone other than a judge (but if not, what?)'. An electric drawing; a radiant oils; a swish water-colour; a gloriously mauve gouache – if Abbott and Holder had had the cataloguing of Velázquez's *Juan de Pareja**, they would probably have called it 'Nice, sombre oils for someone with £2m to blue'.

I paid them a visit on a Wednesday. (On Saturdays they keep open house and you don't need an appointment, but on weekdays *you must telephone first*)†. Castelnau, a Victorian boulevard, takes its name from the Duc de Castelnau, who came over in the early nineteenth century when the beautiful Hammersmith suspension bridge was built. He bought up all the land in that curve of the river, and divided it into plots which in 1832 were put up for auction. None fetched their reserve prices except, as Mr Holder puts it, 'some sold to a poor sucker called Carter, who bought my plot and the one next door. The plan of 1832 shows only my house: it was the first in Castelnau.'

Going round Abbott and Holder's is like being given the run of the house of a rather expansive collector. Mounted drawings wrapped in cellophane lie on every shelf and table; pictures hang on every other inch of wall; but still the impression is of a lived-in house, not a warehouse. Music sits on the piano rest, and perhaps eggs are frizzling in a distant room. Mr Holder does not harry you as you look round, neither does he say maddening things like 'I'm sorry, I haven't priced it yet', like other dealers who aren't quite sure whether they are letting a priceless bargain slip through their fingers by selling it to you.

The way to buy cheaply is to collect sketches, rather than finished paintings; water-colours, in preference to oils; Victorian and modern rather than eighteenth-century works. A collection of sketches can be more revealing of the artists represented than a gallery of their academy paintings.

---

* Sold at Christie's in November 1970 for £2,310,000

† The visitor who lives outside London is advised to write in the first instance; collectors who live in London should consult the local telephone directory

The first thing I found at Abbott and Holder's was a sculpturesque figure study in ink by John Farleigh, well known as a wood engraver in the 1930s. Under it, in the same pile, was a flower study in pencil by James Bolivar Manson (1879–1947). Wasn't he once Director of the Tate Gallery? I asked Mr Holder. 'Yes. He was sacked for crowing at a Royal Academy banquet.' 'Crowing?' 'Crowing: like a cockerel.'

The Manson sketch was dated 16 October, 1944. Dated examples, of course, are more desirable than undated ones. In their catalogue of September 1970, Abbott and Holder advertised a delightfully documented work by Dr William Crotch (1775–1847), a view of Hyde Park inscribed on the back by the artist: 'Handelling my new Camp Stool. Thunder about and like a distant battle, June 9 1832, $\frac{1}{4}$ after 2.' Mr Holder usually has an entertaining anecdote or two about his artists. Of Dr Crotch, he told me: 'He was the first Principal of the Royal Academy of Music. He played "God Save the King" when he was two. He gave organ recitals seated on his mother's knee when he was four. And he had nothing to do with the crotchet.'

Water-colour painting is still largely neglected by the big collectors and this is strange, for of all media it is the one to which the English landscape, misty and undemonstrative, best lends itself. But there are two excellent books on the subject: one is *Early English Watercolours* by Iolo Williams, formerly Museums Correspondent of *The Times* (It was reissued by Kingsmead Reprints in 1970. The original edition now sells for large sums of money in antiquarian bookshops). The other book is *Water-colour Painting in Britain* by Martin Hardie. This is divided into three volumes: *The Eighteenth Century* (such artists as Francis Towne, J. R. Cozens, Blake, Fuseli, Rowlandson and Paul Sandby); *The Romantic Period* (Girtin, Constable, Turner, Cotman, Peter de Wint, etc.); and *The Victorian Period* (the Pre-Raphaelites, Samuel Prout, Birket Foster, etc.). It was published in 1967 and 1968 by Batsford.

On Victorian painting, there are three excellent recent books: *Victorian Painting* by Graham Reynolds (Studio Vista, 1966); *Victorian Artists* by Quentin Bell (Routledge, 1967); and, magnificently illustrated, *Victorian Painters* by Jeremy Maas (Barrie-Cresset Press, 1971). All three are entertainingly written.

A French dealer, M. Gilbert Silberstein of the rue Amélie, Paris, told me: 'In France we often used to laugh at English painting. But now there is a tremendous interest, especially in the Pre-Raphaelites.' The same is true in England. At Robinson and Foster's auction rooms (now, sadly, defunct) in the 1950s one could buy up whole portfolios of Burne-Jones' drawings for a few pounds. I remember a really good Holman Hunt drawing at Abbott and Holder's which was on sale in about 1962 for £20. But the revival of interest, accelerated by such books on the Pre-Raphaelites as the splendid Thames and Hudson work by Timothy Hilton (*The Pre-Raphaelites*, 1970), has put these pictures well beyond the pocket of the modest collector. The 'second division' of Victorian artists – men like Lord Leighton and Sir Edward Poynter – have also risen steeply in value, and a recent biography of Leighton (Yale University Press, 1975) by Mr and Mrs Richard Ormond is bound to cause prices of works by this artist to escalate. I asked Mr Holder which artists he would tip to rise in value over the next few years. He made me a short list: the early Victorian John Mogford (often Pre-Raphaelite in style); the Victorian water-colourists Sir E. A. Waterlow, R.A., and Alfred Parsons, R.A.; and J. R. Reid in oils. He felt that Charles Shannon had been neglected while Shannon's friend Charles Ricketts has become popular: this situation could change. Frank Dobson, R.A. was 'coming up fast'. Undervalued living artists include Carel Weight, R.A., Merlyn Evans and the euphonious Eleanor Bellingham Smith. As a 'long shot' he chose Mildred Eldridge, wife of R. S. Thomas the poet, who 'could become another David Jones – she shares his poetic nonchalance'.

My own tips would be Ethelbert White, a highly original and much underrated water-colourist and wood engraver; James Reeve,* an outstanding modern portraitist who has many top models but not yet many buyers; and, plunging back in history again, Austin Osman Spare (1888–1965), a mystical, slightly cranky painter who could well be made the subject of the kind of West End show the Fine Art Society gave to Maxwell Armfield.†

---

* See profile on pp. 84–87
† Homage exhibition on his 90th birthday, September/October, 1971

From rags to mosaics

When Mr Arthur Gilbert – who now lives in Gatsby-like splendour in sunny Los Angeles – became rich from his successes first in the rag trade in England and later in real estate in the United States, he decided to do what the poor do by necessity, the rich only by discernment or for fun – to collect something that no one else was after, and to form the finest private collection of it in existence. He decided on mosaics.

From the collector's point of view, the life-span of mosaic manufacture was from the late sixteenth to the late nineteenth century, with a few tolerable twentieth-century specimens. The Gilbert collection contains examples of the two main techniques developed in Italy from the sixteenth century onwards – 'Florentine mosaic', or *commesso di pietre dure* (a marquetry of interlocking slabs of hard, semi-precious stone); and 'Roman mosaic', in which minute *tesserae* of coloured glass or ceramics are set in designs in the traditional manner of Byzantine mosaic. The *commesso* technique was popularized by the *Opificio delle Pietre Dure*, which was originally founded by the Medici in the late sixteenth century to supply them with vases, panels and jewellery; as the wealth of the Medici shrunk, the *Opificio* became a source of profit to them by making impressive souvenirs for the grand tourist. The Roman technique was practised at the Vatican school of mosaic, established in 1576 when the St Peter's factory undertook the reproduction in mosaic of the paintings in St Peter's basilica. The school was established permanently in 1727 and, like the Florentine *Opificio*, is still in existence.

Mr Gilbert's collection shows a bias in favour of the Roman micro-mosaics which had been so ignored in comparison with the Florentine *pietra dura* work. The collection contains no work that can certainly be attributed to the greatest of micro-mosaic practitioners, Michelangelo Barberi, although a Roman table decorated with 'The Magnificent Sky of Italy', *c.* 1850, may be by him, and a mosaic of a black and

Mosaics from the Gilbert collection:
(top) eighteen-carat gold-mounted
mosaic brooch and earrings, *c.* 1850;
(left) silver and mosaic box, George IV;
(right) gold and enamel snuff box with
mosaic cover portraying classical head.
Paris, *c.* 1800, by A. Vachette

white spaniel on a Roman tortoiseshell snuffbox, *c.* 1838, is by Aguatti,
who was Barberi's master. Mosaic was an ideal medium for the neo-
classical artist like Barberi, both by its adamantine nature and from
historical precedent.

When Mr Gilbert began his mosaics collection, not only was there
no serious competitor scouring the shops for coloured *tesserae*; there
was also no book on the subject in English. There were books for
collectors of inkwells or Japanese sword fittings, but nothing on
'micro-mosaics' – a term Mr Gilbert invented to distinguish the kind
of mosaics he collected – which are decoratively applied to table-tops,
snuff-box lids, cabinet fronts and jewellery – from the grander mosaics
of Ravenna, Piazza Armerina and Rome, on which there is copious
literature.

The only works he could find on micro-mosaics were in Russian:
E. M. Efimova's *Western European Mosaics from the Thirteenth to the
Nineteenth Centuries* (Leningrad, 1968), and an article by the same
author on the tables of Michelangelo Barberi, published by The Her-
mitage. (With the Vatican, this museum has the only collection of
mosaics to rival Gilbert's.) He had these two works translated into
English, and then began the long, voracious hunt that eventually led
to a picture book of his own, *The Gilbert Mosaic Collection* (Pendulum
Press, West Haven, Connecticut, 1971) introduced by Anthony C.
Sherman.

The Victoria and Albert Museum offers the best education in micro-
mosaics on this side of the Iron Curtain. For would-be collectors,
Sotheby's and Christie's occasionally sell good mosaics, and probably
the best shop for mosaic-decorated snuffboxes and jewellery is Wartski
of 138 Regent Street, London W1.

171

All the Raj

I remember going to school one day in 1947, when I was seven, and hearing another small boy say: 'My dad says we've given away India. Isn't it awful!' The mystique of the Raj period, fed by frustrated Imperialism, is tenacious, and there now exists a large body of Raj relic collectors.

Michael Edwardes, in his introduction to the excellent catalogue of the Brighton Museum and Art Gallery's exhibition *The British in India*, which took place in 1973, wrote: 'Throughout its entire existence, as well as since it finally became "one with Nineveh and Tyre", Britain's Indian empire has been all things to all men. The spectrum of abuse and adulation has ranged from the gaudy vision of "the brightest jewel in the British crown", to the crushing remark that India was "a vast system of outdoor relief for the middle classes." ' That exhibition did not pretend to explore the limits of what it is now becoming fashionable to call 'psycho-history'. Its principal aim was to show something of the texture of British life in India; to illustrate the problems of everyday living and thus paint in the background to the actions of both 'great' and small.

Mrs O'Looney, who organized the exhibition (it was her swansong or, should I say, Indian summer as exhibitions' officer because she later became head of a new applied arts department at Brighton) was born and brought up in India, so the subject was not as exotic to her as it seems to most of us. Some of the exotic comparisons she made were, however, very illuminating: as when, for example, she showed a European painting of the family of Sir Elijah Impey (Chief Justice of Bengal in the late eighteenth century) together with an Indian painting of the same family. The Queen lent one of the most splendid exhibits, the huge ivory throne which was presented to Queen Victoria by the Raja of Travancore, South India, and later displayed at the great exhibition of 1851; shown with the throne was a photograph of Victoria sitting in it and looking hellishly grumpy. Aside from

A late eighteenth-century dish from Government House, Madras

these grand pieces, there were many examples of colonial trivia – *The Hoghunter's Annual*, racing cups, smoking cabinets, ladies' albums, doll's furniture made of porcupine quills, a model of a palanquin, white kerseymere breeches, Viceregal invitations and peacock feather fans.

Giles Eyre, of 39 Duke Street, St James's, London W1, has held a number of exhibitions of Raj drawings, paintings and prints, including one devoted to Thomas Daniell, one of the best known English artists working in India in the early nineteenth century; prices averaged £200. Other shows organized by Giles Eyre have included one of Indian paintings for the British (i.e. 'Company' painting); drawings and water-colours by Europeans working in India; and an exhibition entitled 'Emily Eden in India, 1836–1842'. Emily Eden, who disembarked at Calcutta in 1836 on her 38th birthday, was the sister of George, Lord Auckland, who was sworn in as Governor-General within minutes of their landing. Emily took her place as First Lady and made her home in Government House. 'It is an odd, dreamy existence', she once wrote, 'more like a constant theatrical representation . . . everything is so picturesque and so utterly un-English'. Emily was a gifted amateur artist: 'On the esplanade I hardly ever pass a native that I do not long to sketch.' Nearly 200 of her watercolours were sold at Christie's in 1906. They were bought by Lord Curzon, who presented them to the Victoria Memorial Hall in Calcutta. The Eyre exhibition consisted of miniature copies of her watercolours, made by Indian artists, including Azim of Delhi; and coloured printed plates of them which had been issued by Dickinson and Son of New Bond Street.

Two London dealers specialize in relics of the Raj. Lennox Money, of 68 and 99 Pimlico Road, SW1, stocks furniture. Amongst his stock I have seen a set of eight chairs (of rosewood inlaid with ivory) made in Vizagapatam in the mid-eighteenth century. These were priced at £16,000 (Mr Money had a half-share in them; the other half was owned by Henry Woods Wilson of 103 Pimlico Road, who also has the occasional Raj piece in stock.) The Moneys have also had in stock an ebony sofa-table, which was priced at £900, and a number of Indian toys which represented British soldiers.

If you are thinking of becoming a Raj relics' collector, the following books and publications will give you a good introduction: Dennis Kincaid's *British Social Life in India, 1608–1937* (Routledge, 1973), an extremely amusing and instructive work; the BBC pamphlet *Europe and the Indies* (1970); Hugh Trevaskis's *The End of an Era* (Service Publications, Shoreham-by-Sea, Sussex, 1973); the Victoria and Albert Museum pamphlet *Art and the East India Trade*; a special Indian number of *Apollo* (August, 1970); parts six and eight of *The British Empire* in the BBC/Time-Life series (1971); and volume seven, chapter 107 of the Purnell/BBC *History of the Twentieth Century, India: the Impact of the West* (1965).

With strings attached

I have never been a great one for the cruder manifestations of folk art. Frankly, I prefer civilization. I would have been happy if Cecil Sharp had never pestered those old countrymen, buying them pints in exchange for the performance in a cracked-jar voice of 'So up she went to the maister's room' and so on. My grandmother's expression of horror on seeing Morris dancers perform in Merstham, Surrey ('Grown men!'), seemed to meet the case. Flower dances and well-dressing, or 'The age-old custom of beating the balm-cake at Abbotts Dawdling', to recall Thelwell's delightful cartoon in *Punch*, leave me cold.

But when I recently visited Sicily, I must admit that I was won over by the Sicilian puppet theatre. We had a private showing in the exquisite Chinese Pavilion near the Ethnographical Museum G. Pitrè – the building where Nelson stayed with Lady Hamilton. The performance was preceded by a talk, without notes but in flawless English, by Professor Antonio Pasqualino, a Palermo surgeon, who explained the tradition of this petty pageant, in which knights in shining armour bounce about, drawing their swords and thumping their tin chests with bravado; damsels in distress are saved from dragons and Saracens; and a mermaid with a green tail whizzes through the air and tells the hero to be of good cheer, everything will come right in the end.

Of course, what any good romantic would like to believe is that this puppet theatre has persisted, virtually unaltered, since the days of the Normans, who conquered Sicily about the same time as they did us, and built the great cathedrals of Cefalù and Monreale. But Professor Pasqualino, who looks more like the Christ Pantocrator of Cefalù than one would suppose mortal man could, explained that, although the traditions of chivalry may have lasted right through from the Middle Ages – in living memory the adventures of Charlemagne's knights were ritually declaimed in public squares – the puppet theatre probably dates only from the early nineteenth century. In other words, it was an aspect of the same romantic movement that led to neo-Gothic architecture, novels about medieval heroes and the Eglinton tournament in England.

Professor Pasqualino began to remind me of the moony type of folk-tradition enthusiast when he claimed that one could learn far more about human relationships from these clod-hopping little dramas than from French novels of the Romantic period.

> The personages in the *Storia dei Paladini* are a cross-section of the human race, a paradigm of social and individual relationships used to classify the people one meets in real life. Somebody infamous, a traitor not to be trusted, is a *Gano di Maganza*. A rich and avaricious man who allows himself to be deceived by the wicked is a *Charlemagne*. A very strong, loyal and faithful man, not crafty, very serious and without much luck with women, is an *Orlando*; a strong, rebellious and crafty man, capable of making the best of things, a joker and a wencher, is a *Rinaldo*. A cheerful generous braggart is an *Astolfo*.

We saw only one performance. The young master of marionettes came out afterwards to take his bow and do a lap of honour, parading the brassy little warriors along the aisle and showing us with what dexterous manoeuvres he could cause the sword to flick from the scabbard or the visor to clank down over the pink, painted face. The important spectators, however, are those who come every evening, snared by the cliff-hanging endings into returning again and again. It is a sort of *Crossroads* in armour. The Sicilian spectators often become passionately engaged by the action, and sometimes audience participation goes too far, as when one man, enraged by the duplicity of *Gano di Maganza*, hauled the puppet off, hung him from a tree and riddled him with buckshot. Another man, who could not sleep for worrying, woke up the puppet-master and in tears begged him to accompany him to the theatre to liberate *Rinaldo*, who had remained chained up in a dismal prison at the end of the evening's performance. When his beloved hero had been set free and hung up in a row with the other paladins, he sighed with relief and went back to bed.

As a souvenir, I decided to buy a splendidly armoured *Ruggiero* from one of the leading puppet shops in Palermo: Vincenzo Argento ('Construzioni di Paladini') of 445 Via Vittorio Emanuele. Folk art is rather like African primitive art: provided you buy an example untainted by outside influence or commercial exploitation from abroad, a twentieth-century product may be as acceptable as a much earlier one. Although the specimen I bought for 45,000 lire (then approximately £35) was brand new, still warm from the armourer's hammer, it was little different from those of 100 years before, or those in use on the stage at the Chinese Pavilion.

Making a collection of puppets should appeal especially to people with young children, for, like the best Worcester tea service, the puppets can on occasion be used – and there are few better enliveners of a children's party than this miniature pantomime.

A Wayang Kulit shadow puppet

177

You might begin the non-European section of a puppet collection with some Asian shadow-puppets. An interesting introduction to these is 'Walking Shadows', an article in that well-loved publication, the *British Museum Society Bulletin* (No. 3, February 1970). This describes how in 1969 the Museum bought several collections of Asian shadow puppets, acquired mainly by Miss Shelagh Weir, then assistant keeper in the Department of Ethnography, during her travels in the Far East which were financed by the British Museum Trustees. The Museum's only large holding of shadow puppets previously was the collection of Javanese *wayang kulit*, hide figures, which came to the department on the death of Sir Stamford Raffles's second wife in 1858. (Sir Stamford, who is best known for having founded Singapore in 1819, was Lieutenant Governor of Java from 1811 to 1815.)

The great advantage of Miss Weir's travels was that she was able to meet the puppeteers of Malaysia and with their help identify the different characters by name. In Kelantan, on the north-west coast of the Malay peninsula, she bought a collection of puppets from the puppeteer Awang Lah, who kindly 'took the spirits out of them' so that they would not harm the British Museum staff.

The best general introduction to the subject of puppets is *Punch & Judy* by George Speaight (Studio Vista, 1970). The title of this excellent book is a little misleading, however, for Mr Speaight in fact deals with the whole history of puppets in Europe, from Greek and Roman mimes, which 'remind us that classical art is not entirely represented by the smooth perfection of the *Venus de Milo*', up to the present. The acrobatic buffoonery of the Commedia dell'Arte, with its Pantaloon and Scaramouche, had a powerful influence – though, again, this was a comparatively modern creation, dating only from the seventeenth century.

Speaight deals only with Europe, and especially with England. For a more world-embracing survey of puppets you should obtain *Puppentheater: Figuren und Dokumente aus der Puppentheater Sammlung der Stadt München*. This is a lavishly illustrated paperback by Dr Günter Bohmer, published by Bruckmann of Munich, and a useful supplement to it is *Spiel und Spielzeug aus Aller Welt*, published by the Museum für Volkkünde, Vienna. Another useful book is *The World of Puppets* by René Simmen (Elsevier/Phaidon, 1975).

If you cannot afford to begin a puppet collection at present, you can of course always take example from the recent 'Larry' cartoon, which showed two hands waggling about in a striped booth bearing the notice, 'The World's First *Nude* Punch and Judy Show'.

Taboo subjects

A curious and unique set of rules governs the collecting of African sculpture, as I learnt from two dealers, Alexander Martin and John Kerr-Wilson. 'Old', as far as African sculpture is concerned, means 'before European influence'. So you get the odd situation – quite contrary to that which prevails in the collecting of most European arts – by which a terracotta figure from Lower Bani, Mali, probably of the first century A.D., may be priced at £3,000, while a nineteenth-century Yoruba, or perhaps Lower Niger, bronze with inlaid lead eyes, may cost £9,000. The reason is that the Yoruba figure was produced by an artist still uncontaminated by outside influence, while the ancient terracotta reveals a distinct Egyptian influence, and is not part of a pure African tribal tradition.

Both Martin and Kerr-Wilson know what they are up against in exhibiting and trying to sell such works. 'Art critics don't really like the subject,' commented Kerr-Wilson. 'Yes, they know Picasso relates to it, but that is all they know. There are no documents.' Martin feels that younger people understand it more easily than older. 'The older collectors have a literary approach. They want to read "This is the portrait of a young girl". And of course that's just what Picasso tells them.' There is probably no collecting subject that more tests one's own powers of appreciation.

Again, Kerr-Wilson frankly admits that many of the sculptures are impossible to date. Tribal traditions were tenacious, so that a given piece might have been made in the sixteenth or the nineteenth century. One dealer who will not touch African sculpture told me he dislikes it because it is 'creepy – not the sort of thing you want round the house'. He also felt that wooden sculpture of any age would have been eaten away by termites; and, indeed, one of the most magnificent pieces which I have seen in Martin's gallery, a wooden dance mask of the fertility goddess Nimba, from Baga, Guinea, has had its legs amputated for this very reason. There is also a danger of fakes: even

A Yoruba dance mask from Nigeria

termite damage can be simulated by sand-blasting. But none of these grim caveats will weigh much with the man who is really bowled over by African sculpture. Once the myth and magic have seized him and he has graduated from pretty patinated pieces with 'nice' shapes to votive totems, fetishes, hairy dance masks and phallic witch-deterrents, no mortal argument will frighten him off – except, perhaps, the price ticket. It is still possible to buy genuine but poor quality African sculpture for approximately £50; but a Benin bronze figure of a flute player recently fetched £185,000, and a Gaban wood white-painted mask £20,000, at Sotheby's. Two dealers who regularly stock African sculpture are Lance Entwistle, 137 Hamilton Terrace, London NW8 and Peter Adler, 191 Sussex Gardens, London W2.

The beginner should visit the imaginatively laid out Museum of Mankind (a division of the British Museum) at 6 Burlington Gardens, London W1. I have bought three useful booklets there: *The Tribal Image* and *Divine Kingship in Africa* both by William Fagg; and *Hunters and Gatherers* by James Woodburn, which deals with the culture of the nomadic Hadza. William Fagg, the greatly respected former Keeper of the British Museum Department of Ethnography has co-authored with Margaret Plass what is probably the best possible beginner's book: the Dutton Vista paperback *African Sculpture* (1964). Bois de Rachewiltz's *Introduction to African Art* (John Murray, 1966) is good on the influence of Negro art on European.

Alexander Martin's stock made me think about that relationship. One of the main influences on Van Gogh was Millet – he of the leaden peasants and a far inferior master. Van Gogh transformed Millet's sentimental view of the toiler and moiler and in treating Millet's compositions as a sort of painting-by-numbers set, drained them of their cloying tones and filled the cells with living colour. Millet's peasant scapes, Watts-like allegories of Labour, could only gain by translation into that blazing palette.

We see exactly the reverse process in the paintings of Picasso which have been influenced by African sculpture. The African cult objects gain nothing by joining the Common Market and being Europeanized by an artist of overtly classical background. For the collector, the paradox resolves itself into this practical dilemma: would you rather have an African sculpture or an astronomically expensive Picasso?; the cunning European pastiche or the original wellspring? For putting the frighteners on an enemy, I would rather rely on a Bangwa zoomorphic mask from the Cameroons than the *Demoiselles of Avignon* any day.

Trade descriptions

The purchase of two amusing trade catalogues of the 1870s and the 1880s respectively led me to reflect that a collection of such ephemera, dating perhaps from the first strong impetus of the Industrial Revolution in the mid-eighteenth century, could be a fascinating barometer of taste and social development. One, evidently printed in the early 1880s, is for Müller's Alpha Gas-Making Apparatus. It includes a panegyric on gas lighting, in the course of which scorn is poured on the rival claims of the electric light:

> Much public attention has of late years been given to the best mode of Artificial Lighting. Patent after patent has been taken out for this purpose – most of them, without practical satisfactory result, having to be abandoned after a very short existence – including the Electric Light, which, for all practical purposes, as yet is not applicable for the lighting of private buildings, or the requirements of premises isolated from coal gas centres, as a steam engine must be kept at work if only one single light is in use . . .

The rest of the catalogue – and this is its charm – consists of a series of buildings, ships, and even caves lit with Müller's Alpha machine. A full-page illustration shows 'The Hermitage, Grimsargh, near Preston, A Select Preparatory School. It is lighted with Müller's Alpha Gas 40-light Machine which was supplied in February, 1879'. In the illustration, two wretched boys stand on the croquet lawn before the typical mid-nineteenth century manse, with its barge-board gables and Gothic conservatory.

A testimonial from the headmaster, The Reverend T. Abbott Peters, M.A., says: 'I like your Alpha Gas-making Apparatus very much, and am recommending it to my friends' notice.' Alpha gas also lit the London School Board Training Ship, *Shaftesbury*; the church and vicarage at Claverton, Warwickshire; The Hollins, near Halifax; Clent House, near Stourbridge; Foxearth Church, Long Melford; the

Mourne and Woodside Hotels and Skating Rink, Rostrevor, Co. Down; the Ullswater Hotel, Patterdale; the Whittle Springs Hotel near Chorley, Lancashire, and the Old Roman Lead Mines at Matlock, Bath. The testimonials make entertaining reading. The Revd. J. L. Shepherd, O.S.B., writes from Worcestershire:

> I wish your Alpha Gas-Making Apparatus were known in Italy. Having spent several years there, I know how readily it would be adopted and, if I could, I would publish its advantages everywhere in that lovely country. I have had three years' experience of its lighting power in our Church, and am now going to introduce it into the Abbey of the same, which is a monastery of nuns of the order . . . It is a glorious success. A lay Sister manages the whole Apparatus.

More than one of the correspondents used that nice, nineteenth-century phrase, now almost obsolete, that the machine 'answers very well.' J. B. Holroyde, a gentleman from Yorkshire, wrote: 'I have a large Workshop, where I spend many evenings in mechanical and scientific amusements, which is most beautifully lighted by it, as well as my Billiard Room.' The Duke of Wellington, *per* Walter Mousley, Esq., was more laconic: 'The Alpha Gas Machine in the Hall of Strathfieldsaye House works very well.'

My second catalogue is of American Cooking and Heating Stoves from the American Stove Stores, 155 Cheapside, London (Proprietors: W. Poore & Co.). Here the fun lies in the extravagant neo-rococo designs of the stoves, and the names chosen for them: 'The Mistress', 'The Empress', 'The Victoress', 'The Magnolia', 'The Baroness', 'The Glow Worm', 'The Fire Fly', 'The Egg', 'The Prima Donna', 'The Peasant', 'The Doric Office Stove', and 'The Enchantress', from whose black maw a very disenchanted-looking porker stares out. 'The Enchantress' cost, according to size, from £3 18s. to £6 (complete with utensils). The catalogue also illustrates a 'Prince Alfred Yacht Stove' at £6, a 'New Tailors' Stove' with space for fifteen irons at once, and a 'Little Eva' miniature model for children, complete with utensils and smoke funnel, at 26s.

Martin Orskey, a book dealer of Little Gains House, Elmsted, Ashford, Kent, has a good personal collection of trade catalogues. He told me that apart from early type-face manuals, the first trade catalogue he could think of was a Dutch one of the 1690s which described and advertised fire engines and fire-fighting appliances. From the eighteenth century onwards, the scope is almost limitless. The successful reissue of Old Army and Navy Stores' brochures and other late

Victorian and Edwardian catalogues, full of picnic hampers, servants' uniforms, and spatter-dashes indicates their nostalgic appeal as a collectors' subject.

The best dealers in London for this kind of material are Paul Breman; Paul Grinke; and Ben Weinreb.* The last named has recently had in stock the following colourful examples: *Macfarlane's Castings, Glasgow, c.* 1914 (which illustrates pissoirs, bandstands, and even houses in cast iron); Thomas Brawn, *Catalogue of Medieval Metal Work* (including gas fittings!), late nineteenth century; W. Evans, *Thirty-Six New Original and Practical Designs for Chairs*, Bath, 1840s; Charles Frederick Bielefeld, *On the Use of the Improved Papier Mâché in Furniture in the Interior Decoration of Buildings and in Works of Art*, London, *c.* 1845 – the technique replaced heavy plasterwork in many buildings.

The publishers David and Charles have reissued a number of the most celebrated Edwardian and Victorian examples, including *Edwardian Shopping, 1893–1913* (selections from the catalogues of the Army and Navy Stores, published in 1975), *Gamage's Christmas Bazaar, 1913* (1974) and *Victorian Shopping* (Harrods' catalogue of 1895, published in 1972).

* See pp. 100–101 for addresses of all these dealers

Scientific attachments

There are two kinds of people who collect antique scientific instruments and, like the twins in the song, they look alike, talk alike, and hate each other like poison. On the one side are ranged the devoted students of the history of science, for whom each astrolabe or orrery, sextant or equatorial dial is a stepping-stone of scientific progress to be categorized and gloated over. On the other, we encounter the ritzy interior decorators who think that nothing looks nicer in an aubergine velvet wall bay than one of those quaint old telescopes or microscopes with twiddly bits in ivory.

As a convinced *via media* man (I always think I would have been guillotined early in the French Revolution for being what the *enragés* called a 'moderate'), I side with both groups. It is obviously right that there should be museums, public and private, of scientific instruments of the past, where embryo televisions and 'The Origins of the X-Ray' will be preserved as part of folk tradition; but as one who knows even less about science than Galileo's enemies did, I would still like to possess, for their aesthetic qualities alone, some of those beautiful astronomical skeletons of boxwood and bone, iron and ivory.

Viewed historically, before the invention of the marine chronometer the navigator was unable to determine accurately his longitude at sea. In 1714 the British Government offered £20,000 (today worth about £200,000) for a practical solution. This came in the 1760s, not from an eminent astronomer or mathematician, but from a country carpenter turned clockmaker, John Harrison. He constructed a timekeeper capable of recording accurately the meantime of the place from which a ship sailed (i.e. G.M.T.). As one degree of longitude equals four minutes of time, a ship's position east or west of that place could then be determined simply by comparing the difference between local time (gained by observation of the sun) and the recorded time. This invention led to the evolution of many different types of marine chronometers, many of which have since become coveted collectors' pieces. An exhibition of these was held at Asprey's in July 1972.

Good astronomical instruments offer another rich quarry for the collector. An orrery, for example, is an astronomical clock that records the movements of the planets by turning a handle. It can show the whole solar system, or just the relationship between sun, earth and moon. They were used for teaching in universities, or bought by nobility interested in astronomy. A few were designed for children. I have seen one enchanting example which was made for a small girl: 'Miss Elizth. Parker. Aged 14 of Mettingham near Bungay, Suffolk, as the reward of distinguished merit'. It was made by William Jones of Holborn and still has its original book of instructions and all the accessories – planets being fitted in like the parts of a modern drill.

Another handsome orrery, sold relatively recently and made by George Adams, junior, *c.* 1790, shows Uranus with six satellites. There is an amusing story behind this. Sir William Herschel discovered Uranus in 1781 and two of its satellites in 1787; Adams added another four to his orrery in case more were discovered. But in fact Uranus has only five satellites: Miranda, Ariel, Umbriel, Titania and Oberon. Miranda was only discovered in 1948. But if Adams was over-generous to Uranus, he gave short measure to Saturn: only seven satellites, while Saturn is now known to have ten.

In the eighteenth century, art and science were still in unison; in the nineteenth century they began to diverge. In other words, the eighteenth-century makers of scientific instruments set out to make them beautiful, with engraved cartouches, ivory fittings and so on; the nineteenth-century manufacturers were concerned, for the most part, only with efficient function. This is especially true of the microscope. I have seen an elegant compound monocular microscope by Matthew Loft, *c.* 1725, with oak casing; a later example, by George Sterrop (1745) was cased in mahogany. In the nineteenth century brass became the popular material. Eighteenth-century slides were made of ivory or wood; nineteenth-century ones of taped glass only. I examined a selection of nineteenth-century slides in the lower show room of Harriet Wynter recently. Containing what to the naked eye were anonymous blobs of muddy colour, the slides bore such tantalizing inscriptions in sepia ink as: 'Ferret intestine'; 'Cuticle of obscurus'; 'Tongue of cat 1885'; 'Wing of gnat'; 'Mistletoe'; and 'Egg of bedbug'.

Among the small scientific relics available to the collector, you could buy a pocket sundial, *c.* 1700, for £800; a perpetual calendar with a charming engraving of Amsterdam shipping for £500–£600;

a wooden sundial six inches high by D. Bering *c.* 1750, for £1,200–£1,500. A small pocket globe in a case by Nathan Hill, 1754, might cost about £450.

Early medical instruments and early surveying instruments also fall into this collecting category. One of the oddest members of the latter is the 'waywiser', which resembles a wheelbarrow which has unfortunately lost its barrow. You see them sometimes on eighteenth-century maps, being pushed along bad roads by energetic squireens in knee-breeches. The rotation of the wheel clocked up mileage on a dial. Country aristocracy also bought them to measure the boundaries of their estates. The two best dealers in scientific instruments in London are Harriet Wynter of 352 Kings Road, Chelsea, and Arthur Davidson of 179 New Bond Street, W1 and 78 Jermyn Street, W1.

Circular brass horizontal sundial (*c.* 1820), signed Cox of Devonport and Plymouth. Diameter: 12 inches

Collecting old rubbish

In 1963, the Keep Britain Tidy Group staged an exhibition in London called 'Mess-Age'. It was officially opened by Queen Elizabeth, the Queen Mother. A tape recording of a commentary by Laurie Lee boomed through a loudspeaker: 'This is a Mess-Age, an age of affluent litter, and Britain is fast becoming a giant litter bin. . . . Last year, the average man threw away four times his own weight in rubbish.'

An exhibition at the Victoria and Albert Museum whose title – The Pack Age – exploited the same genre of pun – and which was concerned with the same kind of civilised debris, took place in 1975. The difference was that the V. & A. show took the thrown-out tin cans which the 1963 show had condemned, and put them behind glass as *objets d'art*. One wonders whether Andy Warhol's pop-art glorification of the Campbell Soup can has had anything to do with the new glamour of refuse.

The appeal of antique refuse is more understandable: some well-known artists designed the advertisements which emblazoned these ephemeral containers. The jolly cook of Edward's desiccated soup was drawn by Louis Weierter at the turn of the century. The Bisto kids who rapturously sniff Bisto fumes were immortalized by Will Owen. John Hassall designed the containers (and posters) for Veritas gas mantles; Louis Wain, the cat man, for Mazawattee tea; and Heath Robinson for Peak Frean's biscuits. The obvious challenge of Camp coffee was risen to magnificently by the anonymous artist who depicted a kilted and moustachioed officer being served chicory-coffee by a turbanned native servant.

Mr Robert Opie, whose collection formed the V. & A. exhibition, contributed an amusing and historically shrewd introduction to the catalogue. He wondered whether social historians of the future would look back on the past hundred years as the Pack Age – as archaeologists today refer to the Beaker people of 2000 B.C. Mr Opie believed this would be justified: 'The throw-away carton, the labelled tin, the

Packaging of a bygone era exhibited at the
Pack-Age Exhibition in 1975

jar, the bottle, the food wrapper of paper, foil and polythene have become indispensable to our way of living.' But would our packages survive for as many years as the beakers have done? Mr Opie thought not: 'The patient excavator 4,000 years from now is unlikely to dig up a single yoghurt carton; and certainly he will not imagine that in Britain alone some 460 million yoghurt cartons were being manufactured, filled, purchased, emptied and discarded each year.' The accuracy of history may suffer, but hardly its romance. We might be less impressed by Keats, I suppose, if he had written: 'O for a yoghurt carton full of the nourishing north!'

Mr Opie described how, in the nineteenth century, manufacturers' packaging superseded the old habit of laborious hand-wrapping by the retailer. (Who, fifty years ago, would patronize a store which did not provide chairs for the customers to sit on while they gave their orders?) As late as the 1930s, the better-off continued to look down on those who opened a tin for their salmon, spread 'shop' jam on their bread, or poured sauce from a bottle on to their fish. 'Such people paid dearly for the luxury of their own blend of tea, made up by their grocer; to have their cigarettes specially rolled from their favourite tobacco; and to have a cook living in to provide them with home-made jams and sauces.' Today, branded goods no longer have the same social stigma.

Mr Opie's interest in packaging began one Sunday in Inverness. He was fifteen at the time. In those days you couldn't buy food on Sundays in Inverness. Instead, he purchased some Mackintosh 'Munchies' from a vending machine, and a packet of ginger biscuits. Suddenly he realized that if he didn't keep the packet nobody would. Ever since he has kept the packets of everything he has eaten.

Two stalls in the Chelsea markets specialize in old tin boxes: Stuart Cropper of stall N12 in Antiquarius Market, King's Road; and Ed Carson of stall 85, Chelsea Antique Market (also in the King's Road). Dodo, of 185 Westbourne Grove, London W11, also sells good boxes. Prices range from approximately 50p for a Boracic ointment tin, to £30. For that you can buy a houseboat tin for Jacob's biscuits, or a beehive toffee tin (beehive in shape). Other treasures which I have seen include a Peak Frean Edwardian box in the form of a jewelled casket; a tin in the shape of a revolving book case (dated 1905 on one of the book spines) for Huntley and Palmer's biscuits; canisters and a tin clock – a cheapjack *garniture de cheminée* in *chinoiserie* taste; a 'Lyons tea has stood the test of time' tin incorporating an egg-timer; Sharp's Toffee parrot cages, and a tin in the form of a Jacobean log-box issued in 1910 by Jacob & Co., whose Dublin biscuit factory, six years later, was to play so prominent a part in the hostilities of the Easter Rising.

Short storeys

The Dolls' House Society was founded in 1971 by Mrs Molly Fox as a splinter group from the Doll Club of Great Britain, that Brobdingnagian institution for studying the works of Lilliput. 'We are the Jesuits of the doll world,' Mrs Fox says. 'To qualify for membership, you have to own at least a nineteenth-century dolls' house, and you have to have a skill: woodworking, repairs, needlework and so on. Among our members, for example, Mrs Beryl West has made an exquisite silver Queen Anne teapot. She also owns a lathe for turning miniature furniture, and she makes tapestry carpets. Mrs Winifred Warren, a needlework teacher, makes pillow lace with bobbins. Miss Faith Eaton is a specialist in doll repair, especially wax faces. She has done repairs for Buckingham Palace and many major museums.'

The members' pet name for the Society is 'The Dolls' House Square'. As an American, Mrs Fox is fascinated by the London squares. Each member holds a 'freehold'. Mrs Graham Greene, president of the Doll Club of Great Britain, was honorifically awarded No. 1, while the other members drew their freeholds out of a hat. 'We actually sit in a square at our meetings', adds Mrs Fox.

The annual general meeting is a workshop – a three-day weekend in which members leave husbands, children and doll museums behind. One year they all stayed in a guest house at Shepton Mallet. They visited the American Museum at Bath and 'Titania's Palace', now at Wookey Hole, the famous dolls' house made by Sir Nevile Wilkinson (who also designed Queen Mary's dolls' house) and sold at Christie's in October 1967 for 30,000 guineas. Another jaunt was to Fittleworth, Sussex. On other occasions they visited Lady Samuelson's collection of dolls' houses, and the dolls' house at Uppark.

Mrs Fox, who now runs a training course for executives at I.P.C., was born at Fort Benning, where the My Lai trial was held. Her father, a West Point army officer, was killed in Normandy in the Second World War, and her brother died in Korea, after which she became a Quaker.

'We travelled around so much when I was a child, that I never had a proper dolls' house, though I made room settings in shoe boxes and orange crates. So perhaps my dolls' house collection is a compensation for that, and also for not having had a settled, stable home. It is also escapism – I think all collecting is escapism. I can put a parlour maid, a cook, a nanny into different rooms. If I want a pink bedroom, instantly there's a little pink bedroom – an indulgence one can't afford in real life.'

'Shell Villa – an 1870–75 seaside villa (on the Esplanade) which serves as a boarding-house for cats. In front of the house stand neat park benches and a lobster pot. A notice (too small to be read in reproduction) reads: "Refined Board Residence: the Misses Charlotte and Emily Twitchett." ' (*Mrs Greene*)

She aims to furnish each house with miniature furniture of the right period, in correct scale: not with reproduction dolls' furniture, which is relegated to a display shelf. She began collecting about twelve years ago. One of her earliest purchases was a box of dolls' furniture in the Portobello Road for which she paid £50. The man who sold it to her said 'I'll give you the Georgian house that goes with it'. Mrs Fox was sceptical: genuine Georgian houses are hard to come by. But the Victoria and Albert Museum has verified from samples of the wallpaper that the house is pre-Victorian. She paid £25 for a small-scale model of the first commercially made house (c. 1885–90) with bay windows and a balcony; £50 for a seaside villa (c. 1890–1910); and £160 for the prize of her collection, a 1775 house (perhaps an architect's model) of distinguished neo-classical façade, which she bought in The Lacquer Chest, Church Street, Kensington. The furniture and dolls usually cost far more than the house. In the seaside villa, the dolls alone were priced at £100.

The shop Mrs Fox recommends for collectors is The Dolls' House, 4 Broadley Street, London NW8. They have a wide range of houses, starting with plywood ones at £1 and rising to large, nineteenth-century wooden houses which might cost £150. They specialize in reproduction hand-made furniture, dolls, china and glass; and while this might not be acceptable to purists, it is a good idea for the beginner to furnish initially with reproductions, and then gradually to replace the new with old. Collectors can also subscribe to The International Dolls' House News (41 Manor Street, Braintree, Essex).

One of Mrs Fox's more recent acquisitions is a Quaker dolls' house. Mrs Greene tipped her off about it. It belonged to a Quaker girl born in Reading in 1784. The dolls are being costumed with the aid of a 1901 book, *The Quaker: A Study in Costume* by Amelia M. Gummere, which Mrs Fox borrowed from the library of the Society of Friends.

If you would like to join the Dolls' House Society, and think you qualify, write to Mrs Fox at 55 Marloes Road, London W8 enclosing a stamped, addressed envelope. Recommended books on the subject include *Dolls and Doll Houses* by Kay Desmonde (Letts, 1972) and *Antique Miniature Furniture in Great Britain and America* by Jean Toller (Bell, 1966).

Collaring the market

At the Grosvenor House Antiques Fair in 1975, I saw exhibited a silver dog collar. The dealer had decided to keep it for himself as a reward for having done well in the fair, but the price would otherwise have been in the region of £600. The collar had been made in France for Prince Albert's favourite greyhound Eos and bore the royal owner's name. Landseer painted Eos wearing the collar in 1842 (the painting now hangs at Balmoral); another Landseer painting shows the Princess Royal in her cot with Eos wrapped about her. A silver padlock hangs from the collar; the band, however, opens not with a key but by a trick mechanism which operates when you press the 'A' of Albert.

Later in the same year, a brass dog collar inscribed 'Thomas Taylor Baker, Warwick 1767' was sold for £80. At about the same time I heard that Mr Gordon Wigg, Lord Wigg's brother, owned a collection of dog collars. I therefore wrote myself a reminder note: 'Dog collar.' A friend, seeing this in my flat, asked: 'Are you entering the ministry, Bevis?'

Mr Wigg was celebrating his 67th birthday on the day that I went to see him, and he showed me a birthday card he had just received from his step-daughter – of a dog wearing an elaborate collar, a reproduction of a painting by P. de Vos (1596–1678) which hangs in the Prado, Madrid.

The Wigg collection began over twenty-five years ago when his wife, a breeder of whippets, took the best-of-breed and best-in-show awards at the Ladies' Kennel Association Show, Olympia. There was a bric-à-brac stall at the show, and Mrs Wigg decided to spend her winnings on a handsome dog collar of some age. The stall holder had two others; Mr Wigg telephoned him and later bought them. When Christmas arrived he bought his wife another dog collar. From that time the collection grew steadily, and when Mrs Wigg died it numbered thirty collars, to which Mr Wigg has since added fifty more.

The most he has paid for one of them is £36 for a silver-gilt example. He was recently handed a letter from a woman in Co. Dublin, Ireland, who had heard of his collection, and wanted him to know that she owned a collection of forty-five dog collars. 'That's the first time any-one has ever tried to say "Snap" to me', confessed Mr Wigg. He knows of no other dog-collar collector.

He told me that most of the brass, pewter and silver collars in his collection would have been made for the lord of the manor and his sons, and used by no one else except perhaps their bailiff. He recalled his own boyhood in the village of Ramsdell, Hampshire: 'If anyone arrived in the village with a dog, they were very soon warned off. The gamekeeper would say: "Are you staying in the village long?" and if the man said: "Three weeks," he'd reply: "Not with the dog you're not!" If the game keeper saw an unauthorized dog, he'd dispose of him in no time. They wouldn't stand for poaching. I knew a gypsy who used to work on the estate of my grandfather's farm. He owned a lurcher – a poaching dog which was a cross between a whippet and a greyhound. George Bath, my grandfather's coachman, told me this dog used to slink off once they reached a village; he would rejoin the gypsy at the other end of the village. No one could ever catch that darn dog!'

As you might imagine, there is no vast literature of the dog collar. The best account is an article by Charles Beard in *The Connoisseur* of 1933. Beard traces the history of the dog collar from its earliest ex-amples (Mr Wigg believes his earliest collar, an iron one, is probably of fifteenth-century origin, and pointed out that the locking mechanism on some early collars was identical to that of contemporary chastity belts).

Eighteenth-century metal dog collars elaborately engraved with scenes and inscriptions

Beard illustrates a sixteenth-century suit of dog-armour in the Armoury of Wartburg, but the earliest dated example he shows was made for 'Judge Powell' in 1701 – probably Sir John Powell (1645–1713), whom Swift described in 1711 as 'the merriest old gentleman I ever saw' and who was famous for having reassured an alleged witch accused of flying that 'there is no law against flying'. The article also illustrates a brass dog collar with toothed edges inscribed 'The Right Honble. Lord Byron' – possibly made for Byron's ferocious bull mastiff, Nelson.*

He quotes from Burns's celebrated poem *The Twa Dogs* to indicate the social status which the right collar could confer:

His locked, lettered, braw brass collar

Showed him the gentleman and scholar.

And he laments that the collar given by Alexander Pope to Frederick, Prince of Wales, is apparently no longer in existence. This bore the legend:

I am his Highness' dog at Kew.

Pray tell me Sir, whose dog are you?

Beard adds: 'A well known boxer of recent years modified this couplet to adorn the neck-wear of his own animal. The query on this occasion was, however, couched in language more forceful than polite.' New scope for the poetic talents of Mr Muhammad Ali perhaps?

---

* Sold at Sotheby's on 14th December, 1976 for £600

The 1890s recaptured on vellum

In his poem *On Seeing an Old Poet in the Café Royal*, Sir John Betjeman put these words into the old man's mouth:

> Where is Oscar? Where is Bosie?
> Have I seen that man before?
> And the old one in the corner,
> Is it really Wratislaw?

Theodore Wratislaw (1865–1933) was one of the authors whose works were on show in an exhibition of 1890s' books which took place at the National Book League in 1973; appropriately, it was Sir John Betjeman who opened the show. 'I remember some of these authors', he commented. 'Anthony Hope, who told me that the favourites among his books were *The King's Mirror* and *Tristram of Blent*, not *The Prisoner of Zenda*; Arthur Machen, when he was living at Amersham; and of course Bosie, Lord Alfred Douglas.'

Sir John added that the exhibition was 'full of books I longed to touch', and that certainly was one of the main attractions of the books on show, although the desire to touch cannot be gratified through showcase glass. The books that such publishers as John Lane, Elkin Mathews, Leonard Smithers and Grant Richards produced often have impressed *gauffrage* designs on the covers, by artists of the stature of Aubrey Beardsley, Charles Ricketts and Gleeson White. 'The feel, the broad margins, the good paper, the joy of the smell of them, particularly vellum: that has all disappeared as a result of paperback books', said Sir John wistfully. Even when the Laureate's words do not fuse into verse, they hover on the brink; one could see the lines being formulated:

> A joy to smell 'em
> Espec'ly vellum.

The exhibition was organised by Dr Gutala Krishnamurti, who has made a study of that very 1890s' poet, Francis Thompson, and in 1963 founded the Francis Thompson Society. I was interested to meet him

197

because I own an extraordinary book which he edited in 1967: a commemorative volume on Thompson's poem *The Hound of Heaven*, which contained reproductions of letters from the Pope, the Dalai Lama, and His Holiness Jagadguru Shankaracharya Maharaj. The letter from the Vatican informed Henry Williamson, who is President of the Francis Thompson Society, that the Holy Father had learned with pleasure of the Society's intention to celebrate the 75th anniversary of *The Hound of Heaven* with a special exhibition.

> His Holiness is well aware of the spiritual and moral good to which this poem in particular, and the other works of Francis Thompson, have given rise; and He nourishes the prayerful hope that wider and more profound knowledge of his literary productions may be a source of ever-increasing graces to his many readers.

Henry Williamson was present at the opening of the 1890s' exhibition. Spry as a twenty-year-old, he ran up the curved staircase at the National Book League to give an impassioned rendering of a Thompson poem.

Dr Krishnamurti came to England from South India in 1962. I asked how his interest in Thompson and the '90s began. In 1954 he was in his final year at university, reading English language and literature. He was writing one-act plays in English. In the course of writing one called *The Love of an Artist*, he got stuck when trying to describe the implements of the artist. He met a Greek artist who was able to help him with this. The Greek's father had married an English woman and it was she who first suggested that Krishnamurti should research into Francis Thompson, of whom he had never heard. His university library did not have the works of Thompson, but the librarian ran *The Hound of Heaven* to earth in an anthology.

'I made eight or ten attempts to read the poem, but then gave up', said Dr Krishnamurti. 'I did not like it.' He became a lecturer in Vizagapatam. In December 1955 he was asked to represent the university at a conference at Cuttack, N. India. There he sat next to an English woman who was the Professor of English at Calcutta University. 'She was the examiner in old English – the subject of which we were all afraid.' The two got talking, and Dr Krishnamurti asked her if she would take him as a Ph.D. student. She said certainly, and suggested, out of the blue, that he might tackle Francis Thompson. 'Thompson was nowhere in my mind at that time.' She said: 'Perhaps you are haunted by him, as he was haunted by *The Hound of Heaven*.'

Unfortunately he could not afford to take up the offer, although by now he was smitten with the subject. He began teaching in a central Indian university and while there was asked by Radio Bombay to talk on Francis Thompson. 'I did so; and when I returned, the chairman and all the members of the faculty were at the railway station to greet and congratulate me. The head of the faculty pestered me to research into Thompson and to study for a Ph.D., as he said I could never become a professor without a doctorate. It reached the stage where I tried to avoid meeting him.'

Eventually, Dr Krishnamurti decided he must go to England to do research. The Indian Government said that Francis Thompson was not a subject of value to the nation, and refused to allow for foreign exchange. But the *Times Bookshop* offered him a job at £9 a week, so he left India with £5 in his pocket and the intention of staying for two months. He was disappointed to find that much important Thompson material was in America; but he decided to extend his stay in England. In 1963 he founded the Francis Thompson Society. He worked at Routledge and Kegan Paul's bookshop opposite the British Museum, and later obtained a teaching post from the G.L.C. At present he is teaching in a primary school in Brixton, which leaves him little time to organise literary exhibitions.

He spent the years 1968–72 in America, lecturing at Providence College, Rhode Island, Bridgewater, Massachusetts, and at the University of South East Massachusetts, where he also organized an 1890s' show. He is now planning a bibliography of Thompson. He has already written a life of the poet, but he plans to revise and extend it. He would also like to edit a six-volume edition of Thompson's complete works. 'Unfortunately, as a schoolmaster I don't have much status with publishers. The other irritating thing is that they want me to write books on India, which I left so long ago and about which I am not well qualified to write – one publisher sent me a £200 advance for such a book. Although I know a lot about the 1890s, I am not apparently considered suitable to write about the period.'

I have written at some length about Dr Krishnamurti, because he illustrates very well the kind of devotion the 1890s can inspire in those who study and collect books of the decade. Many of the books in the exhibition were from his own collection, and he told me that several more, including some of the finest examples, are still in America.

The exhibition began with anthologies of the 1890s, including Oscar Wilde's own copy of *Primavera* (1890) which contains poems by Laurence Binyon, Manmohan Ghose, Arthur Cripps and Stephen Phillips; a presentation copy of *The Second Book of the Rhymer's Club*

(1894), given to Gleeson White (first editor of *The Studio*) by John Todhunter, who with Lionel Johnson, Yeats, Le Gallienne and A. C. Hillier was one of the contributors; and *An Anthology of ''Nineties' Verse* (1928) compiled and edited by A. J. A. Symons, author of *The Quest for Corvo*. A 1948 anthology of the 1890s, chosen by Martin Secker, contained an introduction by John Betjeman, from which one passage had been extracted as a wall-text for the exhibition: 'Draw the curtains, kindle a joss-stick in a dark corner, settle down on a sofa by the fire, light an Egyptian cigarette and sip a brandy and soda, as you think yourself back to the world which ended in prison and disgrace for Wilde, suicide for Crackanthorpe and John Davidson, premature death for Beardsley, Dowson, Lionel Johnson, religion for some,

A stylish 'uniform' edition of 1896 in high *art nouveau* style: *Gryll Grange* by Thomas Love Peacock (Macmillan; illustrations by F. H. Townsend)

drink and drugs for others, temporary or permanent oblivion for many more.'

The exhibition included one interesting pairing: Grant Allen's *The Woman Who Did* (1895), with a title page and cover design by Aubrey Beardsley, and the perhaps inevitable rejoinder by Vivian Griffin, *The Woman Who Didn't* (1895). A large collection of works by the unspeakable T. W. H. Crosland, whom Siegfried Sassoon described so amusingly in his autobiography, was on display, including his best-known work, *The Unspeakable Scot*. Another, *Lovely Woman*, drew this comment from an angry Australian girl in Melbourne: 'Unfortunately it belongs to a library, so I can't hurl it out of the window or make abusive marginal notes.' I also saw a copy of Robert Smythe Hichens's novel *The Green Carnation*, a skit on Oscar Wilde, Lord Alfred Douglas and other aesthetes, which was first published anonymously in 1894. 'Robert Hichens I did not think capable of anything so clever', Wilde wrote to Ada Leverson, the Sphinx. The second edition of *The Green Carnation*, which bore the author's name on the title page, was withdrawn from sale after Wilde's trial, at the request of Hichens, as it seemed to him 'in very doubtful taste to continue selling such a "skit" on a famous man who had got into trouble.' Dr Krishnamurti had seen to it that a large vase of green carnations (dyed in ink) was on display in the exhibition room.

The gems of the exhibition, artistically speaking, were *Silverpoints* by John Gray (1893), with its delicate cover design by Charles Ricketts, *Poems* by John Cowper Powys (1899), the cover design in Japanese style by the versatile Gleeson White, and Jane Barlow's *The End of Elfin Town* (1894), cover design by Laurence Housman. Dr Krishnamurti emphasized that a great number of good artists were working on book design. When he asked me to guess the cover designer of Mrs G. Hudson's *Ivory Apes and Peacocks*, I guessed Beardsley, which delighted him because in fact the designer was Paul Woodroffe, an example of an excellent yet little known talent. One of the best dealers from whom to buy this kind of book is Sebastian d'Orsai, of 8 Kensington Mall, London W8.

In his opening speech, Sir John Betjeman quoted from Dr Krishnamurti's introduction to the catalogue of the exhibition: 'They were writers. Let us look for them. Let us feel their pulse. If there is no more sign of life in them, let us at least give them a decent burial.' To this Sir John added: 'The best burial of all is a beautifully produced book. And the best place to look for a beautifully produced book is a second-hand bookshop.'

Rescued from the rubble

I have just about given up the ghost on the subject of architectural preservation. I used to write anguished letters to the press when I heard of an impending demolition, and even more furious letters when the demolition was carried out. But with the combination of governmental indifference and local philistinism, one finally has to accept the hopelessness of the situation. The prevailing complaisant and accommodating attitude was perfectly illustrated by a caption in *The Sunday Times* which described as 'a very honourable solution' the plan to turn an early nineteenth-century Baptist church into an extension of a Fine Fare supermarket. 'This kind of re-use should happen much more often,' chirped the *Sunday Times* writer. It does, sir, it does.

One consolation for the aesthete, however, is that, when fine buildings are demolished, he can get his hands on the best architectural details: a chimney-piece full of William de Morgan tiles; a grotesque corbel; carved panels; stained glass windows; Art Nouveau door handles and fingerplates. I discovered that such things are usually 'builders' perks' when I bought for £10 in 1964 a frosted glass door bearing an Art Deco profile of Gertrude Lawrence from the rubble of Maison Lee Coiffures in the Finchley Road. When Joe Lyons ruined the Strand Palace Hotel, they graciously allowed the Victoria and Albert Museum to remove, for the price of carriage only, the gloriously prismatic entrance, which will eventually be set up in the museum beside the old shop-fronts and Georgian porticos they already show. When exotic tiling was stripped from the Ideal Standard Building, next to the London Palladium, the designer Bernard Nevill acquired a handsome chunk for his home.

Comparatively few public houses have been demolished; here at least the interest of the public is engaged. One Sunday I retraced the steps of Thomas Crofton Croker, who in 1860 wrote *A Walk from London to Fulham*. His route ran from the junction of Sloane Street and Brompton Road to Fulham Church. I found that, whatever else

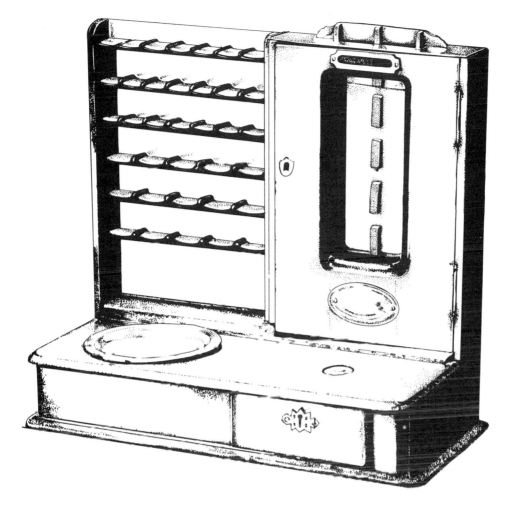

The pub till with Tunbridge-ware change-tray and Edward VII crown set into the base

had disappeared, the pubs had remained. But what has been happening in the past few years is an appalling desecration of pub interiors. As big groups with a mania for standardization and 'house style' take over the pubs, the old richness of engraved glass and 'Queen Anne'-style mahogany is replaced with plastic and blue leatherette. In deference to some perverted form of democracy, the divisions between private, saloon and public bars have been torn down. (I wish H. M. Bateman had drawn a cartoon of the man who entered the private bar of the Pig and Whistle without an Introduction, whilst a dozen or so scandalized eyes glared up at the door.)

The Victorian interior of the pub once used as *The Times*'s local, the Baynard Castle, has been gutted and refurnished in a style accurately described by a *Times* man as 'stripped Pinewood Studios.' The air of the Markham Arms, Chelsea, is horrid with jukeboxes: the worst time was when a hotted-up version of Mozart's 40th Symphony was the current favourite – *Private Eye* suggested the sweet, if expensive, vengeance of putting twenty coins in the box and pressing the button twenty times in succession for the same request.

Several pubs have also become skittishly extrovert, tricking out their forecourts or the pavement outside with Parisian-style metal tables and chairs. James Laver wrote, in his introduction to *Nineteenth-century French Posters*:

> Paris lived in public... At the hour of the apéritif half the population was sitting at little tables on the pavement watching the other half go by ... Perhaps nothing could be more typical of the contrast between French and English life than the difference between the café and the public house. The 'pub' is an attempt to create a kind of cosiness, even, sometimes, a sphere of privacy. It looks inward towards the bar; the café looks outward towards the street.

This spoliation, however, means that some delightful pub fittings have come on to the market. You can, for example, buy engraved glass in the Portobello Road. I bought an attractive pub till in Antiquarius Market, King's Road, Chelsea. (At least, I was assured it was a pub till, although for all I know it could be a haberdasher's). It has a Tunbridgeware change-tray and an Edward VII crown set into the base. Old beer-pulls are also available, ranging from the traditional wood pulls to those made in Staffordshire pottery, ivory or even in the style of Wedgwood. A Wedgwood beer-pull? Almost as incongruous as Meissen false teeth bearing the crossed swords mark.

If you do want to collect pub fittings and become, as it were, a kernoozer of the boozer, three books currently available will suggest fine pubs to keep an eye on. In addition to *Victorian Public Houses* by Brian Spiller (David and Charles, 1972), Mark Girouard, author of that splendid book *Victorian Country Houses* (Oxford University Press, 1971), has written a book on pub architecture called *Victorian Pubs* (Studio Vista, 1975). I can also recommend *The English Pub* (Collins, 1976).

Fired with enthusiasm

I know what fire-marks are for two good reasons. First, my father's career, until his recent retirement, was in fire insurance. While other children had their blood curdled by bedtime stories about the man who couldn't shudder, even though they put his grandma under a steam hammer, my flesh was made to creep by horrid tales of spontaneous combustion, of arson in hayricks and of shady businessmen who poured paraffin over their declining businesses.

On country walks I had pointed out to me the little signs, of lead, copper, tin or iron, which identified houses insured by particular companies against fire. The signs were put up for various reasons: to identify the property in the days before precise, numbered addresses; to advertise the insurance company; or (when bearing a number below the company's device) to indicate the policy relating to the building. These signs were fire-marks.

The other reason I know about fire-marks is that, as a child, I was a member of the *News Chronicle* I-Spy Club, even attending, on one occasion, an I-Spy rally at Chessington Zoo, where I secured the autograph of a robust journalist known as Big Chief I-Spy, and was given a special commemorative feather to add to my head-dress. Members of the I-Spy Club went round with small I-Spy books, in which one was awarded twenty-five points for a ha-ha at the bottom of a stately garden; twenty points for a thatched cottage; ten points for a hammer-beam, and so on. When you had identified all the things in a given book, you sent it off to Big Chief I-Spy and, in due course, received another feather through the post. Unscrupulous kids cheated and put a tick against the village stocks or the eighteenth-century lock-up without having seen them. I think one probably scored fifty points for a fire-mark – an indication of the rarity of these relics.

I had never before this moment thought of one good thing to say about the demolishers of ancient cottages, but I suppose there is this: they make the old fire-marks available to collectors – an avid and increasing breed. As a former employee of the Commercial Union Insurance group, my father continues to receive its 'house magazine', *Concord*. The winter 1975 issue contained an article by D. M. Griffiths, 'Committee Member, The Fire-Mark Circle', about a meeting of the circle held at St Helen's, Bishopsgate, by permission of the directors of the Commercial Union. The first guest speaker, Mr E. Nugent Linaker, chairman of the Fire-Mark Circle, who owns the finest private collection of British fire-marks, spoke about the fire insurance offices founded between 1680 and 1720. The second speaker, Mr Henry Russell, gave an 'amusing account of his experiences in collecting fire-marks', which he modestly described as 'those hunks of rather ugly lead or bits of rusting iron'.

Later in the proceedings, an auction was held which disposed of ninety-eight lots, including not only fire-marks but a Merryweather silver-plated fire captain's helmet of the design introduced by Captain Shaw to the Metropolitan Fire Brigade in 1866, and a blue glass Harden Star grenade fire extinguisher, *c*. 1884. Ah, blest bidders! The total realized by the auction was more than £1,100, which gives us an average price of approximately £11 a fire-mark. Phillips are now predicting £20–£40 as an average price for a number of individual fire-marks, and £80–£100 for some of the earliest examples. (Price is determined not so much by age as by the rarity of the company.)

Lead fire-marks of the Royal Exchange Assurance (founded 1720) and of the Hand-in-Hand (founded 1695)

206

The oldest known fire-mark is that of the Friendly Society of London, which was founded by William Hale of Kings Walden, Hertfordshire, in 1683. The Amiable Contributorship of 1696 became known as the Hand-in-Hand from the device of its fire-marks (clasped hands surmounted by a crown). The Sun Fire Office, the largest and most successful of the eighteenth-century insurance firms, began in 1710. The Sun Office produced twenty-nine variations on its mark – more than any other company; some collectors, for this reason, specialize in the marks of the Sun company alone.

The Westminster Fire Office was founded in 1717; the Bristol Crown Office, the first of the provincial companies, in 1718; the Edinburgh Friendly Society and the London Assurance in 1720. Then followed a long period with no new establishments, because after the bursting of the South Sea Bubble, which revealed the existence of many fraudulent joint-stock companies, the so-called 'Bubble Act' was passed to prevent the raising of capital stocks by transferable shares. No new fire insurance offices were opened until 1767, when the Bath Fire Office was founded.

I recall a cartoon which depicted an A.A. (or could it have been an R.A.C.?) man standing arms akimbo and coldly surveying a motorist who had driven half way up a lamp-post. 'Are you a member, sir?' read the caption. (Or it may have been, given the prejudices of the past, a female driver.) I had always imagined that the fire-mark system worked in a similar way; but I now have the assurance of Mr Vince that 'tales of firemen arriving to find a blazing building bearing the mark of another "office" and sitting down to watch it reduced to ashes are entirely apocryphal.'

Anyone interested in collecting fire-marks should read the brief but informative paperback book, *Fire-Marks* by John Vince (Shire Publications, 1973). Vince gives a short bibliography. In addition to this, one should consult the article on collecting fire-marks by Peter Johnson which appeared in the January, 1976 edition of *The Antique Collector*, and the article by B. Chamberlain in *The Connoisseur*, 1914, vol. xl.

Dedicated to blurb lovers everywhere . . .

I was amused to read in a Sunday newspaper that Desmond Elliott, the literary agent turned publisher, was offering a prize for the worst book-jacket blurb of the year. Elliott maintains a not very affectionate vendetta against Auberon Waugh, and is the author of the clerihew:

Auberon Waugh
Is a bore;
I'd rather
Read father.

He stipulated that the prize would not be awarded in any year in which Waugh published a novel.

I was especially taken with Elliott's scheme because I had been collecting chronic and curious blurbs for some time. I will give extracts from my three prize winners of all time (none of them describes a novel by Auberon Waugh) at the end of this article; but first I want to descant on the more general subject Elliott's prize suggests: collecting books, not for their contents but for their extraneous attractions, including dedications, portraits of authors and blurbs.

One of the best introductions to book collecting is P. H. Muir's *Book Collecting as a Hobby*. My copy is printed on cheap wartime paper and the book is long out of print. It is still possible, however, to pick up a second-hand copy. Muir recommends beginners to pick up the small volumes of The Book Lover's Library, issued towards the end of the nineteenth century and edited by H. B. Wheatley. Muir adds: 'In this "Book-Lover's Library" he wrote a volume called *The Dedication of Books*, and I have often wondered why no one has formed a collection of books solely for their dedications'.

Dedications began as tributes to patrons. The first book printed in English, Caxton's translation of the *History of Troy*, is dedicated to his patron, Margaret, Duchess of Burgundy; one of the few surviving copies contains a copper engraving showing Caxton presenting the book to her. Then there is Shakespeare's dedication to Mr W. H., of which we hear so much from Dr A. L. Rowse. Muir considers Milton's *Lycidas* to be 'one long dedication'. Irresistible dedications may be found in books which might otherwise bore you stiff: that of Sir Humphrey Davy to his wife in *The Elements of Chemical Philosophy*, for example. The supreme prize of the dedication-collector is to be found in *Counsel and Advise to all Builders* by Sir Balthazar Gerbier, 1633, which has forty-one separate dedications.

Muir feels that, although it is not strictly a dedication, Johnson's reply to Lord Chesterfield, first published in 1790, should be included. He cites two other good examples of the anti-dedication, both addressed to Oliver Cromwell: an indictment by Denzil Holles in 1647, beginning 'To the unparalleled couple Mr Oliver St John and Oliver Cromwell', and Colonel Titus's *Killing Noe Murder*, ten years later. He suggests that one should also hunt down dedications which Johnson composed for other less felicitous authors: these are listed in Courtney and Nichol Smith's *Bibliography of Samuel Johnson* (Muir recommends the Oxford University Press edition of 1925).

My most pleasing discovery in dedications is that in *Historic Fancies* (1844) by Mr George Sydney Smythe, M.P.. 'To the Lord John Manners, M.P., whose gentle blood is only an illustration of his gentler conduct, and whose whole life may well remind us that the only child of Philip Sydney became a Manners, because he is himself, as true and blameless, the Philip Sydney of our generation'. Smythe, later Lord Strangford, who fought in the last duel on English soil in 1852, was a great friend of the young Disraeli (a friendship well described in the *Autobiography* of Sir William Gregory, who knew them then); and Disraeli cribbed part of this dedication for the tribute to Prince Albert that finally endeared him for ever to Queen Victoria — as his equally cribbed tribute to Wellington had previously outraged her. Possibly, therefore, no book dedication has had a greater historical effect. The biter, however, was bit, as Muir points out: 'Disraeli's pretty dedication of *Vivian Grey* (1826) was adapted with the minimum of alteration, and a complete lack of acknowledgment, by the anonymous author of *Journal of a Tour through the Highlands of Scotland* (1830).'

Among more modern dedications, Muir suggests the notable one in Bentley's *Trent's Last Case*. I would add those in Jonathan Franklin's *Two Owls at Eton* (1960): 'To my Mother, who bravely put up with my owls for many a long and troublesome day when I was absent'; in Sterling North's *Raccoons are the Brightest People* (1966): 'To the one girl and the many raccoons in my life'; and in James Pope-Hennessy's *Sins of the Fathers*: 'To my bank manager, to whom I owe so much'.

One could also collect authors' titles or 'styles'. I recently visited the superbly stocked bookshop of Colin and Charlotte Franklin at Home Farm, Culham, Oxford, and was shown there a book on rat-catching whose author gloriously styled himself: 'Rat-catcher in Ordinary to Her Royal Highness Princess Amelia'. Authors' photographs would be another good subject: such a collection would have to include the portrait of Mrs Frances Simpson and her silver male 'Cambyses' from her turn-of-the-century book on cats which, incidentally, is dedicated 'To the many kind friends, known and unknown, that I have made in Pussydom'. This book carries an advertisement for another, *The ABC of Poultry*, by E. B. Johnstone – 'A capital addition to the many books devoted to the outdoor life . . . careful classifications of . . . the diseases to which the fowl is heir.'

One would also like to have the dust-jacket of Evelyn Waugh's *Ninety Days*, of which a copy was sold at Christie's in 1969 for £30: it shows him in tropical shorts. Auberon Waugh used the head of Michelangelo's *David* in place of his author's photograph on the jacket of his novel *A Bed of Flowers* (1971). Which brings me back to Desmond Elliott and his blurb's prize. High marks must surely go to this blurb, for *Crab Apple Jelly* (1944):

> In his new book of stories, Frank O'Connor has made a tasty jelly out of the crab apples of Irish life . . . Two monks who have renounced the world, the flesh and the devil imperil their immortal souls by a weakness for racing news. An anti-clerical Town Clerk tells his daughters the story of his own life under the guise of a romance about a certain Grand Vizier who has had a disagreement with the Grand Mufti of a Turkish town; while a fastidious, sensitive curate is compelled to explain the grotesque activities of the local Vigilance Society to an incredulous French sea-captain. An old woman who has spent her life in the city dreams of leaving her bones 'on a high hilltop in Ummera', the village she had left forty years before . . . 'O'Connor,' said the late W. B. Yeats, 'is doing for Ireland what Chekhov did for Russia.'

You can say that again.

My second prize goes to the blurb of *Hallucinations* by Reinaldo Arenas (1971).

> This novel is the hallucinatory history of Friar Servando Teresa de Mier, a Mexican friar whose famous heretical sermon on Our Lady of Guadalupe (now seen as an outburst of the passion which led to the independence of Mexico early in the nineteenth century)

resulted in his lifelong persecution. Ingeniously merging fact and fantasy, the novel records the friar's wildly improbable exploits as he escapes from prison to prison, narrowly avoiding immolation, rape and marriage, travelling Europe on foot, a witness to the excesses of debauched clerics and corrupt revolutionaries. He voyages in the three lands of love in Madrid, is caged by a wealthy jewess in Bayonne, witnesses the triumph of Napoleon in Paris, meets Lady Hamilton and Virginia Woolf's hermaphrodite Orlando in England's 'remote and misty land', picks cotton in the American South and finally returns to applause and welcome in newly liberated Mexico.

Sounds quite exciting.

As for his award, I think Mr Elliott would find no better candidate than this tantalizing description of *Full Moon* (the novel, written by Caradog Prichard, was published in 1973):

A young man is walking up an empty village street under the full moon, his world in his pocket, and out toward the dark lake on the Welsh mountainside that was the boundary of his childhood. As he walks he remembers how that same full moon marshalled a drunken Will Starched Collar to salvation and the transvestite Em to the asylum, smiling like a collie who's been killing sheep. Here, he and Moi and Huw dug for pig nuts and discussed the mechanics of crucifixion; there the visiting choir sang for funds to sustain the pit strike in the mysterious distant South. And in the reassuring centre of the world there was his mother, a lulling presence in the big bed, who contrived to keep the two of them from Friday to Friday on the parish money, and fought the remorselessness of life until it became an unequal struggle against the fury of the moon.

If the *New Statesman* were to set a competition for the most off-putting blurb, I think nobody could better that.*

* They did; and no one did. B.H.

Forging ahead

It has long been obvious that most people are far more interested in a good fake than the real thing. Nothing captures the headlines so easily as a big museum hoodwinked by a spurious Greek bronze horse; it is akin to the alleged pleasure of seeing a bowler-hatted businessman slip on a banana-skin.

Elmyr de Hory's forgeries of Picasso and other modern masters revealed that anyone can do it. The Louvre's experts became so accustomed to passing de Hory's fakes of Matisse as authentic that when a real Matisse was shown them they said: 'Not in his usual style: a palpable fake'. If someone could have proved that the Tutankhamun treasures at the British Museum were an elaborate hoax, the queues would have stretched to Islington.

Fakes used to be spurned by collectors: now they are avidly bid for when they come up (*as* fakes) in a saleroom – fakes by Sampson of Paris, the best-known forger of ceramics, have been sold at Christie's. Even a whiff of forgery can add value to a saleroom item. A silver tea service made in the 1860s by Cortelazzo, an Italian faker of Renaissance metalwork, was sold for £3,500 at Sotheby's in 1972; Cortelazzo had been persuaded by Sir Austen Layard, the English connoisseur, to give up his profitable trade in Renaissance fakes and to make wares of his own, of which these were examples. Forgeries of antique silver, however, are in a special class because they are automatically illegal.

Literary forgeries also enjoy a kind of vogue. The famous mountebank Psalmanazar, whose company Dr Johnson preferred even to that of the novelist Richardson, claimed to be a native of Formosa. Rescued – he alleged – by missionaries from an appalling heathenism, he had trained himself to eat raw meat to sustain the myth. Psalmanazar forged a colourful history of Formosa. Another great forger was Annius of Viterbo, whose name Pope borrowed to satirize the eighteenth-century English collector Sir Andrew Fountaine:

But Annius, crafty Seer, with ebon wand,
And well-dissembled em'rald on his hand,
False as his gems and cancer'd as his Coins,
Came, cramm'd with capons, from where Pollio dines.

Up to now, the principal literary forgeries that have come into the sale-room have been by Thomas Wise, whose spurious rare editions of such poets as Elizabeth Barrett Browning were brilliantly exposed in the 1930s by two young scholars, the late John Carter and Graham Pollard. An even more outrageous forger was Constantine Simonides. 'Of all the names that belong to the darker side of literature,' wrote J. A. Farrer in *Literary Forgeries* (published in 1907 and still the best introduction to the subject), 'none is more famous or interesting than that of Constantine Simonides, the Greek, who claims the year 1820 as that of his birth.'

Simonides first came to England in 1853, bringing with him a number of genuine manuscripts of no very great antiquity and about twenty of his own production, including miniature scrolls of Homer, Hesiod and other classical poets purporting to be centuries older than any known manuscripts of the same texts. He offered the fake manuscripts to Sir Frederick Madden, Keeper of Manuscripts at the British Museum, who unhesitatingly rejected them. On the following day he offered Madden the genuine works, and these were bought. Simonides then met Sir Thomas Phillipps, the obsessional bibliophile, whose vast collections have been sold at Sotheby's. Phillipps knew Simonides's reputation, yet so powerful was the wishful thinking of this besotted collector that he bought, between September 1853 and August 1854, almost all that Simonides had to offer: eight genuine manuscripts, five forged ones, six forged rolls and three forged 'chrysobulls'.

The way in which Phillipps acquired the Homer scroll was fortunately witnessed by a visiting German traveller, Johann Georg Kohl, who wrote of Phillipps: 'The object obviously fascinated him; the vellum attracted and charmed him as a piece of jewellery would a woman.' When Kohl came downstairs the following morning Simonides had left, and Kohl congratulated Phillipps on having withstood the Greek's blandishments. Phillipps ironically produced the scroll, for which he had paid £50. He said to Kohl:

I kept revolving the matter in my mind all night long. Should I allow the earliest manuscript of a Homeric rhapsody to escape me? The Greek may possibly prove once again to be a rogue and to have brought me merely a remarkable forgery. But it is also

Congreve matchbox and two fake scrolls by Simonides

possible that the document may be genuine. This morning he threatened that if I did not close with him he would take it away and let the British Museum have it. Should I risk that? I preferred to risk my £50.

Mr Gladstone, an expert on Homer, was approached about the scroll and 'proved evasive'. Dean Gaisford contemptuously dismissed the Hesiod as a fraud. But mad Phillipps remained obstinately convinced of the genuineness of the Homer and the Hesiod. He mumbled to himself on paper: 'Cicero records that he once saw a copy of the Iliad enclosed in a Nutshell and Aelian mentions the circumstance of an artist writing a distich in letters of gold, which he was able to deposit on the rind of a grain of corn.'

In 1972 the miniature Homer roll fetched £750 and the Hesiod £550. The Odes of Anacreon on four rolls of fine vellum with Pythagoras's Golden Verses on a vellum roll in a cylindrical Congreve matchbox also fetched £550.

The Simonides of our own times has been Mr Tom Keating, who after an investigation by my colleague on *The Times*, Geraldine Norman, admitted that he had forged some 2,000 paintings, many in the manner of Samuel Palmer. Like the Dutch faker Van Meegeren, whose forgeries of Vermeer bamboozled the *Burlington Magazine* in the earlier part of the century, Keating claimed that he had faked not for personal gain but to expose the false standards of the art world. Van Meegeren had never won recognition by painting in his own style, so he had decided to prove that he was as good as one of the universally acclaimed masters. Keating, for his part, alleged he was concerned about the commercial exploitation of great artists ('my brothers') and that he wanted to show up the art dealers as more greedy than discriminating. Both forgers thought they had proved their points. Yet both were eventually exposed through no open confession of their own; though Van Meegeren might have got away with it had he not been accused of collaboration in selling 'Vermeers' to Goering (his defence, naturally, was that he had sold the Nazi a walloping fake, and had therefore committed a thoroughly patriotic act).

What gives away the fake? First, there is the 'methinks he doth protest too much' aspect. Just as historical novelists destroy verisimilitude by overlarding their narratives with 'period' touches – perruques, "Tis he's', nankeen breeches, patches, jabots, red heels – the faker is prone to add just one quirk too many, to make sure that the gullible will accept the authenticity of one of his counterfeits. An even more common giveaway is the straight 'borrowing' of many elements from different works which are fused together in the fake. This was true of the Keating 'Palmers', in one of which there could be detected a group of cows from one original Palmer, clouds from another and a barn from a third. The same kind of mistake can expose fake autograph manuscripts, where the forger has relied too slavishly on the quirks of the author's calligraphy or phrasing. Forged memoirs can be rumbled, quite simply, if a date fails to tally with that recorded in a contemporary's letters or diary: if a spurious Tom Moore journal says Byron was in Venice on 23 April, for example, when we know from Byron's own letters that he was in Genoa on that date. A specimen of china is often proven a fake by holding it up to the light: the faker may have caught the outward appearance of Chelsea or Worcester but he will not have managed the patches of lighter paste known in Chelsea as 'moons', or the greenish glow of Worcester by transmitted light. Patina – the bloom of antiquity that accretes on old bronzes or is given to ivory netsuke by generations of handling – is another *pons asinorum*. It is no mere pun to say that glass fakes are the easiest to see through: the correct quotient of bubbles, the right degree of flintiness, must not only be achieved, but manifestly be seen to have been achieved.

Antiques without fakes would be like a world without wickedness: in theory paradise, in practice rather spiceless. People prefer to read about crimes and follies; Chaucer is more engaged by his bad characters than his virtuous ones. Collecting would be less enjoyable, and there would be less pride in the attainment of expertise, without the possibility of a pitfall. The Keating saga *proved* that the public is more interested in a fake than the real thing. When the story broke, Michael Leapman, *The Times*'s diarist, gormlessly wrote: 'Hands up those who had heard of Samuel Palmer before this exposure.' Speak, hands, for me.

The best books on the subject of fakes are: *Fabulous Frauds*, by Lawrence Jeppson (Arlington Books, 1972); *The Gentle Art of Faking Furniture*, by Herbert Cescinsky (Eyre and Spottiswood, 1970); and *Antique or Fake?*, by Charles Hayward (Evans Brothers; 2nd ed. 1970). I would also recommend an article on china and glass fakes by J. B. Kiddell of Sotheby's, who keeps a 'black museum' of forgeries, in the *Journal of the Chartered Auctioneers' and Estate Agents' Institute* (February 1952).